Dean Dixon

African American
Cultural Theory and Heritage
Series Editor: William C. Banfield

Dean Dixon

Negro at Home, Maestro Abroad

Rufus Jones Jr.

ROWMAN & LITTLEFIELD
Lanham • Boulder • New York • London

Published by Rowman & Littlefield
A wholly owned subsidiary of The Rowman & Littlefield Publishing Group, Inc.
4501 Forbes Boulevard, Suite 200, Lanham, Maryland 20706
www.rowman.com

Unit A, Whitacre Mews, 26-34 Stannary Street, London SE11 4AB

British Library Cataloguing in Publication Information Available

Library of Congress Cataloging-in-Publication Data

Jones, Rufus, Jr., 1968–
Dean Dixon : Negro at home, maestro abroad / Rufus Jones, Jr.
pages ; cm. — (African American cultural theory and heritage)
Includes bibliographical references and index.
ISBN 978-0-8108-8855-5 (hardback : alk. paper) — ISBN 978-0-8108-8856-2 (ebook) 1. Dixon, Dean, 1915-1976. 2. Conductors (Music)—United States—Biography. 3. African American conductors (Music)—Biography. I. Title.
ML422.D54J66 2015
784.2092—dc23
[B]
2014045493

Printed in the United States of America

To Ritha Dixon,
a woman of great intellect,
extraordinary strength,
and exemplary courage.
Your unconditional love and unwavering devotion
to Dean is inspirational.
Be blessed.

Contents

Foreword

It would have been an absurd fantasy had Edward Anderson or Harrison Ferrell given thought to conducting any ensemble other than the groups they established within their own communities on the East Coast. Whatever training they managed to secure, no matter what scores they studied, they had to be thankful they were able to realize their ambitions just with the players they were able to assemble. There could be no complaints about inexperienced players, the absence of contrabassoon or English horn instruments or players—fill in the missing parts at the piano! The audience might be excited by the new experience of this repertoire, comforted by their participation in the elevation interests of the Harlem Renaissance. But the conductors had no organizational structure to care for funding, no hall for rehearsals or concerts, no administration to address operations, even too few music stands; everything was ad hoc. It is unlikely any of those involved were granted ready access to the professional concerts presented in the cities where they lived: Philadelphia, New York, or Chicago—and Ferrell had earned his Ph.D. in 1928 (but in German) from Northwestern University. He might have founded an orchestra in Chicago in 1923, but he turned to linguistics for a profession.

Dean Dixon changed that, even if as a pioneer he did not properly benefit from his efforts, certainly not in the United States. Rudolph Dunbar and Everett Lee, Dixon's contemporaries, shared his fate, with even less success.

But on Dixon's shoulders stood the next generation of African American maestri, most notably Henry Lewis, Calvin Simmons, and James DePreist, who are no longer with us, and Paul Freeman, now retired, whose nine LP recordings for Columbia helped awaken the musical world to three centuries of Black composers. And now we have a new crop of outstanding talents, some of whom have yet to reap the full benefits of Dixon's labors: Leslie Dunner, Alfred Duckett, John McLaughlin Williams, and Dr. Rufus Jones Jr.

The dramatic story of Dean Dixon had to be told by a conductor with firsthand insight into the extensive steps from sheer motivation to the podium, and it was critical this evolution be traced by one who was sensitive, not only to the social barriers, but also to what Leontyne Price said was "the luxury of being Black." Dixon's student, the late conductor and composer Coleridge-Taylor Perkinson, told me that when studying with Dixon in Hilversum, the subject of race was never brought up, yet Dixon wrote me some years before his death, eager to have news of the recent activities of Black composers back in his native land. I was struck by what was more than nostalgia.

Dr. Jones has gone well past the synthesis of available data by meeting with Dixon's survivors and exploring the riches hidden within the holdings of the Schomburg Center. One might think his Ph.D. was in musicology, not conducting. He does not hesitate in providing information on the problems Dixon faced in music, but also those of his personal life. The result is a compassionate, vital documentary on the life of a major force in music and Black history—one whose readership must embrace a larger public than might be initially expected.

—Dominique-René de Lerma

Acknowledgments

When I started this project more than seven years ago, I was an assistant professor of music at Georgetown University in Washington, D.C. During that time I was very fortunate to have three of the finest minds on the planet to help me understand all that was involved in writing a book. Dr. Carole Sargent, director of the Office of Scholarly Publications at Georgetown, offered sound advice on how to write an effective book proposal and the importance of time management. She was a reassuring voice in my life as I began to map out how this book was going to be written. Dr. Anna H. Celenza, the Thomas E. Caestecker Chair in Music at Georgetown, was instrumental in helping me secure two consecutive summer academic grant awards, which allowed me to spend those summer months in Harlem, New York, to research at the Schomburg Center for Research in Black Culture. Dr. Anthony R. DelDonna, associate professor of musicology at Georgetown, served as my mentor on this project and taught me the meaning of hard work and integrity. When I first approached Anthony about the story of Dean Dixon, he encouraged me to move forward on this project with due diligence because this story needed to be told. He believed in me like no other colleague I have ever encountered in my life. To those three I give my sincerest gratitude.

Navigating my way through the Dean Dixon Papers would have been an overwhelming undertaking without the help of the wonderful staff at the Schomburg Center. Ms. Diana Lachatanere, curator of the Manuscripts, Archives, and Rare Book Division at the Schomburg Center (retired), was an invaluable resource on every aspect of the collection. Mr. Steven G. Fullwood, assistant curator of the Manuscripts, Archives, and Rare Book Division at the Schomburg Center, seemed to always remember my topic of research and which box of the collection I was using during my sporadic visits to the second floor. Ms. Mary Yearwood, curator of the Photographs and Prints Division at the Schomburg Center, went beyond the call of duty to answer any questions I had about using photographs from the collection in my book. To those three and the countless other staff members at the Schomburg Center, you have my respect and heartfelt appreciation.

From the very beginning of this project, it was always my intent for this book to read more like a novel than a dissertation. I was so blessed to find a copy editor who understood my vision and kept me honest whenever I strayed. Ms. Caryl Fantel is a music director who served as piano accompanist for my middle school chorus for almost two years before I discovered she had a background in copy editing. She is a gifted musician with a sense of humor that made for a wonderful collaboration. I could not have done it without you, Caryl. Thank you.

To the family of Dean Dixon (Ritha, Nina, Nora, and Lavi and Kelan Daniel), I want to thank you for allowing me to invade your personal space during this process. I recognized that there were times when my questions ventured into uncomfortable topics. But it was necessary in order to gain insight that thousands of documents in a collection could not adequately provide. I learned from you that Dixon was not just this gifted conductor who had a fascinating professional life, but also someone's father, grandfather, and husband. Words cannot fully express how that realization changed my perspective and caused me to rethink how I needed to tell this story. You have my deepest appreciation and love.

I want to give a special acknowledgment to the late Kaj Kristoffersen and his wife, Christa. Kaj Kristoffersen's research is the reason that so many of Dean Dixon's own words were available for this project. His taped interviews with Dixon (which took place in Frankfurt, Wolfsburg, and New York from 1967 to 1970) were later transcribed and now are a part of the Dean Dixon Papers at the Schomburg Center. Information from those interviews served as the foundation for this book. I was fortunate to have an opportunity to communicate with Mr. Kristoffersen before he passed. I thanked him for his significant contribution and made sure that he knew his work was the reason that the Dean Dixon story could be told with such depth and personal insight.

To my mother, Helen Bonner, I want to thank you for nurturing my talents as a musician by not allowing anyone or anything to get in the way of my studies. When others thought I should become a football player or a real estate tycoon, you saw my true calling and gently pushed me in the right direction. I love you!

To my wife, Felicia Ford Jones, I want to thank you for your sacrifice during this very difficult season. Even with all the issues of life that we could not avoid (as much as we would have liked to), you never stopped encouraging me. Your continual affirmation throughout these seven years of research and writing confirmed in the depths of my soul that this book is a gift from God and so are you! All of my days . . .

Introduction

My fascination with Dean Dixon started more than twenty years ago while matriculating as an undergraduate music education major in Austin, Texas. I was studying to become a high school band director. One Saturday afternoon while visiting my family in Dallas, I came across, on the local PBS station, a rebroadcast of Maestro Zubin Mehta conducting the Israel Philharmonic and New York Philharmonic in a joint concert at Avery Fisher Hall. Maestro Mehta seemed to have the orchestra transfixed with his passion, his piercing eyes, and his fluid baton technique. I could not take my eyes off the television. I was transfixed! I had no idea what the orchestra was playing, but I was blown away at the size of the orchestra and the sounds that were being produced. I knew then that being a high school band director was no longer my destiny. I wanted to be an orchestral conductor.

I confided in a number of friends about my career change both expecting and anticipating their unwavering support. To my utter surprise, it seemed that no one believed I had the ability to be an orchestral conductor. I vividly recall when one of my friends took me aside to explain to me why orchestral conducting was not my destiny. I was amazed as he rattled off pronouncements like, "You're no Leonard Bernstein; you don't have the physical build for this profession; and you don't have enough knowledge of the orchestral repertoire." We were only second-year undergraduates at the time trying to find our way in this ever-expansive field! How could someone so easily and permanently label me a failure before I even began this journey? Not too long after this encounter I met for coffee with a close and dear friend who unfortunately has since passed away. Her name was Marsha Henderson. She was a classically trained pianist and mezzo-soprano who exuded charisma. Her energy was contagious. People loved to be around her. Marsha was a true diva. She earned her bachelor's and master's degrees in piano and voice performance from Indiana University in Bloomington. Marsha stood six feet tall and was a lovely, full-figured, mocha-skinned woman with a voice that could melt your heart. She could sight-read anything on the piano. What an amazing talent! After sharing with her my experience, she responded by saying with great clarity that it was not my ability they questioned but their perception of what or who an orchestral conductor should be. I did not realize until sometime later that she was not only speaking of my situation but of her own struggles in the profession she loved so much—opera. Could this really be a race issue? Could the fact that I was a Black man trying to pursue a career in which I would lead mostly White men and women in performances of the great masterworks be the reason for the discouragement? I simply did not know the answers to these very disturbing questions that were racing through my head.

Perhaps I was naïve to think that my race would not be a factor in pursuing a career in conducting. I simply believed then as I do now that one's musical gifting was supposed to transcend how one looked in the mirror. My dark brown skin should not have adversely persuaded anyone that I would not be able to achieve my goal. I was determined more than ever not to let these discouraging words and events keep me from my destiny. I needed to know more about my history and more about how others in my profession coped with the sobering reality of racial discrimination.

In 1989, I was reading through the February issue of *Ebony* magazine (a magazine devoted to African American issues and culture) and discovered an article that forever changed my life. It was entitled, "The Maestros: Black Symphony Conductors Are Making a Name for Themselves." This article cited a number of incredible accomplishments by extraordinary people that I never knew existed. It told the story of Black orchestral conductors who persevered against the most overt acts of racial discrimination and went on to become highly successful in their field. I was introduced to conductors like James DePreist, Paul Freeman, Isaiah Jackson, Henry Lewis, James Frazier, Kay Roberts, Willie Waters, Leslie Dunner, Michael Morgan, and Denis de Coteau. No one, however, stood out more prominently to me in this article than Dean Dixon. Why? Because he was the first!

In the early twentieth century, White European-born classical performers were the accepted norm in concert halls across America. Black singers and instrumentalists were accepted in limited ways and often only because of their extraordinary talents. The thought of accepting a Black conductor, however, who could assert musical authority over White male instrumentalists, was offensive to many and opposed at every corner. This intolerance was based on the understanding that beyond the innate musical gifts a conductor exhibits on the podium, he must also possess a musical intellect equal, if not superior, to those he is leading and instructing on how best to perform Beethoven, Brahms, Mozart, and so forth. In other words, many could not live with the prospect of a Black conductor actually having the intellectual dexterity needed to lead a professional orchestra. It would mean that, potentially, all Blacks, if given the proper training and opportunity, could succeed at the same level as their White counterparts.

Despite this pervasive environment of intolerance, Dean Dixon (1915–1976) became the first Black American to lead the New York Philharmonic and NBC Symphony orchestras in 1941. After successful guest conducting engagements with the orchestras of Philadelphia and Boston, a number of newspapers and popular magazines began to write about Dixon as someone to watch; a leading figure among a new breed of American conductors who would no doubt become leader of one of the major symphony orchestras. Author and music critic David Ewen thought so much of Dixon's accomplishments that in 1948 when he revised his book *Dictators of the Baton*, he expanded it to include, among others, a chapter dedicated to this "conductor for tomorrow." In it he wrote: "Another young conductor whose work gives us every reason for faith in his future is Dean Dixon. . . . [His] career is the triumph of talent over the greatest obstacle which can be placed in the way of a young musician acquiring [conducting] assignments: race prejudice. . . . It is not an easy road that has brought a Negro to the conductor's stands of two great American orchestras. That the road has, at last, been traversed speaks well both for Dixon's capabilities and for the capacity of true talent to assert itself."[1] Unfortunately, these accolades did not lead to an appointment with a major orchestra. Dixon became increasingly disillusioned by the apparent disinterest of American orchestras in his abilities as a conductor.

Dixon left the United States in 1949 painfully realizing that if he remained, the color of his skin would prevent him from achieving his ultimate goal. He acknowledged this reality in poignant terms, noting: "My goal [is] to develop myself to my highest capacity as a serious, mature American artist and thus to make my contribution to society in the field of symphony conducting. Through this I hope to contribute to the reduction of America's disinclination to accept Negroes in this and like categories, thus opening up many fields to Negroes who are bent on serious and profound contributions to society."[2]

That same year, Dixon was invited by the French National Radio Orchestra to guest conduct for several upcoming broadcasts. Once in Europe, his career blossomed. He went from sparse appearances during 1944–1949 in the United States, to a full roster of prestigious guest conducting appearances across Europe. Additionally, he went from no major conducting appointments in the United States to two permanent appointments in Europe: Gothenburg Symphony Orchestra (1953–1960) and the Radio Symphony Orchestra in Frankfurt, Germany (1961–1974). His success in Europe also led to an appointment in Australia, where he served as principal conductor of the

Sydney Symphony Orchestra (1964–1967). Dixon's success abroad was unprecedented for an American conductor, and he did not return to the United States for twenty-one years.

One of the real tragedies in the life of Dean Dixon, which will serve as the narrative thread throughout this book, is that as he began to achieve notoriety in Europe, very few American papers were writing about him, and from 1949 to 1966 no serious invitations were presented to Dixon to appear with a major symphony orchestra in America.

While hurt beyond words from what he would characterize as the cruelest form of abandonment, Dixon had long ago resolved that he would achieve success not only for himself but also for those who would have the audacity to believe that their dreams were not too grandiose to bring to fruition. Dixon eventually returned to the United States in 1970 with an invitation to conduct the New York Philharmonic.

Despite his public pronouncements that he had no desire to live or be recognized in the States after his success in Europe, personal letters reveal a different story. He was pleased when the invitation came from the New York Philharmonic in 1969. He also sought out numerous opportunities to stay in the States for longer periods of time by writing American universities to inquire about visiting professorships. He wanted to return home not just to show the world that a Black conductor succeeded in this last bastion of elitism, but to experience a true sense of acceptance by his fellow countrymen.

When I began my research of Dean Dixon, I quickly discovered that no major document had been produced that provided a detailed account of his extraordinary life. After Dixon died in 1976, his wife, Ritha Dixon, discussed writing his life story with a number of family friends. She believed that his life could be an inspiration to those who find obstacles all around them but refuse to give up their dreams. When no one followed through on their initial interest to tell Dixon's story, Ritha donated most of her husband's personal effects to the Schomburg Center for Research in Black Culture, which is part of the New York Public Library System in Harlem. The collection is a literal treasure trove of unpublished primary and insightful secondary sources including reviews of his numerous European performances. How incredible this process became when at first what seemed to be obscure bits of information, to my surprise, would help usher in a whole new world of germane and exciting discoveries.

Through my research I concluded that a number of the earlier published biographical sketches were incomplete and filled with misinformation. The biography of Dean Dixon is intended to address those published inaccuracies and introduce a new generation to the life and work of a great, virtually forgotten Black American musician. This story will address the painful issues of racism, abandonment, self-imposed exile, health issues, spirituality, and financial difficulties. In the end, all of these issues will serve as a back-drop to Dixon's unquenchable thirst to achieve the American dream— abroad.

Prologue

Just tell the story . . .
—Susie C. Owens

It's July 21, 1970, a beautiful summer evening. The New York Philharmonic is hosting its annual Parks Concert series. For a number of years the Philharmonic has presented summer outdoor concerts in city parks representing all of the five boroughs: Manhattan, Brooklyn, Queens, Staten Island, and the Bronx. The No. 10 buses along Central Park West in Manhattan are doing extra business today, dropping off people of various ages and persuasions. They're pouring in by the thousands and making themselves comfortable on the plush green grass at the Sheep Meadow in Central Park. Some observers are reporting that at least seventy-five thousand enthusiastic and curious concertgoers are in attendance for this momentous occasion. [1]

The anticipation of something great is in the air but does not remove the lingering questions in the minds of many who have come out to witness the return of Dean Dixon. Who is this conductor from Europe? Why did the Philharmonic bring in an "unknown"? Is he any good?

Few remember his first appearance with the Philharmonic in the summer of 1941 at Lewisohn Stadium, where five thousand attendees witnessed the first Black conductor to lead the oldest orchestra in America. Even fewer remember his triumphal appearance with the NBC Symphony Orchestra in its summer subscription concert that same year.

As thousands of spectators settle in with family and friends—arranging their pillows, blankets, and picnic baskets—a subtle cue from backstage signals the orchestra that all playing, warming up, or last-minute run-through of that tricky musical passage must cease. A faint applause, which emanates from stage right, begins to trickle throughout Central Park. It quickly strengthens as everyone now realizes that the concertmaster has entered the stage and is walking to his designated position to signify to the principal oboist that it's time to tune. That all-important "A" resonates throughout the city park three times—one for the woodwinds and brass, one for the low strings, and one for the upper strings. After the tuning has concluded, the concertmaster takes his seat.

Then it happens. Dixon enters the stage in the same dignified manner he has done for more than thirty years. His five-foot-nine-inch stocky frame gracefully approaches the podium as the orchestra stands to acknowledge the maestro of the evening and the thunderous applause of the audience.

There he is on the podium, immaculately dressed in his custom-tailored white dinner jacket, looking out at an enthusiastically responsive audience. In his right hand, Dixon is holding a fifteen-inch molded fiberglass baton, which was given to him by the principal violist of the Sydney Symphony Orchestra during his tenure as music director there. Dixon is a soft-spoken man, who looks the part of a maestro—calm, self-assured, experienced, and focused. Not to mention his beautifully trimmed Afro—a hairstyle he sported in Europe long before it was popular in America.

After acknowledging the audience with an appropriate bow, Dixon turns to the orchestra to signal that they may take their seats. With precision and great subtlety, he quickly surveys the ensemble to establish eye contact. Feeling comfortable with his assessment, Dixon raises his baton and sets his heart, mind, and body to the compositions of Henze, Sibelius, and Brahms.

One journalist who attended the outdoor concert wrote in *Newsweek*: "The 55-year-old Dixon came home to mount the podium before an American orchestra for the first time since 1949. . . . This was a ripe Dixon, authoritative and precise. He is not a showboat conductor, yet he showered his program with lilting lyricism and controlled grace. And he gave Brahms's Second Symphony a rich romantic sweep that brought the great throng to its feet in a standing, especially thrilling ovation."[2]

The return of Dean Dixon to his homeland after a twenty-one-year self-imposed exile is news heard around the world. His is a story of triumph from years of disappointments in the United States to success abroad beyond anyone's imagination. But there is something the public does not know about Dixon. His years of struggling to reach his goals were not without a heavy price. Dixon's energetic countenance on the podium belies the fact that he is a man of great frailty. Over the years, his body has fought serious bouts of asthma, life-threatening allergic reactions, and hypertension. Despite his overwhelming infirmities, Dixon knows that he must savor his sojourn home. He is soberly aware that his life's journey has brought him full circle.

Although recognized throughout Europe, South America, Asia, and Australia as one of the shining stars in the world of classical music, this West Indian American from Harlem, New York, is a stranger to most Americans.

Chapter One

West Indians in Harlem

On September 6, 1905, the S.S. *Cantanio* left the port of Barbados for its journey to Ellis Island. The port of arrival manifest recorded eight passengers who decided to take this journey with the captain and his crew. One was from Trinidad; the rest were from Barbados. Three were White and the remaining passengers were Black. Their ages ranged from six to forty-nine. Their occupations varied from teacher, tailor, and clerk to seamstress. All but one could read and write. McClara Dean Rolston was one of the eight passengers.[1] She was born near Sam Lords Castle in St. Phillips, Barbados, on January 1, 1880, to Ida Fitzgerald and Elizabeth Burgess Rolston. McClara was twenty-five years old when she arrived at Ellis Island on September 14, 1905.

She came to New York City with only $10 to her name, but an eagerness to begin her new life in America. She arranged to stay with her brother as a live-in housekeeper. E. C. "Cliff" Rolston came to the States a few years earlier. He lived at 207 West 33rd Street in Manhattan—the heart of the "Tenderloin District." The Tenderloin was a Black and Irish American community encompassing West 20th to 39th streets and extending to 9th and 10th avenues. It was not an exaggeration to say that the living quarters were substandard in every way. There were no formal lease agreements for these dwellings, but in some cases if you agreed to reside in them for a year, you received free rent for one month. That enticed many families to endure until the end of the year.[2] McClara eventually settled in a place of her own a few miles from her brother at 627 8th Avenue. She continued to keep house for Cliff and took in laundry to satisfy her creditors.

McClara was a woman of regal bearing. There was no mistaking her Barbadian speech and British-influenced culture. She wore her hair up, which always accentuated her round face and piercing brown eyes. Dignified in every aspect of her persona, it was not a surprise that Henry Charles

Dixon, who lived in the next building at 625 8th Avenue, took notice. Henry arrived in the States in the early 1900s. He was born in Kingston, Jamaica, on March 3, 1877, son of Horatio Charles and Martha Dennis Dixon. Henry was trained as a lawyer in England, but was unable to find work in his chosen profession in the States.[3] He settled on a bellman position at the Navarre Hotel on 38th Street and 7th Avenue. During this time, most West Indian immigrants received an elementary-level education in their homeland. They were then expected to learn a trade. Once they arrived in the States, many typically worked as domestics, porters, waiters, and janitors. While some continued their education in America, going to trade school or college, very few arrived in their new homeland with the level of education Henry had attained. One would think that would have put him in a much better position to succeed than most. It did not. Henry's failure to realize his dream of practicing law in America was quite troublesome. While he accepted that most, if not all, White establishments in Manhattan would likely not accept his credentials to practice law, he was perplexed as to why his "own people," both foreign-born and native-born Blacks, did not see fit to recognize his credentials and support his career. He accepted the fact, albeit reluctantly, that his life would not be what he had originally hoped for in America.

After a long courtship, Henry and McClara were married on February 17, 1914, in the St. Chrysostom Chapel at 550 7th Avenue with the Reverend V. D. Ruggles serving as the officiate. They moved to a larger apartment at 331 West 35th Street, but did not stay there long. Their family of two was about to become three.

Dean Rolston Dixon was born on January 10, 1915. The doctor who delivered him lived next door to Henry and McClara at 329 West 35th Street. Dean was a healthy baby, delivered to this world with physical features more akin to his father than his mother. With dark mocha skin, deep rich brown eyes, and a broad nose, no one could deny Henry's intimate role in this creation. Dean was baptized the following month at St. Chrysostom Chapel on February 14, 1915, three days shy of Henry and McClara's one-year anniversary. His name on the baptism certificate read Charles Dean Dixon. Henry and McClara preferred Charles Dean to Dean Rolston, seeing more of an equal compromise by using both of their middle names.

Life became harder for Henry with another mouth to feed. He was heavily dependent on his job at the Navarre Hotel, trying to bring home extra money through tips from generous hotel guests. His dreams permanently deferred, Henry began to focus more on what his family needed, and less on what he desired. This new focus would eventually have devastating consequences for the Dixon household. Besides trying to make more money, Henry knew he needed to find another place more suitable for raising his son. He and McClara heard about a community uptown that was steadily making a name for itself as a residential and business haven for Blacks. Cliff was opening a saloon in the same area, so it is likely they heard about this bustling neighborhood from him. The opportunity to move into a community with better housing, away from racial tension that was ever-present in the Tenderloin, was too much to pass up. Four months later, the Dixon family moved to Harlem.

Harlem was originally a predominantly White community that experienced a major real estate expansion in the 1890s. However, the demand for real estate in this vibrant community was overestimated. White owners were left with vacant rental property throughout Central Harlem. Black realtors convinced a few of the owners that despite the negative backlash that was inevitable, it was in their best interest to lease their vacant buildings to them. The agents then turned around and rented the property to Black tenants.[4] Blacks from crowded West 53rd Street, the San Juan Hill section, and the 34th and 35th streets of the Tenderloin District were pouring in to Central Harlem in the early 1900s. By 1915, as more and more White residents realized that no form of objection could quash this unwanted "invasion," they slowly but steadily moved out of Central Harlem, while Blacks, both native and foreign born, took over most of 130th to 139th streets.

The Dixon's new apartment at 143 West 138th Street was a "railroad flat," meaning the apartment was laid out similarly to that of a railway car. The kitchen and dining area were the first section of the apartment Henry and McClara saw as they opened the door to their new home. What followed was a narrow corridor that spanned the length of the apartment. The first room had two large windows, facing 138th Street, which became the study. A piano would later be placed in this room. Further down the narrow corridor were one bathroom, one guest room, and a master bedroom. The last room in the back of the apartment was originally designed as the maid's quarters. That room was given to Dean.

Although situated on the same street, albeit a few blocks away, their new place was not in as affluent a neighborhood as the so-called Striver's Row. Striver's Row was a collection of beautiful brownstones and apartments situated on parts of West 138th and 139th streets. White owners restricted Blacks from buying these buildings until 1919. It seemed that almost immediately following the release of these properties to the community-at-large that "the Negro press was plastered with advertisements for their sale; within eight months practically all were sold to well-to-do Negroes."[5] In the 1920s, Black intellectuals, businessmen, and entertainers lived in these fashionable row houses "striving" to live the American dream, hence the name Striver's Row.

Henry and McClara had never lived in a place this spacious. What started out as an exciting new launch for this West Indian family, became in just a few short years a financial hardship. "Rents, traditionally high in Harlem, reached astounding proportions in the 1920s—they skyrocketed in response

to the unprecedented demand created by heavy Negro migration and settlement within a restricted geographical area."[6] Moreover, the rent for Blacks
throughout Harlem was disproportionately higher than Whites who resided in
the same community. Depending on the number of rooms you had, Black
Harlem renters paid as much as $10 more than their White counterparts. This
resulted in many families who resided in three- to five-bedroom apartments
renting out their vacant rooms to extended family, friends, and strangers.
While this would have been a solution for Henry and McClara's financial
woes, there was no record of them ever taking on boarders.

The Dixons' rent averaged around $20 a month. Henry's job as a bellman
only brought home $7 every two weeks. The expected tips from those gener-
ous hotel guests rarely materialized, but when they did, McClara saved every
penny. She was able to pay the rent and other household expenses by supple-
menting Henry's income with her either doing laundry or working on behalf
of small businesses as a secretary or bookkeeper. McClara had a keen mind
for numbers and organization.

Henry began to withdraw emotionally and physically from his family.
Not only did he find himself working a job that he believed was beneath his
station in life, he was unable to support his family without the help of his
wife and possibly Cliff, McClara's brother. McClara witnessed Henry's
interest in being the patriarch of the family fade away. While she understood
the cultural dilemma he faced, she had no choice but to take charge of the
household. Her son's future was at stake. Although Henry stayed in the
house during this period, and worked to support his family, McClara, by
default, became mother and father to Dean.

Dean was exposed to classical music at an early age. Having taken piano
lessons in her youth, McClara was very serious about making sure that classical music was a central part of Dean's life.[7] One day, following one of their
visits to the top gallery of Carnegie Hall, McClara swore she saw Dean
walking around their home pretending to play the violin with two sticks. She
wasted no time procuring a full-sized violin for $15 at a Harlem pawnshop
for her young virtuoso-to-be.[8] This was no small purchase for a family with a
steady monthly income of approximately $14. McClara said about this huge
sacrifice, "[We] saved from Monday's vegetables; Wednesday's washing,
and from Saturday's roast, in order to buy [our] son a violin."[9] At age three-
and-a-half, Dean could barely hold on to the violin due to its size and weight.
It was almost as tall as he was. The schedule of three lessons per week began
immediately.

Dean's first teacher was a Russian violinist who had a large studio in
Harlem. Most of his students were from the neighborhood and Black. Mr.
Fagen was his name. He was an elderly man, confined to a wheelchair.
McClara was impressed that a man in Mr. Fagen's physical condition found a
way to make a respectable living. McClara accompanied Dean to his lessons

at Mr. Fagen's home. On their first meeting, Mr. Fagen allowed Dean to use one of his more appropriately sized violins, until he grew into his own. For the first few years, Dean's lessons were "pure technical work." Mr. Fagen spent most of his time with Dean making sure he had perfect bow strokes, accurate fingering positions, and correct posture.[10] McClara observed carefully during the lessons, taking in all that was said, so that she could properly supervise Dean's practice time at home.

Initially, Dean hated practicing the violin. His mother created her own practice regime for him, insisting that he practice every day. He started out practicing one hour a day and slowly worked up the stamina to five hours a day. Playing the violin also brought on never-ending ridicule from the neighborhood kids because many of them viewed playing classical music as effeminate. Dean's "boyhood" was further called into question when McClara sent him to his lessons wearing dress shorts and knee-high white socks. He endured the teasing up to a point.

One Saturday morning, while on his way to Mr. Fagen's home for a lesson, one of the neighborhood boys began to tease him. Dean was old enough to walk to Mr. Fagen's home on his own and therefore no longer had the protection of his mother to shield him from these unmerciful verbal attacks. In addition to being called "sissy" and other effeminate names, he was an overweight child and called names like "fatso" quite often during his childhood. Out of all of the derogatory names he was called, the one that he had no tolerance for was "Crisco." This all-vegetable shortening, which was used in many homes as early as 1912, strongly resembled the texture and look of that equally used animal fat, "lard." To Dean, Crisco was code for lard, meaning, "you're fat."

He had had enough! In his mind, this was the ultimate insult. Dean calmly set down his violin case and proceeded to have what he called a "knockdown fight" with his verbal tormenter. The vigorous scuffle drew blood on both sides. After the fight ended, Dean picked himself up, wiped the blood off his face, picked up his violin, and continued to Mr. Fagen's home for his lesson. Dean won that fight, and no one bothered him in this way again. In looking back on this moment when he was much older, he realized that being called Crisco, in and of itself, was not the reason he lost his temper and fought. It just happened to be the newest name to accompany a long list of insults, which had finally reached its breaking point. Dean also recognized the violence in his neighborhood that caused him to develop a mindset of survival:

> Living in filth and having violence around you, you begin to protect yourself—you have to. I learned as a youth that the first law in protection is not to fall down . . . because if you fell down you were gone . . . so you learned to stand on your feet no matter what happened . . . this was a part of living. It had

nothing to do with practicing violin five hours a day. That was upstairs in my
house. I was therefore safe. When I was down into the street, I had my eyes
around and back, all over. I had to. Had I been a little angel with my head in
front of me, see nothing, do nothing, I wouldn't be here today. [11]

He often talked about the violence in his neighborhood and how over time it
was just simply accepted as the "jungle" he lived in. There was one incident
where Dean awoke one early morning from the sounds of an earth-shattering
explosion. When his parents investigated, they learned that in their building
lived a questionable character that was independently making his own liquor.
While making your own booze during the prohibition era in the 1920s was a
common occurrence, it was swiftly dealt with if you were discovered to be
producing without the blessing of the local crime boss. The explosion was
clearly a deadly message sent by an organized crime syndicate whose territory was being infringed upon. Scenes like this were as normal a part of the day
as waking up in the morning, eating breakfast, and leaving for work. After
the incident subsided, Dean, his family, and the neighborhood went on about
their daily lives as if nothing extraordinary happened a few hours earlier.

McClara was as committed to Dean's formal education as she was his
musical training. She believed the earlier he was in school the better. At age
five, Dean was still too young to enroll in the New York Public School
system. McClara did not find this acceptable at all. Dean was very much into
his violin studies and improving at great strides, and as a result, McClara
believed he had the intelligence and preparedness to start learning his ABCs,
now rather than later. In 1920, McClara found a nearby Catholic school that
accepted Dean into their program. Its location was ideal at 55 West 138th
Street, and its values exceeded all of McClara's expectations. Later that year,
he began his formal education at St. Mark the Evangelist School. [12] Sister
Katharine Drexel founded St. Mark the Evangelist School in 1912. This was
one of many schools she and her organization, Sisters of the Blessed Sacra-
ment, started to fulfill their mission to help those who were underrepresented
and discriminated against. In this case it was Black children in Harlem. She
and her supporters believed that everyone deserved a quality education. St.
Mark's was the first Catholic school in New York City for Black students
and it was open to all denominations. [13]

Religion was an important part of Dixon's upbringing. Dean's parents
were practicing Catholics, but it was from 1917 to 1919 that McClara converted the family to the Episcopalian faith. They began attending the St.
Philip's Protestant Episcopal Church, which opened its doors in Harlem in
1910 on 134th Street. In 1922, the Dixons and a small number of West Indian
families moved their membership to the St. Luke's Episcopal Mission for
Negroes. It was St. Luke's Protestant Episcopal Church, located on 435 West
141st Street, which established the chapel. This humble edifice, which was

renovated from an old row house at 28 Edgecombe Avenue near 136th Street, had a seating capacity of three hundred. Kenneth Clark, a childhood friend of Dean, was a member of one of the families that moved to the mission and remembered the transition well: "This was [a] small church. My mother was a founding member of that church, because the church that we first went to, when my sister and I were very young was St. Philip's Church . . . and they had Indians [who] broke off and formed St. Luke's Church."[14] Kenneth and Dean served as altar boys until they both turned sixteen. Kenneth recounts those years "on the altar" with Dean as less than pleasurable: "[My mother] insisted I serve on that altar with Dean Dixon as my partner, till we were sixteen. In fact, one of the reasons I didn't want to go to college in New York City was because I knew if I stayed at home and went to college, my mother would want me to continue serving on that altar, and I was damn sick and tired of it."[15]

Dean had little to no exposure to White children during his two years at St. Mark's and no personal experiences with racial discrimination beyond the discussions he had with his mother, father, and neighborhood friends. McClara was careful in monitoring Dean's exposure to family and friends, hoping to thwart any stories that might corrupt her young child's sensibilities toward what was right and wrong. Cliff was the unfortunate exception. It was through ill-fated encounters with his Uncle Cliff that Dean developed his "first complex" regarding his skin color. Uncle Cliff was a very light-skinned man with hair and physical features that gave no evidence of his African heritage. He could pass for White if he wanted. One day, Dean was asked by McClara to deliver a meal for Cliff at his saloon in Harlem. Once there, Cliff proceeded to make fun of Dean's skin color by saying things like, "Hey, why don't you wash? What do you mean by coming here with these dark spots? Why don't you take a brush—go home and clean yourself." Dean later admitted: "That was the first concept I had that I had different coloration within me and that I was evidently dirty. [Therefore], I went home and I brushed until all my skin became raw . . . my uncle had put this little seed into me that I could scrub out my heritage. I could wash the color off."[16] McClara was obviously aware that something happened to Dean at her brother's saloon, given the physical evidence on his hands later that day, but there was no evidence that McClara confronted Cliff about this encounter.

Dean was prohibited from listening to the radio. McClara believed that this new form of media was unsuitable for her son and did not want him to be negatively influenced by it. When Dean protested, saying that all the other neighborhood kids were allowed to listen to popular music, McClara responded by saying that "someone has to play the music on the air and that if [you] studied hard [you] might be the person to do so."[17] While Dean didn't find McClara's explanation acceptable, he later discovered those words of encouragement and admonition to be seemingly prophetic. In 1924, Dean's talent on the violin was discovered and he began playing on the local radio station, WNEW. He achieved celebrity status in his neighborhood: "Those same youngsters [who called me sissy and fatso] were using crude crystal sets to hear the broadcasts and were stopping me in the street to ask, 'Can I carry your violin? Will you take us to the radio station so we can see what it is like?'" [18] He realized after his time on the radio that his status with even those individuals who teased him unmercifully had changed for the better. Things were looking up.

In 1925, when Mr. Fagen became too sickly to continue his studio, he recommended that his son David Fagen (also a violinist) take on Dean as one of his students. David agreed. He came to the Dixons' home for violin lessons, where he was always greeted with traditional Barbadian cakes and tea. David's approach to teaching violin had obvious similarities to his father. However, what differed was that more times than not he was on the piano accompanying Dean, making comments on his playing only when absolutely necessary. David was not a taskmaster like his father. While McClara was not impressed with the younger Fagen's more relaxed style of instruction, Dean found the lessons with David refreshing and musically illuminating. As a result, his outlook on music became more than mastering the basic rudiments of violin playing. Dean began to appreciate the joy of music making, and although he did not have any understanding of the art of conducting at that time, he learned to appreciate various timbres from the piano that were akin to instruments of the orchestra. Unbeknown to him, this early exposure to orchestration would have a profound impression on his development as a conductor.

In 1926, Dean was concluding his fourth year at P.S. 5 elementary school on West 143rd Street and Amsterdam Avenue. The principal of his school was asked to nominate a number of outstanding students to attend Speyer Experimental Junior High School. Named after its main benefactor, James Speyer, this experimental school was headed up by a number of instructors from Columbia University Teacher's College. Speyer was located near Columbia University on 124th Street between Amsterdam Avenue and Broadway, which was in a predominately White neighborhood.

The school emphasized as an alternative "small classes, extracurricular activities, early introduction in foreign languages and a degree of self-government most unusual in the public school of that day. There was no tuition and the selection process paid no heed to ethnic origin, race, religion, or color." [19] The self-governing aspect of this experimental school was most intriguing to Dean and was instrumental in helping to develop his keen sense of right and wrong and how one should feel comfortable, almost duty-bound to publicly denounce inequalities on every level.

There were six Harlem boys accepted into the program. Dean and his five classmates from P.S. 5 traveled to and from this experimental school together, both for morale and for safety. Almost every day on the way to the Speyer school, Dean and his friends stopped on 8th Avenue in Harlem to consume several freshly made jellyrolls at the local bakery. These pastries, the aroma of which could be savored several blocks away, were hot, greasy, oval-shaped concoctions with powdered sugar on the outside and red jelly on the inside. The boys ate on the way to school each morning until they got to Morningside Park. Dean and his friends never forgot that this park, which extends from approximately West 110th to 123rd streets, unofficially represented the border that separated the White neighborhood from the Black neighborhood. They were on their guard from this moment until they made it to Speyer. While racial tolerance was emphasized and enforced in school, outside of school a number of students expressed their true feelings on integration. It never failed that after their anxious march through the park, Dean threw up. This involuntary purging was a reaction to his fear of what he just experienced in the park and what was to come after school: "Emptying myself in the morning from those greasy jelly rolls was subconsciously designed to prepare me for the Olympic style running I would have to do in the evening."[20]

Three to four times a week, Dean and his classmates from Harlem had run-ins with White kids who did not welcome their presence at Speyer. They chased Dean and his classmates from the schoolyard at Speyer to the borders of Central Harlem. While the White kids never ventured into the Black section of Harlem, they continued to show distaste for their presence by throwing rocks until Dean and the others were no longer in sight. Dean became quite skilled at dodging those deadly, albeit primitive, weapons. Running down those stairs at Morningside Park, skipping three to four stairs at a time, like "wild mountain goats," the boys developed this zigzag technique, which made it much more difficult for the White kids to get a direct hit.

At home, his everyday routine was becoming more difficult to manage. Dean left for school at approximately seven in the morning, came home around three in the afternoon to discuss with McClara, usually over a glass of milk, how his day at school was, "asking me what had happened in geography, what had happened in geometry, what had happened in algebra, and what the various teachers had said,"[21] and then on to his violin. He paused for dinner and afterward completed his five-hour practice regimen. If there were time left in the day without any homework, he usually went out for a few hours of leisure with his friends. But even with that, he felt the overbearing presence of his mother in his head, never letting up, and always the demanding, unforgiving taskmaster. When he did have homework, it was not uncommon for Dean to be up as late as one in the morning finishing his assignments. McClara was always with him, no matter how late. Dean became increasingly resentful toward his mother at maintaining this torturous schedule. He often lamented that he rarely had time to enjoy his childhood:

> When I had to practice, all of my buddies were out playing stickball or sitting and talking, or across the street in a lot building a fire (before the YWCA dormitory was built). . . . So I was practicing. I had a passage that I had to go over, over, and over again, until I walked to the window, still making the exercises, and watched my buddies playing stickball. . . . I am practicing, and watching the stickball game, but I'm practicing and that's all that's needed. . . . [Then here] comes McClara. . . . That shade went down—the other shade went down, and an hour was added to my practice time. After that, I practiced with the shades down so I wouldn't look out and be distracted. [22]

For Dean, his encounters with his mother escalated into what he character- ized as psychological warfare. He believed his childhood was held hostage. He wanted to be free of McClara's psychological leash but was unable to articulate his concerns without a verbal confrontation. And there were many. There were also many physical punishments throughout Dean's childhood. He remembered most vividly those physical punishments associated with bad habits developed during his practice time.

> I'd be practicing and standing in the fiddle position working on something. I'd have the rhythm going in my knee. That, my mother didn't like. Why? No whys. No wherefores. She didn't like. So they had at that time small black canes—[with a] Charlie Chaplin head and long body—that were sold on pa- rade days, with a small replica of the flag attached so you could wave the flag. She took one of those and stood in the back of me, and every time the back of my knee started—Tack! I got one of those. I guess [it] lasted for a week. Then it hurt so much, the leg stood still. [23]

In 1928, the Dixons' association with David Fagen ended and McClara sought out an instructor who could help Dean achieve a higher artistic profi- ciency on the violin. She discovered Samuel Gardner, who at the time was an established concert violinist and composer teaching privately out of his home on West 119th Street near Columbia University. Gardner was also four years into his tenure as a violin instructor at the Institute of Musical Arts. An arrangement was made for Dean to start lessons with Gardner in March. McClara paid for three lessons in advance ($15) to ensure Dean a spot in his studio. His lessons took place right after school. He was completing his last year at Speyer. In order to make it to his lesson on time, Dean had to catch a trolley immediately following school.

Dean never felt comfortable with his new teacher and sorely missed his musical encounters with David Fagen. One particular encounter with Gard- ner after one of their lessons reminded Dean of uncomfortable moments spent at his Uncle Cliff's saloon.

[After] putting my violin away in the big studio, I came down. He had come down the hall already, [and] was in the bathroom on the washbasin washing his hands. When I came up to him we were facing each other and as he was saying goodbye, it was something to this effect, "Dixon, I do wish you'd wash your hands before you come to your lesson. You know there are times when I might have to touch your fingers and I can't afford to go all day long with dry hands." He was washing his hands after my lesson and he read the riot act to me. At the time I tried to explain to him that I just did make it from school, [and] that in school all day they had nothing but cold water. . . . So, at the time I apologized and mumbled I am very sorry, sorry there's no way for me to wash before I come. "But try to do something about it," [he said]. Here he is washing in warm water with soap, towel, and everything. [Yet] he asks me to arrive at my lesson with clean hands instead of what I have felt ever since I thought it through, of offering to let me wash my hands [in his home].[24]

Dean was not given a chance to explain to Gardner the reason he came to his lesson with dirty hands. Before hopping on the trolley to Gardner's home, Dean was in his gym class engaged in a game of tossing the medicine ball. He normally washed up before leaving school, but that particular day the hot water was not working, and if he tried to find another place to wash, he would miss his trolley and be late for his first lesson with Gardner. Clearly recognizing that no excuse would be acceptable if he came to another lesson with unwashed hands, Dean brought knit gloves with him to gym class. While he succeeded in coming to his second lesson dirt-free, it was not without unceasing ridicule from his gym teacher, followed by laughter from his peers.

We used to have to play ball on an entrance foyer floor (no gym) and the boy's toilet was just across and gradually the wet shoes would be all over the floor and the drinking fountain was a long horse trough type of thing and I remember. . . . I went one day for the medicine ball. I wore gloves so my hands wouldn't get filthy and I got the balling out of my life from my gym teacher. "This is no sissy game, where do you think you are, who do you think you are etc., etc." But I went through this all day in school, grabbed my violin, dashed on to the trolley car, and went up for my lesson.[25]

Dean endured the ridicule because he was well aware of the significant financial sacrifice his mother made in order for him to continue his violin studies. He also did not want word to get back to McClara about his unclean hands preventing Gardner from doing his job properly. This would surely not be acceptable to his mother.

While Dean did not have the close relationship with Gardner that he had with David Fagen, McClara was thrilled that such a highly regarded performer, composer, and instructor took Dean on as one of his pupils. Her excite-

ment was short-lived. On March 15, 1928, sometime after Dean's second
lesson, Gardner wrote McClara to deliver devastating news:

> My Dear Mrs. Dickson [*sic*],
>   After a very thorough trial I feel it is my sincere duty to inform you that I
> can not conscientiously continue teaching your son because he is not fitted by
> nature to be a real violin player. The little he does can be done by any intelli-
> gent child (and he is one) but that does not mean having a definite violin talent.
> Therefore, I cannot continue accepting your hard working money for a work,
> which will not bring good results. Enclosed you will find my check for $5.00
> for which one lesson was still due.
>
>   Yours truly,
>   Samuel Gardner[26]

McClara believed she knew the real story behind the letter. It was suspected that Gardner was receiving complaints about Dean from the tenants in
his building. They were disturbed at seeing a "colored boy" coming up and
down on the elevator. When McClara informed Dean of the letter, he asked
his mother what would be their next move. Although somewhat relieved that
he would no longer be taking lessons from Gardner, Dean was concerned by
his former teacher's assessment of his musical abilities. Not missing a beat,
McClara declared with confidence and authority, that Gardner "is not God"
and that she would find another instructor for him.[27] Dean was deeply moti-
vated by his mother's declaration and determined to continue his studies.
Unfortunately, McClara was unable to afford another instructor of Gardner's
artistic caliber. Dean would not take private lessons again until after high
school. But this would not be his last encounter with Gardner.

Chapter Two

Dean Dixon School of Music

Financially, things were beginning to spiral out of control for the Dixon family. There is no evidence of Henry making any consistent financial contributions to the household. It is not clear whether he was still employed as a porter or employed at all during this time. But there was clearly a need for additional income. Dean tried to fill the financial void. He started his own teaching studio and called it the Dean Dixon School of Music. At age thirteen, he began taking in local boys from the neighborhood to teach violin and piano. He wasn't as proficient on the piano as he was on the violin, but it's likely he picked up enough from David Fagen and McClara to teach beginners. It's during this time that Dean seemed to be desperately searching for a father figure to help him manage his new, albeit unwanted responsibilities as "man of the house." He had no innate sense of how to fulfill these daunting, unfamiliar tasks. The only other male figure outside of school was his Uncle Cliff, and given Dean's past experiences with him, seeking his advice was not an option. Dean found that father figure in the person of Dr. Jim Copeland.

Dr. Copeland was a local medical doctor in the Harlem community who attended to Dean whenever he had issues with asthma. From an early age Dean suffered from severe asthma attacks, and they were usually triggered from allergic reactions to dust, animal dander, stressful situations, and cold weather. During the winter months there were times he spent a number of weeks in bed recovering from attacks due to the cold weather. Dr. Copeland saw Dean a number of times for treatments and their relationship developed beyond doctor and patient. Dr. Copeland clearly saw something special in Dean, beyond his musical talent, and noticed the absence of Henry in his life. He saw in Dean a determined young man committed to providing for his family, by using a skill set that his mother insisted he master—music. The good doctor also recognized an all too familiar situation in Harlem, where the son, for various reasons, had to prematurely take on the financial role of "bread winner." Dr. Copeland did what he could to guide Dean in this new uncharted territory of life. Dean described Dr. Copeland as a man with a heart of gold "who really took care of me like a son."[1] Dean saw in Dr. Copeland a decent man, a father figure, a successful professional, who despite the racial difficulties within and outside his community succeeded, and as a result he provided an ideal model for Dean to follow into adulthood.[2]

Dixon's new responsibilities not only represented his rite of passage into manhood, but they also represented a slight relinquishing of the psychological leash that McClara held. Because of Dixon's much-needed financial contribution, he exercised a bit more assertiveness on those things he could heretofore only dream to do. McClara allowed Dixon to go out more often with his friends for leisurely activities. The daily five-hour practice schedule was relaxed to make time for his teaching schedule, given the slow but steady expansion of his "school of music." He and his friends would spend time going to the movies on Saturday afternoons and playing stickball whenever there were enough boys around to make a team. He particularly enjoyed swimming, even when the environment was not its best. They spent a great deal of their time at the Hudson River. Sporting their standard swimwear of cut-off jeans, they found themselves diving into waters that were strewn with condoms, banana peels, cantaloupe shells, and cigarette butts. They developed their diving and swimming skills by trying to avoid these and other foreign objects. "Living in that jungle, such a thing was quite normal,"[3] Dixon told an interviewer. With this newfound freedom, Dixon slowly began to experience pockets of normalcy in his childhood. The "hooks" were still there, but it was better.

This freedom also exposed him, for the first time, to dealings with the police in Harlem. These encounters were never pleasant, and as a result Dixon built up a hatred for the police that would be with him throughout his life. Dixon and his friends were constantly at odds with the police. It started during the summer months when he and his friends hung out on the steps of Abyssinian Baptist Church on 132 West 138th Street.[4] The church was only a few blocks from Dixon's home. This was where he and his buddies spent their leisure time when it was too "hot and muggy" for stickball and it was too late for swimming in the Hudson. They would sit on those steps or sometimes venture across the street from the church to the steps of selected row houses to talk, sing, and joke. They were often rewarded for their loud verbal expressions with a head full of water thrown on them from out of a window of an anonymous disenchanted resident. There were also evenings during the month of August "when the breezes began to blow between the two rivers." On those unobstructed nights, Dixon and his cohorts walked around the neighborhood looking for something to do or something to get into—whichever came first. They usually found themselves flirting with the neighborhood girls or contemplating a game of stickball. But there were other times when they ventured into mischievous endeavors, which sometimes resulted in satisfying their hunger by stealing sweet potatoes, then finding an empty lot to build a fire to cook their delicious, albeit ill-gotten, spoils. "[These] special long sweet potatoes which we had to throw into the fire and wait until everything looked like black coals down bottom and [then] get them out . . . were the most wonderful tasting things that one could eat anywhere. No mother could cook like that; no home could cook like that."[5] On any given evening, Dixon and his friends were always on the lookout for the police. They were frequently chased off the streets, preventing their stick-ball games from taking place. Even on the steps of the iconic Abyssinian Baptist Church, which became their regular hangout during the summer, they kept an eye out for the police. One person positioned himself in the eastern direction toward Lennox Avenue and another positioned himself in the western direction toward 7th Avenue. If one of the lookouts saw the police he gave the word: "'Jeeze, it's the cops' . . . [and] everyone would stand up and run like bats out of hell as though we were being chased."[6]

No crime had been committed by anyone in the group. They were simply sitting down and enjoying each other's company. But it was the fear of being caught and beaten, if not worse, that prompted the survival instinct of fleeing from the scene. The escape routes were many. Some took to the alleyways and then up the escape ladder to the roof, where they jumped from one roof to the next. One of Dixon's friends went down in his heroic efforts of trying to jump a six- to seven-feet distance from roof to roof. These drastic, and sometimes dangerous, measures of escape were drilled into Dixon and his friends, as well as most neighborhood kids in Harlem, from an early age. No matter the danger of injuring yourself during the escape, it was clear that if you wanted to live, you were not to be caught. It wasn't uncommon for bottles to be thrown and guns to be fired by police for no reason—sometimes hitting their mark. "The whole aspect was anti-police." As Dixon grew older, his reaction when spotting the police changed. Instead of running away, he walked away. He questioned why he had to leave a public place, having done nothing wrong, just because the police appeared. That sense of justice, which was instilled in him at Speyer, and his growing argumentative nature, which he believed was inherited from his "West Indian blood," overrode the fear placed within him as a Harlemite. "Why were we running, what are we doing here that's wrong[?] Why can't we sit and talk here, because we were talking quietly and not disturbing anybody, just a group of five, six, eight boys sitting on the steps of the church and talking[?]"[7]

Dixon's argumentative spirit and sense of justice escalated to a point where he placed himself in harm's way. He was tired of running, tired of walking, tired of avoiding the police as a preemptive measure. He was ready to state his case. He believed that a discussion between him and the police would result in a reasonable solution. Despite hearing reports from friends and neighbors of a number of Harlemites who were beaten or even shot to death for the subtlest exercise of civil disobedience, he prepared himself to face the police officers. When his friends saw the police a few blocks away, heading in their direction, they slowly stood up stretching, pretending they didn't see them coming, and walked away in the opposite direction. Dixon stayed. It's likely that his friends, fearing for his life, strongly encouraged him to follow suit. But he was determined that he would, on this night, stand up for what was right. As a policeman approached Dixon, the officer's body language and facial expression gave no foreshadowing of what he was about to do to Dixon. With no warning, the policeman hauled off and slugged Dixon on the jaw. The officer followed this unexpected physical assault with language that cemented Dixon's belief that his life would truly be in danger if he did not acquiesce and leave the steps of the church as his friends had earlier: "You dirty Black son of a bitch! Get the hell out of here!"[8] For Dixon, "it was another nail in the policeman's coffin. I began to understand better how people learn to hate policemen. It went into my blood [that] policemen are bastards."[9]

Life continued as usual in Harlem for Dixon and McClara. His "school of music" maintained a modest but steady flow of neighborhood kids interested in learning either the violin or piano. He began to understand his role in the Dixon household, and more importantly he began to understand his mother's role. Dixon freely admitted later in his life that while he still believed his mother robbed him of his childhood, he concluded, with more of an appreciative and understanding nature,

> Now after thinking it through until I have arrived at a conclusion I would say—if anyone asked me—that I admire her and what she did for me very much. . . . From her standpoint, this is what she felt; this is what she honestly believed in; this is what she invested all of her eggs into one basket for; this is what she sacrificed for. She didn't know better. She didn't have the modern pedagogic techniques, or learning techniques, or childrearing techniques, or the appreciation of playtime, or leisure time, or relaxation time, or balance. She was part of the jungle, and considering that she brought me up in the jungle, if we look at it that way, she did a fantastic job. . . . Because no matter how she did it, with hands or without hands, with suffering or without suffering. From her point of view she achieved her objective. [10]

That same year, Dixon began his studies at DeWitt Clinton High School.

From its inception, DeWitt Clinton was a fully integrated school, which was not a common occurrence in most public schools in the state of New York. This was bolstered by the fact that in 1900, Theodore Roosevelt, who was then governor of the state of New York, was responsible for the enactment of a law that made it illegal for public schools in New York to deny any person an education on the basis of race. The law, on paper, ended segregation in the public schools of New York.

Dixon successfully auditioned for the DeWitt Clinton Symphony Orchestra and joined the first violin section. Harry A. Jennison was head of the music department at DeWitt Clinton. For many students, he was affectionately referred to as "Pops" Jennison. "In the manner of the old school teacher we read about now but rarely see, he directed people into paths that served them well for the rest of their lives."[11] Jennison encouraged Dixon to continue his violin studies and find as many opportunities as possible to perform outside of school. "He became a very great motivating force in my life, without my knowing that he was. He was one of those who had, I think, an early faith in me. He treated me as a normal student . . . a gentleman of the first water."[12]

There was one incident that happened during a rehearsal at school that would serve as a "prophetic challenge" manifesting itself on numerous occasions throughout Dixon's career. His stand partner, who was already frustrated that a "Negro" sat ahead of him, refused to turn pages, which of course was the customary thing to do. Feeling frustrated and embarrassed by this incident, but at the same time not wanting to cause a scene, Dixon decided to resolve this issue the only way he knew how. Later that night, he memorized his part to all the pieces that would be on slate for tomorrow's rehearsal. Unbeknown to him, his stand partner had the same idea and memorized the same pieces. It was a modern day "face-off." Both boys believed that they had the moral high ground and would prevail in the end. Unfortunately for Dixon's stand partner, he faltered after five minutes of playing from memory and had no choice but to reach over and turn the page. Dixon prevailed and gained the respect of Jennison, who obviously knew what was going on between the two rivals but did not interfere. He knew Dixon had to handle this situation on his own because, unfortunately, this was his fate in life as a young Black man. Dixon quickly learned that it was not enough to be better than your White counterpart was. You had to be prepared to prove yourself worthy of every achievement through continuous challenges.

Dixon followed Jennison's advice and immersed himself in the local music scene, playing in a number of community orchestras along with his good friend Fedele Bonito. Fedele was also a violinist. They met at DeWitt Clinton and quickly became running partners. They spent most of their Saturday afternoons together, playing various duets by Viotti and the like. Dixon loved visiting Fedele's home in the Bronx, because it was yet another opportunity to get away from the pressures of life at home. Fedele had this unique old stand that they used when playing their duets. Candles could be placed on top of the stand and the way it was constructed allowed for two people to use it while facing one another.

During their musical excursions throughout the city, Dixon began to notice an unfortunate trend: "There was a group of us, who used to go from orchestra to orchestra, building up our experience to get into the profession. Never did I meet another Negro on any of these trips. I remember sessions in particular at the Steuben Society in Yorktown, the German section in New York. There I was, playing in the Steuben Society Orchestra and this went on day after day, and I had tremendous experience by that time, but I wasn't meeting any Negroes in these areas."[13] Dixon did not know at the time what could be done to provide more Blacks the opportunity to perform in orchestras, but he concluded the noticeable absence of Blacks playing in orchestras of all levels was unacceptable.

Dixon, his teachers, and friends believed that a career in music was his destiny. McClara, however, wanted him to pursue a career in medicine. She was already making plans to send Dixon away to study medicine at McGill University in Canada. There he would become a pediatric doctor; then he would come back to Harlem and have a successful practice. While she supported all of his musical endeavors as a child, due to the current social climate, she did not believe Dixon would be allowed to make a comfortable living in music. Her concerns were understandable given the scarcity of successful Black classical musicians in Harlem. Another concern McClara had was how he would make a living as a musician given his health issues. Because Dixon suffered from severe asthma attacks, if he pursued a music career as a performer and something happened to him as a result of his asthma, would he be able to perform? And more importantly if not, how would he be able to make a living? These were questions that occupied McClara's thoughts when it came to Dixon's future in music.

Once Jennison discovered the career path chosen for Dixon, he requested a meeting with McClara to convince her that music, not medicine, was Dixon's true calling. Jennison was sure that Dixon would be able to make a living in the field of music. He was obviously very persuasive, because McClara allowed Dixon to move forward in his pursuit of a music career. There was one catch. Being reminded of the elderly Mr. Fagen, Dixon's first violin instructor, McClara wanted to make sure that wherever Dixon studied music, the focus would be teaching, not performance. If Dixon found himself in bed for weeks at a time due to an asthma attack, McClara believed that having a violin studio, where students would come to his home for lessons, would be more financially sustainable than eking out a living as a performer.

Jennison wrote a letter of introduction to Walter Damrosch, a friend, conductor, and brother to Frank Damrosch, who was the founder and director of the Institute of Musical Art (IMA). Jennison also asked McClara to meet with the director of music for the New York City Department of Education, George H. Gartlan. Gartlan knew the Damrosch family and likely assured McClara that she was making the right decision in allowing Dixon to pursue music. On the strength of Jennison's letter and Gartlan's connection with the IMA, Dixon was invited to audition.

Chapter Three

The Damrosch School

Frank Damrosch started the Institute of Musical Arts (IMA) in 1905. His goal was to produce an American conservatory that modeled the comprehensive curriculum and artistic integrity of the established European conservatories. Unlike many American conservatories that were already producing promising young musicians, Damrosch wanted a comprehensive music program that included not just instrumental and vocal training, but "music history, music theory, ear training, orchestration,"[1] and so on. Damrosch remained at the IMA long enough to help usher in the merging of his school and the Juilliard School in 1926. From the inception of the IMA until his departure in 1936, Damrosch auditioned every prospective student. In 1932, it was Dixon's turn. Accompanied by McClara, and violin in hand, Dixon made the trip to 120 Claremont Avenue. Moments after he and McClara entered the building, they were met by this very petite, stern-looking redhead, who seemed a bit surprised to see them. Her name was Helen A. Frank. She served as Damrosch's secretary for forty years and was very protective of her employer's time. Dixon nervously announced to Miss Frank that he was there to play for Mr. Damrosch. McClara waited outside as Dixon was escorted to the director's office. There was a brief introduction and then Dixon was asked to play his prepared piece, which was the Violin Concerto No. 22 in A minor, by Giovanni Battista Viotti. After his audition, Damrosch sat down with Dixon and commented, "You took that tempo a bit fast, didn't you?" To which Dixon responded, "Yes, sir, I guess I was a bit nervous." Damrosch responded by saying, "You have great talent. I congratulate you; you are accepted."[2] While Dixon still had two more entrance exams to take before his acceptance was official, the nervousness he experienced upon entering the director's office was gone. As he left Damrosch's office, the petite, stern-looking redhead that met him as he entered the school showed her true colors. Dixon recalls seeing Miss Frank looking toward him with a newfound respect. As he passed Miss Frank's desk to tell McClara the good news, she spouted with no preamble, "You must have been damned good!"[3] Dixon smiled at the remark and knew he had a friend in Miss Frank. He successfully completed his music theory and ear training exam, and was officially accepted into the IMA music program.

In the fall of 1932, Dixon was faced with a dilemma. As he was preparing himself to begin his matriculation at the IMA as a violin major, McClara reminded Dixon that she allowed him to pursue a music career on the condition he would study to be a music teacher, not a music performer. Moreover, because there was no degree offered for violin majors, McClara saw this as a total waste of time and effort. The only degrees given at the IMA during this time were public school music, music supervisor, and music pedagogy. Dixon honored his promise to McClara and changed his major to public school music. But the most pressing issue that plagued Dixon throughout his time at the IMA was how he would pay for his education. In the 1930s, tuition at the IMA for those majoring in public school music was $330 a year.[4] McClara was in no position to help, and the school did not provide any financial assistance. This financial burden fell squarely on Dixon. Not knowing how he was going to fulfill this financial obligation, Dixon approached his new best friend for help—Miss Frank. She used her considerable influence to allow Dixon to pay in very small installments—meaning whenever he could with whatever he made that previous weekend teaching. "I paid $3.00 one day, 75 cents another day, $1.50 another day, and $5.00 after a bonanza weekend. That's the way I paid."[5]

Now that Dixon had the financial aspect of his education under some control, he began focusing on his course load. While his course work was focused in the public school arena, meaning academic, scientific, pedagogic work; his performance studies continued unhindered.

This full and comprehensive schedule left little time for anything else:

Monday: English Diction, Chorus, General and Education Psychology
Tuesday: Singing, Wind and String Instruments
Wednesday: Violin, Piano, Dalcroze, General and Education Psychology
Thursday: No class
Friday: Singing, Ear training, Rhetoric, Methods I, Elements of Conducting, Orchestra
Saturday: Piano, Methods I, Junior Orchestra

As Dixon settled into being a full-time student at the IMA, he often reminisced on those days when he and his musician friends went on their musical excursions throughout the city performing with different orchestras. This was a bittersweet memory, because he also recalled the disappointment in discovering that with each orchestra he played in, no other Blacks could be found. He was the first and only.

Now was the time to follow through on a dream that stayed with him since his time at DeWitt Clinton.

It all started when Dixon discovered that the local Urban League and the NAACP were beginning to question segregation practices in the workplace throughout New York City. In Dixon's mind, looking into the hiring practices in the field of classical music had a clear "double-edged sword" implication. On the one hand, putting pressure on these music organizations to be more inclusive to non-Whites was admirable. On the other hand, what would happen if these civil rights organizations actually succeeded in their efforts to break through this bastion of elitism? Dixon believed the results would be catastrophic, because there were simply not enough Black classically trained musicians who could win an audition with a professional orchestra. Dixon knew you could find some of the greatest jazz and popular instrumentalists in the world right there in Harlem, but you would be hard-pressed to find any who were classically trained. He clearly understood the difference. He believed that the professional orchestras in the city also understood the difference, but were prepared to appease the civil rights groups by extending an invitation to these jazz musicians to audition, fully aware that they would not succeed. Although still very young, Dixon had acquired a wealth of experience as a teacher and performer and wanted to give back to the community that supported him from the very beginning. He didn't know if it would succeed, but he wanted to create a training orchestra in Harlem whose primary mission was to develop the classical repertory and performance practice for those aspiring Black musicians whose experience fell under blues and jazz. With two of his students, one a pianist and the other a violinist, he founded the Dean Dixon Symphony Orchestra. His first rehearsal took place in a theater located in the basement of the local Harlem YMCA on 180 W. 135th Street. Dixon was fortunate to secure space in this new building when he did. The "135th Street Branch YMCA" opened its doors on January 1, 1933. Three years later the name was changed to the "Harlem YMCA." This eleven-story edifice was the hub of Harlem. Numerous entertainers, politicians, and athletes made it their business to stop by the "Harlem Y" for various events.

The musicians of the Dean Dixon Symphony Orchestra were made up of men and women of all ages drawn from the neighborhood and beyond. His initial intent was to create an all-Negro orchestra. He believed that the success of such an orchestra would do wonders to break many of the pervasive stereotypes that plagued his community when it came to the acceptance of Blacks in classical music, particularly instrumentalists and conductors. Dixon quickly discovered that there were two big problems with this idea. First, because so few Blacks were given the opportunity to play classical music in an ensemble setting, he would not only have to teach prospective members how to play an instrument from scratch, but he would also have to re-train those prospective members who played an instrument well, but not in the European classical tradition. This prospect would take too long to yield the kind of results that he dreamed about. Secondly, Dixon was a true integrationist. What if this "separate but equal" ensemble was successful? Dixon did not want to do anything that supported, directly or indirectly, the philosophy of keeping the "races" separate. In this case he believed that the end would not justify the means. So the idea of an all-Black orchestra was abandoned. Dixon's only requirement for entry into the orchestra was "some technical proficiency and a sincere desire to make beautiful music."[6] All were welcomed. But it was very tough in the beginning. "In those lean years, getting the necessary music meant going without lunches for months on end. We would buy the music for the violins one month and the music for the horns the next. . . . I guess you could say we rehearsed Schubert's Unfinished Symphony on the installment plan."[7]

In his first year at the IMA, there were a group of boys that Dixon gravitated toward. They were five out of the approximately sixty-nine students that started the same year in the public school music program. Louis Valentino, Herbie Fine, Phil Kessler, Herbie Schiffmiller, and Dixon were virtually inseparable because they shared a paradigm that was predicated on the belief that the course curriculum was neither intellectually nor musically stimulating. They set their own goals of expectation that, to them, far exceeded the school curriculum. For example, if the curriculum in instrumental methods stated that they had to learn how to play one woodwind, one brass, one percussion, and one string instrument, they took it to another level and learned two woodwind, three brass, four percussion, and all the string instruments. It became a friendly, but serious, competition on who could learn the most instruments and play them well. Dixon found himself on many occasions heading home on the train working on his embouchure with a tuba or French horn mouthpiece. The Five learned how to play every instrument in the orchestra well enough to sit in on rehearsals playing an instrument of their choosing. They tested their newfound proficiency every Tuesday and Friday in Mr. Adolf Schmid's wind and string methods class. The Five were constantly eyeing one another during class to see who might be getting the upper hand on any particular instrument. Dixon recalled, "You knew that wherever the five were sitting they had eyes on you. They were watching to see what you didn't play; they were watching your fingering, how high you went in the position, starting in first position [on the cello], suddenly you flip up to the third. Aha! Bastard, he's got the third position! When did he get that?"[8]

In 1932, Dixon began presenting "music appreciation hour" at the public library on Lennox and 135th Street. Those sessions consisted of games and recordings. Dixon and his local colleagues demonstrated the sounds of orchestra by playing various instruments, which brought a large number of kids from the neighborhood in from the streets to see what the commotion was about. Dixon's philosophy for his "school of music" was not only to present great music through quality performances, but to find innovative ways to educate and inspire kids of all ages in his neighborhood about the joy of classical music. For many in his neighborhood, classical music was something far removed from their everyday life. Dixon believed that exposure to classical music at the earliest age was the key to true appreciation.

Dixon had a great relationship with the instrument caretaker and music librarian at the IMA. His name was Felix Gottlicher. He took a shine to Dixon from the very start. "Felix loved me as I loved him. It was with him that I was able to go so far with the instruments because I could take whichever instrument I wanted home."[9] Dixon described Gottlicher as a short, stout German with a very short temper. That temper was demonstrated on a number of occasions when dealing with faculty and students who seemingly showed little respect for him and his commitment to keeping his instrument inventory and music library intact. Dixon, who could often be seen perusing the instrument inventory, or looking at orchestral scores, experienced his temper firsthand. On one particular morning, Dixon came in early to return an instrument he borrowed the night before and to check out another. Gottlicher trusted Dixon so completely that he provided him a key to come and go as he pleased. Shortly after Dixon arrived that day, Gottlicher came storming into his caged domain, his face red with anger, speaking half English and German, both of which were barely understood. However, Dixon clearly understood the expletives spewing from his mouth like flowing water as he entered the room. He was impressed that such a large man moved with grace and efficiency, even in the midst of being enraged. But it was those volatile moments that Dixon knew not to say a mumbling word. "I knew when not to speak to him, not to bother him. I was a piece of furniture."[10]

It was only when Gottlicher calmed down that he realized Dixon was in the room. "Oh, it's you," he said to Dixon. But before Dixon could respond, Gottlicher remembered what he was upset about and mumbled with great intensity, "Oh, that bastard . . . he comes in at the last minute . . . he always . . . "[11] Dixon never found out the details behind this outburst and wisely decided not to investigate the matter.

Dixon had to expand his teaching load to pay for his studies at the IMA and to fund his new orchestra in Harlem. Learning those new instruments came in handy. He taught cello, viola, piano, singing, and composition. His Saturdays and Sundays were devoted to teaching from 7 a.m. to 11:30 p.m. In some cases he finished with his last student past midnight. These were all Harlem residents, so it was easy to continue his teaching in his home. The same room that he was forced to practice in every single day was now the room in which he taught his students. The neighbors in Harlem were very accommodating to the strange sounds that were emanating from his apartment. McClara was very understanding with her home being turned into a private studio every Saturday and Sunday. Dixon was able to meet all of his financial obligations as a result of his teaching, and that made McClara both happy and relieved. No longer did she worry as to how her son would survive in the music profession.

Of all the courses that Dixon took at the IMA, the one that had to be the most interesting, if not awkward, was his violin lessons with Samuel Gardner. This was the same Samuel Gardner who wrote McClara back in 1928 to inform her that Dixon had no future as a violinist and that he would no longer be teaching him. Because of the bitterness Dixon had for Gardner, it was almost certain that he had no say as to who would be his violin instructor. When McClara found out the predicament Dixon was placed in, she simply told him to forgive and forget. Dixon neither forgave nor forgot Gardner's premature assessment of him in 1928, but he had no choice but to move forward. By all accounts, things seemed to work out well. Gardner's semester reports on Dixon were consistently positive. In 1934, Dixon's lessons with Gardner led to his first solo recital at the YWCA in Harlem. This recital was not designed to fulfill any requirements at the IMA, given Dixon's major. It's more likely that he presented this recital for his current students, demonstrating concert preparation and etiquette. It was also a clever way to recruit for new students. Dixon invited all of his friends from the neighborhood, his friends from the IMA, students from his studio, and anyone else with a passing interest to attend his debut recital. Curiously, Dixon did not invite Gardner. When McClara found out her son was performing one of his teacher's compositions, she wisely corrected the intentional omission. When Dixon performed Gardner's *From the Canebrake*, op. 5, McClara told her son that Gardner was very pleased with his performance, saying to McClara, "I will make a Russian violinist out of him yet!" [12]

Dixon experienced many racial encounters in New York that changed his perspective on life and humanity. But nothing compared to his first encounter with racial bias in the Deep South. One summer, Dixon agreed to travel to Ft. Lauderdale, Florida, with one of his best friends, Sylvanus Hart III. They were going down to pick up a car from Hart's grandfather. The plan was to make their way down to Ft. Lauderdale and drive the car back to New York. As Dixon and Hart set out to New York in their newly acquired car, something happened that could have easily cost them their lives. Dixon pulled up to a gas station in Ft. Lauderdale to fill up the car for the journey ahead. He asked the attendant if there was a restroom he could use. The response from the attendant was "not for you." Dixon, who had just paid to have the car serviced, was livid that he could not use the restroom in the same place that just took his money and he was about to let the attendant know exactly how he felt about this unacceptable treatment. Hart, knowing Dixon well, quickly went over to the driver side of the car and with no preamble pushed him inside. As they drove a few miles away from the station, Hart spotted an area where Dixon could relieve himself. It was clear that Dixon had no idea of the consequences for objecting to this kind of treatment in the Deep South. Hart explained to Dixon in very clear terms that he was not in New York and if he had made a scene, their lives would have most definitely been in danger. Hart tried to calm Dixon down, but with no success. As Dixon took the wheel again, he had no idea he was speeding. It didn't take long for a police car to show up. Dixon was given a $20 speeding ticket, payable immediately. He explained to the officer that he didn't have the money. Dixon was arrested, taken down to the station, and placed in a roach-infested jail for eight hours, while Hart rushed to his grandfather's home to get the money needed to bail him out. Decades would pass before Dixon ventured back to the Deep South.

Dixon's fascination with teaching music to children was encouraged by Miss Lucy Morrison. Miss Morrison was the chorus instructor at P.S. 103 in the Bronx and worked with a number of the public school music students at the IMA. Dixon was one of her favorite students, and she was one of his favorite teachers. Dixon described her as a true intellectual. She knew her craft, but was open to new ideas in teaching. She allowed her students from the IMA to think outside of the box. She was enthusiastic about her work. She did very little teaching from a formal lecture point of view. Instead, she allowed teaching moments to come in the form of observations of her "student teachers" in the classroom. Dixon flourished and learned a great deal from Miss Morrison. On one occasion, Miss Morrison was giving an overview of the music curriculum for elementary students in New York City. It all sounded fine to Dixon, until Miss Morrison got to the section that talked about what grade you were supposed to teach part-singing. Dixon was surprised when she said that the third grade was the accepted grade level that students could learn this skill and understand it. Dixon was in total disagreement with this conclusion. He had obviously experienced something different in his community with younger children who were able to comprehend and demonstrate the concept of part-singing. When Dixon asked Miss Morrison why kindergartners could not experience this, she responded by saying that it had never been tried with kindergartners. Dixon asked Miss Morrison if he could try it with her class. Intrigued, Miss Morrison allowed Dixon to experiment with her class. He quickly moved to action by separating the class into three sections, one section on the left, one to the right, and one in the middle. Dixon took a few moments to explain to the excited kindergartners what he wanted them to do. He navigated from section to section with very specific instructions. He then asked them all to sing "Row, Row, Row Your Boat." Dixon moved from section to section like a mad man with a mission cueing each section's entrance! After a few rehearsals, Dixon was successful in creating simple harmonies to accompany this very familiar song. Miss Morrison was so impressed with Dixon's successful demonstration, that she invited all of the public school music students from the IMA to observe Dixon's experiment. The students at the IMA were surprised to see Dixon sprinting from one section to the next starting the young singers to create the three-part singing. It was unlike anything they had seen in the classroom, but it worked!

During his last year at the IMA, Dixon attended a concert next door at the Juilliard School. He had a chance to see graduate conducting students for the first time. He was very interested in the program but wasn't convinced he had enough experience or talent to apply. It had been three years since he started his own orchestra in Harlem. Dixon's impetus for creating the orchestra was to provide an opportunity to educate, not to become a professional conductor. But something happened along the way as the orchestra began to flourish. He realized he had an affinity for the art of conducting and believed that he was able to convey his musical intentions more effectively as a conductor than as a violinist. After the concert Dixon felt a sense of relief overtake him. He realized that none of the graduate students he saw were doing anything that was beyond his comprehension. He decided at that moment to apply to the graduate program in conducting.

Chapter Four

Pursuing the Dream

Dixon recalled inquiring with Oscar Wagner (who was then the assistant dean at Juilliard) as to what was needed to apply for the graduate program. According to Dixon, as Wagner went through the audition process, he focused a great deal on the piano requirements. Knowing Dixon's limited ability on the piano, Wagner discouraged him from auditioning, believing that he would not get beyond the first round. Not at all fazed by the discouragement, Dixon inquired further about the piano requirements. He was told to prepare a Beethoven sonata of his choosing and a Prelude from Bach's *Well-Tempered Clavier*. Dixon spent the entire summer preparing for his piano exams. He was determined not to allow his piano deficiency to prevent him from getting on the podium. As luck would have it, Wagner was wrong on the order of the audition. The first round of the audition was the conducting portion. Dixon was relieved to know that he would at least get an opportunity to conduct before the impressive panel of judges: Ernest Hutcheson (dean of the Juilliard School), John Erskie (president), Oscar Wagner (assistant dean), and Albert Stoessel (director of the orchestra and opera program). Dixon quickly realized that this was a big deal to have all these dignitaries in one place to select the next batch of conducting students. Once Dixon entered the examination room and began to conduct, he knew that this was going to work out. "The conducting exam went so well that I could have gone in without knowing what the piano looked like."[1] Dixon believed he impressed the entire panel with his conducting. This was confirmed when he later discovered from members of the Juilliard orchestra that he was the only student from the audition invited to come and speak to Ernest Hutcheson and the rest of the panelists. As Hutcheson read through Dixon's list of accomplishments at the IMA, while impressed with the fact that he could play every instrument in the orchestra, nothing in those reports gave them any indication of what they had just experienced from the young maestro on the podium. They were very interested to know how Dixon could be so proficient and calm on the podium, with very limited exposure to conducting at the IMA. Dixon modestly responded, "I don't know. It's the way I feel the music."[2] It is unknown whether Dixon informed the panel of adjudicators that at the time of the audition he had been developing his conducting skills with an orchestra, albeit amateur, for the last three years. In the end Dixon was accepted into the graduate conducting program at Juilliard. This entitled him to a fellowship, which Dixon referred to as "getting honey from heaven. . . . No tuition, practice rooms, lunch cards, and a bit of pocket money."[3] In fact, as a fellowship recipient, Dixon received $2,500, which was renewable each year.

While McClara was pleased with Dixon's acceptance into the graduate program at Juilliard, she felt he could do much more in the field of music education. She strongly encouraged him to continue his academic studies by applying to Teachers College, Columbia University (a prominent graduate school of education). Dixon tried to explain to McClara that the fellowship at Juilliard was a full-time job, and to add on another full-time graduate program would make it nearly impossible to continue with his full-time teaching schedule (which was the only source of income at the time for him and his mother), his orchestra in Harlem, and his new chorus society. McClara, once again, got her way. In the fall of 1937, Dixon was a full-time graduate student at the Teachers College, majoring in music education. In Dixon's house and even within his culture, it was not unusual to have more than one job or pursue several interests at the same time. He was "multi-tasking" long before the word was a popular saying in the American lexicon. These multi-tasked goals represented something that Dixon often spoke privately about and that most Black parents told their children: "You have to do more than anyone else in order to get half of the credit."[4]

Dixon studied conducting with Albert Stoessel. Ernest Hutcheson brought the protégé of Walter Damrosch to Juilliard to help develop a string orchestra he had organized in 1927. In 1930, Stoessel left New York University, where he served as chair of the music department, to direct the orchestra and opera program at Juilliard. That same year he created a conducting course. Hutcheson knew Stoessel from their collaborations at Chautauqua.[5] It was clear from the beginning of their complex relationship that Stoessel recognized Dixon's talent. Dixon desired so much to have a mentor that could help him navigate through the extensive orchestral repertoire, as well as someone who could advise him on how to best further his career as an orchestral conductor. While Dixon did not find Stoessel to be the mentor he so desperately longed for, he managed to learn from him through observation. Most of his observations were done while playing in the Juilliard Orchestra. Although Dixon's primary instrument was violin, he was asked on occasion to play viola, which seemed to impress both Stoessel and members of the orchestra, given the high level of artistry in the ensemble. Dixon's stand partner was also a conducting fellow. They got along nicely and used their time together to critique what Stoessel was doing on the podium.

Those informal chats helped to form in Dixon's mind very clear philosophical views on the art and psychology of conducting. Dixon used Stoessel's successes and failures on the podium as a way of developing his craft, experimenting on what he observed with his Harlem orchestra. On rare occasions, Stoessel allowed Dixon to take the baton and conduct the orchestra when he needed to listen to the group from afar for balance and overall flow. During those moments, it was imperative that Dixon maintain the exact tempos given by Stoessel. He ran a very efficient rehearsal and had a metronomic mind, both of which fascinated Dixon. Stoessel was able to beat out a tempo marking without the use of a metronome. And it was expected that all of his students develop this skill. When Dixon was asked to beat out the metronomic marking of 76 for a movement in some Tchaikovsky symphony, he was shocked by the request, but "I wasn't going to say I don't know 76, so I went Bup, Bup, Bup up to 76 and he just sat there listening to me."[6] After a few seconds of silence, which seemed like an eternity, Stoessel responded, "Close enough." Well, this was a failure in Dixon's mind. He was determined that if asked again, he would be prepared to answer without having to guess. For the next month everywhere he went he carried alongside him, in a huge brown paper sack, his pendulum-driven metronome. Whenever there was a moment to think about music, he had his metronome out ticking away. Dixon learned a valuable lesson from this encounter. Music was not just about playing the right notes, balance, good ensemble, and warm sounds. In addition to all of those things music had to have a clear sense of pacing. You needed to possess a clear idea of what tempo worked best with a musical phrase, not to be confused with adhering to a metronome marking (quarter note equals . . .). Dixon believed that music needed to "breathe" and one has to understand how tempos vary based on the organization of the music and the composer's intent. For Dixon, this became an essential part of the conductor's métier.

According to Dixon, he had heated disagreements with Stoessel on many philosophical issues related to conducting. One in particular that Dixon noted was the axiom that the conductor was always right. Dixon observed a number of major mistakes made by Stoessel, only to see him either not acknowledge his mistake or blame someone in the orchestra for a mistake that was not their fault. The belief for that generation of conductors was that if you admitted you were wrong at any level, you would be considered weak or, worse, incompetent. Dixon believed it was a sign of strength and confidence in one's ability to admit when you made a mistake on the podium. While he didn't condone Stoessel's refusal to admit his mistakes, he understood the misguided psychology behind it.

Dixon's relationship with Stoessel was tested to its breaking point on two recurring occasions. In addition to his duties at Juilliard, Stoessel was the musical director of the Chautauqua Institution and conducted the symphony orchestra. Each summer, Stoessel selected a number of his top players at Juilliard to accompany him to Chautauqua, New York. This was a great opportunity for young instrumentalists to get experience playing with a professional orchestra and receive a good wage for their services. While Dixon was one of Stoessel's top violists at Juilliard, he was never extended an invitation to perform at the summer music festival. He clearly could have benefited from the experience and money. Although never stated by Stoessel, Dixon believed he was concerned that the people of Chautauqua would not be accepting of a Negro performing in their orchestra, not to mention the backlash Stoessel could suffer if such an invitation were extended. Stoessel knew Dixon was frustrated by this decision. But instead of sitting down and speaking with Dixon directly, he asked a mutual friend to speak with him, Felix Gottlicher. Gottlicher prepared all of the music to be performed at Chautauqua and helped with the logistics of selecting those students who would accompany Stoessel to Chautauqua. Gottlicher told Dixon that Stoessel felt bad that he was unable to invite him, but that his hands were tied. Dixon understood the reason behind the decision, but still believed that Stoessel could have advocated more for his inclusion. Dixon was further dejected on those occasions when Stoessel convened with his conducting students to discuss job vacancies at various universities and symphony orchestra societies. These institutions and organizations wrote to Stoessel on a regular basis, requesting his recommendations for conductors. As Stoessel disseminated the inquiry letters to the students he felt best suited, Dixon was left empty-handed each time. He didn't understand why the school accepted him into the graduate program, if they were not going to follow through and help him achieve his goals outside of the protective walls of Juilliard.

For five years, Dixon and his Harlem orchestra struggled to stay afloat. But in 1937, things took a turn for the better. Dixon was approached by a group of women in the Harlem community that were impressed with his mission and what he had accomplished thus far with no outside financial assistance. They offered to help him raise money and to get the word out about all aspects of his "school of music," which now encompassed his private studio, music appreciation hour, his orchestra, and his chorus society. Things began to really look up. With the participation of his Juilliard colleagues, the orchestra grew in size and performance ability; so much so, that Dixon planned to perform a Beethoven symphony every year. Dixon also began plans to take his Harlem orchestra outside his neighborhood for performances.

Some of the Juilliard players in Dixon's Harlem orchestra also played in a professional chamber orchestra called the League of Music Lovers Chamber Orchestra. The chamber orchestra was made up of twenty-two string players. The group was planning a performance at Town Hall, when their conductor left due to a disagreement with its director, Eddie Shine. The Juilliard students spoke to Shine about Dixon and persuaded him to give the young maestro a chance.

On May 7, 1938, Dixon made his professional conducting debut with the League of Music Lovers Chamber Orchestra at Town Hall. The program was clearly a Baroque affair, including Bach's *Brandenburg Concerto* in G, Concerto in D minor for piano and orchestra, Suite in B minor for flute and strings; Handel's Concerto Grosso in B minor; and Corelli's Concerto Grosso in G minor.[7] By all accounts the concert was a success. Dixon approached this concert like any other event. He understood that success was the only outcome. His colleagues at Juilliard put their reputations on the line by recommending him for the guest post. He was not going to let them down. He took control of the rehearsals in the same calm, self-assured manner he had become known for at Juilliard and with his Harlem orchestra. His conducting was matter of fact, but with purpose. Dixon was never the "showboat" conductor that so many in his field were infamous for. His score preparation was impeccable and his rehearsal technique was efficient, clear, and meaningful. He knew exactly what he wanted from the orchestra. The orchestra appreciated these traits, which were usually attributable to someone much older, and played for him without hesitation from the very beginning. According to music critics of the *New York Times* and *New York Sun*, the highlight of the concert was Bach's Concerto in D minor, with Vivian Rivkin as the solo pianist. This was the first of many collaborations between Dixon and Rivkin.

Word quickly got out about this Negro conductor from Juilliard. His knowledge, talent, professionalism, and charm were a surprise to all who heard about the young maestro from Harlem. He was back in Town Hall a year later to conduct another professional chamber orchestra that he founded. The New York Chamber Orchestra was made up of musician friends from Juilliard, the New York Philharmonic, the NBC Symphony, and other professional orchestras in New York City. Dixon invited Rivkin to perform concertos by Shostakovich and Mozart.

In the spring of 1939, Dixon graduated from the Juilliard Graduate School "on advice." To graduate "on advice" was an honor granted to the most gifted of students. They were allowed to come back and seek advice from their teachers as they began their music careers. That same year, Dixon also finished his graduate studies at Columbia University, graduating with a master of arts degree in education. Soon after Dixon enrolled at Columbia to study for his Ph.D. in education.

Dixon's Harlem orchestra grew into a seventy-two-piece orchestra with a complete instrumentation. The tradition of one rehearsal a week and one concert a year was just the right speed for this amateur orchestra. The civic-minded women who joined forces with him in 1937 to help bring money and more publicity to his organization succeeded. On April 2, 1939, Dixon celebrated his fifth season as founder and director of the Dean Dixon Symphony Orchestra, performing works by Haydn and Beethoven and featuring pianist Lydia Mason (a young Black pianist who taught privately in New York), who performed the Bach D minor Piano Concerto. The Dean Dixon Choral Society made its debut that same evening, performing works by Handel, Elgar, Shaw, Schubert, Nikolsky, and Rachmaninoff. Tickets for the event were very reasonable, ranging from $0.50 to $1.50. Dixon made sure that there were always at least three hundred free tickets set aside for students in the Harlem community. Even as his reputation grew throughout the city, Dixon never forgot about his first orchestra and the community he grew up in that made it all possible.

Dixon's career was on the rise. He was a respected conductor, educator, and public speaker. But someone came along to assist Dixon in a way that ignited the trajectory of his career in a way no one could have imagined— First Lady Eleanor Roosevelt.

Chapter Five

Eleanor Roosevelt

In 1936, Marian Anderson, the internationally acclaimed contralto, presented a benefit concert for Howard University's School of Music. This became an annual affair and by 1939 the organizers of the event needed to find a bigger venue to accommodate the growing support of this cause and the growing reputation of Anderson. Sol Hurok, Anderson's manager, requested the use of Constitution Hall for a benefit concert scheduled that year over the Easter weekend. There was only one problem. The Daughters of the American Revolution (DAR) owned the concert hall. The DAR was founded in 1890 and made up of a select group of women who could trace their lineage back to patriots of the American Revolution. Constitution Hall opened its doors in 1929 and was the crown jewel of the DAR. This architectural masterpiece was an ideal facility for Anderson's benefit concert, given that it was the largest auditorium in the District of Columbia, with a seating capacity of four thousand. Hurok was told by the DAR that the date requested was booked. He later discovered that it had nothing to do with scheduling, but everything to do with Anderson being Black. Paul Robeson (singer, actor, civil rights activist) was another Black artist that was prohibited from performing at Constitution Hall in 1930. Harold Ickes, who was secretary of interior with the Roosevelt administration, was pressured by Hurok and the newly formed Marian Anderson Citizens Committee (MACC) to try and convince the DAR to change their mind. Ickes was unsuccessful. When Mrs. Roosevelt discovered the decision made by the DAR, she had no choice but to act. She publicly resigned her membership. In a letter to the president of the DAR, she stated, "I am in complete disagreement with the attitude taken in refusing Constitution Hall to a great artist. You have set an example which seems to me unfortunate, and I feel obliged to send in to you my resignation. You had an opportunity to lead in an enlightened way and it seems to me that your organization has failed."[1] This public display by Mrs. Roosevelt ignited out-rage from politicians, entertainers, and dignitaries throughout the country. Meanwhile, Mrs. Roosevelt, Ickes, and others quietly began organizing a concert and finding a venue that would meet all of Anderson's needs. Once the logistics were worked out, Ickes, who himself was a past president of the Chicago NAACP, requested permission from President Roosevelt to move forward with the event. The president approved the request and on April 9, Easter Sunday, Marian Anderson performed on the steps of the Lincoln Memorial to an enthusiastic, integrated crowd of seventy-five thousand. Many more heard the concert over the radio. Fearing that her presence would overshadow Anderson's historic moment, Mrs. Roosevelt did not attend the outdoor celebration. In supporting Anderson's civil rights, Mrs. Roosevelt brought national attention to this country's racial divide like no other before her. This would not be the last time Mrs. Roosevelt reached out to a Black classical musician.

The rising notoriety of Dixon and his orchestra in Harlem caught the attention of Mrs. Roosevelt. She made it possible for Dixon to fulfill one of his dreams for the Harlem orchestra—to perform outside the borders of his neighborhood. On May 18, 1941, Dixon gave a performance with his orches-tra at the Heckscher Theater on 5th Avenue and 104th Street. In attendance were Mrs. Roosevelt and her close friend, Major Henry Hooker. While she did not make a speech at the concert, she allowed her name to be used to promote it. The concert program consisted of Haydn's Overture to *L'Isola disabita*, Holst's Fugel Concerto for flute and oboe, Bach's Arioso transcribed for strings by Sam Franko, the finale from Tchaikovsky's Sere-nade for Strings, and Beethoven's *Eroica* Symphony. Mrs. Roosevelt stayed for the entire concert. As warmly as the audience responded to the respect-able performance of Dean Dixon and his orchestra, they equally responded to Mrs. Roosevelt as she departed the theater. After the concert, she met Dixon at a party given in his honor to congratulate him for a job well done. Mrs. Roosevelt later penned her thoughts on the concert in her "My Day" column. She wrote, "My brother, Major Henry Hooker and I enjoyed the Dean Dixon concert last night very much. It was remarkable that a group, largely made up of amateurs, could be brought together through the conductor's ability and achieve such a good performance."[2] This syndicated column, which was published widely, reached millions of Americans. Dixon's rising notoriety in New York soared to national recognition after Mrs. Roosevelt's endorsement of his talents. Longtime music critic and composer Virgil Thomson's review both praised Dixon's performance at the Hecksher Theater and served as an indictment of those who continued to refuse Negro classical musicians the opportunity to perform.

It is not possible to make any generalizations of moment about Negro conducting from the work of one conductor, nor to say which of his qualities are personal gifts and which are racial facilities. That Mr. Dixon is a good musician and a gifted conductor not without experience is evident. That Negro musicians have for a long time lacked opportunities to play in classical orchestral ensembles is well known. That there is such an opportunity now available to them is cause for rejoicing. Because it is absurd that colored people of good musical education should be constrained by mere organizational defects in our society to working always in the folk and popular styles.[3]

Days before the concert, Oscar Wagner, who had been promoted to dean of the Juilliard School by this time, was in communication with Samuel Chotzinoff, music director for the National Broadcasting Corporation (NBC), trying to convince him to give Dixon an opportunity to conduct Toscanini's orchestra. Chotzinoff was intrigued by the prospect of having Dixon conduct the orchestra, especially given Mrs. Roosevelt's support of the young maestro. But there were major risks involved with bringing a Negro conductor to NBC. So before any decision was made, Chotzinoff spoke with David Sarnoff, the head of the Radio Corporation of America (RCA) and NBC, and they both agreed to attend the performance the night that Mrs. Roosevelt was in attendance, before making a decision. Both Sarnoff and Chotzinoff were impressed with Dixon's musicianship and authority on the podium. After discussing the matter with Maestro Toscanini, the decision was made. Dixon was engaged by the NBC Summer Symphony to conduct two of their Saturday night concerts. The performances occurred on June 21 and 28, 1941. It was broadcasted over the NBC-Blue Network from 9:30 to 10:30 p.m. The program on June 21 was Brahms's *Academic Festival* Overture, Strauss's *Don Juan*, Tchaikovsky's Overture to *Romeo and Juliet Fantasy-Overture*, and Saint-Saens's *Danse Macabre*. The program on June 28 was Von Weber's Overture to *Oberon*, Haydn's Symphony No. 88 in G-Major, Bach's Arioso, and Dello-Joio's Sinfonietta.

As Dixon was preparing for his first rehearsal with the NBC Summer Symphony, he was called into Sarnoff's office. As they got closer to the radio broadcast, it seemed that both Sarnoff and Chotzinoff were becoming increasingly concerned about how people would react to Dixon's appearance. Specifically, Chotzinoff was concerned about the orchestra's reaction to Dixon and Sarnoff was concerned about the sponsor's reaction. Sarnoff explained to Dixon in no uncertain terms that he must succeed. He was taking a huge chance with his Southern listeners by having Dixon on the radio program, but he was also impressed with Dixon's talent and demeanor on and off the podium. Sarnoff believed that Dixon deserved this chance. Chotzinoff's concern about how the orchestra would respond to Dixon was put to rest after he observed Dixon's first rehearsal. "The guest conductor stepped to the podium, raised his baton and the men gave him everything he

asked for. He knew exactly what he wanted and wasted no time talking.
From the beginning he was the master of the situation."[4] Another observer
noted Dixon's salutation before he started his first rehearsal with Toscanini's
orchestra: "I hope when I have finished, you will think as highly of me as I
do of you."[5] Dixon did, however, encounter some resistance from members
of the NBC Summer Symphony, originating with the associate concertmaster. The orchestra had the same personnel as in the regular season, with one
exception. The concertmaster did not have to participate in the summer concerts and therefore the duties of concertmaster were given to his associate.
The incident took place during a rehearsal of Strauss's *Don Juan*. It was
normal for the musicians to comment or to ask questions about tempo, balance, and so forth. It was also normal for Dixon, as the conductor, to correct
the orchestra when what they played did not correspond with the composer's
wishes. As the rehearsal progressed, the orchestra came to the section in *Don
Juan* where it called for *un poco agitato*. Dixon noticed that the first violins
were playing more of a *tranquillo* style than the *agitato* style requested by
Strauss.

> And when I finally stopped the orchestra and asked for my correction one of
> the points was, "Is it possible that at letter or bar whatever that you could play
> a bit more *agitato* rather than too calmly." At this he [associate concertmaster]
> flared up, he blew a gasket so to speak, and sort of turned it right away; "What
> do you mean? You don't like my playing?" I replied, "It has nothing to do with
> that. It's just that Strauss has written *agitato*, and I would like to have a bit
> more *agitato*."[6]

Dixon realized that soon after his verbal exchange with the associate concertmaster, some members of the orchestra were visibly disturbed by what had
just happened. He later discovered that there were a number of musicians in
the orchestra who were vehemently opposed to him being allowed to conduct
Toscanini's orchestra. There was also a clear sense of those in the orchestra
who were supportive of Dixon, and that was his saving grace. While there
were no further incidents of this type with the orchestra, it was clear that if
there was any chance at winning over those musicians who were "anti-
Dixon," his performance had to be flawless. There was no evidence that
Dixon won over those who were opposed to his presence on the podium, but
it was clear the concerts were a resounding success. Critics, friends, and new
admirers wrote directly to the NBC office offering congratulations to Dixon
for a fine performance and to NBC for having the courage to support the
talents of a Negro conductor. While Dixon was grateful to all of the wonderful reviews and letters of congratulations for his successful engagement with
NBC, none seemed to give him more satisfaction than the letter he received
from Alain LeRoy Locke. Locke was widely recognized as the founder of the
Harlem Renaissance, with his groundbreaking book, *The New Negro: An*

Interpretation, in 1925. Locke's love for classical music was quite evident in this letter, dated June 21, 1941.

Dear Dean Dixon:

Allow me to extend heartiest congratulation on your triumph of tonight. Although I would gladly have attended, I had the satisfaction of hearing it at home as I have the other N.B.C. concerts and of being able to make comparable comparisons. The concert came over beautifully with all the subtleties of shadings and dynamics clearly evident. You deserved the ovation you received, and in addition I think you must have convinced the critics. I shall look forward eagerly to reading the comments. I hope this means a break-through to guest conducting during the regular season. Certainly from the point of view of our cause, you have rendered a great service, which of course, I realize is only the result of long hard work and steady persistence. The orchestra sounded enthusiastic; you have won them, for them to have given you such marvelous responsiveness. I particularly liked the restraint of the Don Juan. It made the forte passages so much more effective. That too was a masterly piece of programming, the contrast of the Berlioz with the Saint Saens. To take the Sylphes out of the cradle rocking valse tempo in which it is usually played and make it shimmer the way you did was a real achievement; also you did wonders descriptively with the Danse Macabre without descending to claptrap. I wish you many seasons of real recognition; it seems to me that among the younger men you have the post, as they say in racing.

Cordial best wishes,
Sincerely,
Alain Locke[7]

Locke's hope for Dixon to receive an invitation to conduct the NBC Symphony during its regular season became a reality. After the successful completion of his two concerts with the NBC Summer Symphony, Dixon was quickly engaged to conduct the orchestra during the regular season in 1942. Chotzinoff said about this engagement, "I then felt justified in engaging him for the regular NBC Winter Symphony Series, along with such conductors as Stokowski, Mitropoulos, and Fritz Reiner."[8]

With a glowing recommendation from Chotzinoff, the New York Philharmonic took advantage of the immense popularity that Dixon was receiving at the time and without hesitation engaged him to conduct America's oldest orchestra at Lewinsohn Stadium of City College on August 10, 1941. Dixon conducted Brahms's Symphony No. 1, Daikeong Lee's *Prelude and Hula,* Bach's Arioso from Cantata No. 156 for Strings, Mendelssohn's Scherzo from *A Midsummer Night's Dream,* and Liszt's *Les Preludes.* The concert was a success. Dixon was recalled to the stage twice before the intermission and four times at the end. At the end of the concert, the orchestra paid him an even greater compliment by refusing to stand at Dixon's request to acknowledge the applause of an enthusiastic audience. Instead they joined in with the audience applauding his performance. While McClara, Vivian Rivkin, Wal-

ter White, and other friends and family were in attendance for this momentous occasion, one person was missing. Dixon's father died before his
groundbreaking appearances with NBC and the Philharmonic. Dixon did not
publicly speak of his father until much later in his life. And even then, very
little knowledge of their relationship was revealed. McClara, on the other
hand, was there for Dixon from the very beginning. And leave it to McClara
to bring Dixon back to earth after being on cloud nine throughout the summer of 1941. Dixon could not celebrate too long. He had to get back to his
studies at Columbia University Teachers College.

Dixon took on an ambitious topic for his dissertation: "The Desirability of
Making Adjustment in the Symphonic Scores of Beethoven in the Light of
the Development of Orchestral Instruments."[9] He had gone through most of
the symphonies, piano concerti, and overtures of Beethoven, writing all of
his thoughts and conclusions on 3x5 cards that filled several file cabinets. As
he went deeper into his studies, he concluded that the frustration Beethoven
felt dealing with limited range and flexibility of the winds and brass, resulted
in compensations that make his music unique and groundbreaking. This conclusion made it increasingly difficult for Dixon to continue with this topic. In
his words,

> How can I remove the frustration without removing the compensation? Then I
> would have to really change Beethoven drastically. . . . I cannot change Bee-
> thoven. Beethoven as a human being, as a man, had his strengths and his
> weaknesses. What kind of thinking is it to show only the strengths? We have
> to see the weaknesses also, we have to see where he fell on his face, we have to
> see where he didn't know where to get out, and therefore he changed key, etc.
> We have to see the whole man preferably; therefore why muck around with
> taking this and making that better. . . . No, I can't do this thesis; I won't do it.[10]

After speaking with his advisors, they agreed that if he felt so strongly about
not moving forward, he should choose another topic.

It so happened that during this time, Dixon began to solidify his philosophy on educating young people through the use of the orchestra. He was so
focused on trying to fix Beethoven that he never considered what became his
new thesis topic, "Music Education Through the Use of the Symphony Orchestra."[11] Dixon worked out this innovative approach to making music
accessible to the very young while he was a student, but was unable to test
his theory until much later in his career. Dixon completed all of his course
work and his thesis, but was unable to graduate due to financial obligation
associated with the publication of his work. "When they asked me to publish
my own thesis for a $2,000 fee, my hair rose. So I refused. I couldn't begin to
think of paying out such a sum at that time in my career."[12]

Dixon tried to capitalize on his success with the NBC Symphony and the
New York Philharmonic by seeking someone to manage his career. He was

well aware that succeeding in this business was not won on talent alone. Dixon needed someone who was established with deep connections and a staunch advocate and nurturer of one's talent. That person was Arthur Judson.

Chapter Six

The Plastic Carrot

According to Dixon, Arthur Judson had a monopoly on all the recognized conductors and major orchestras in the northeast. If you were under Judson's management, your career was set. If you crossed him, your career could be in jeopardy. From the start, Judson questioned Dixon's ability to make it in the profession. After every triumphal conducting engagement, Dixon made his way to Judson's office, accompanied with newspaper clippings that were strewn with praise of Dixon's performances. Nothing Dixon presented seemed to impress the powerful impresario. He was led to believe that if he met all of Judson's expectations, representation would soon follow. It never did. Dixon felt the only way to win Judson over was to have him come to one of his performances. Everything was arranged for Judson to come and see him conduct the New York Chamber Orchestra that Dixon founded in 1938. At the last moment Judson had a conflict and was unable to attend Dixon's performance. No reason was given, but Judson did send in his place one of his assistants to report back to him what he observed. It was not favorable. Dixon met with Judson a few days later to find that his assistant reported that the concert was uninspiring, and that Dixon himself did not have the charisma needed to be a world-class conductor. Dixon was shocked at what he heard from Judson, because his numerous reviews spoke to the contrary. Descriptors like uninspiring and lack of charisma were never used to characterize Dixon's conducting. It was at that moment that Dixon came to the realization that Judson was never really interested in managing him. "This promise, this carrot had been in front of my nose now for six years, and suddenly I realized it was plastic."[1] Judson's parting words to Dixon was that instead of pursuing a career in conducting, he should take his family down South to some "Negro College" and teach "his own people" music. Dixon, of course, found this last remark insulting, but it served as confirmation that if

43

there were any chance of succeeding in this business, it would have to be without the support of one of the most influential men in classical music. Judson's rejection did not discourage Dixon in the least. He still had his Harlem orchestra, his regular speaking engagements throughout the city, and a few guest conducting opportunities with community and youth orchestras. In addition, Dixon spent a few summers in Wingdale, New York, conducting an amateur chorus at Camp Unity.

He secured the job because of his successful work with the Dean Dixon Choral Society. While his extensive knowledge of the orchestral repertoire was well known to the public, few knew that his choral repertoire was just as impressive. Camp Unity was recognized as a "left-wing" getaway for those who were either communists or sympathetic to the cause. Dixon was neither. While he clearly was aware of the type of camp he was involved with, it was all about eking out a living the best way he could. According to Dixon, summer festivals like Chautauqua and Tanglewood were not interested in him, so he was willing to take the risk of being associated with this organization. Dixon spent eight weeks at the camp. The chorus was not an auditioned group, but instead recruited from within the general populace of the camp. To ensure that there would be a chorus, Dixon had to convince a number of enthusiastic campers to participate in his group. He was allowed to give a quick spiel about the chorus and how much fun anyone who joined would have each night: "Come down whether you can sing or whistle or you'd like to meet some boys or some girls or if you'd like to sit and watch others work."[2] The spiel worked. Dixon had an estimated seventy people each week. It was all about "drilling, drilling, hard" every night after dinner from 7 p.m. to 8 p.m. They rehearsed in an outdoor facility overlooking the lake. Every weekend they performed some oratorio and various Spanish war songs that were very provocative for that time. The success at Camp Unity introduced Dixon to a tight-knit group of celebrities that were associated with the communist cause. Dixon shared the rostrum at events like "Russian-American Evening" with silent screen icon Charlie Chaplin and writers of various genres who were sympathetic to the cause. Continuing to state his disinterest in communism, while attending numerous events by communist-leaning organizations, created a sense of suspicion on both sides, those who were trying to recruit him and those who were anti-communist. Because of his continued association with these organizations, Dixon was labeled a communist in anti-communist publications such as *Red Channels*. The list created from this tract was designed to inform the public of those in television and radio who were either communists, sympathetic to the cause, or merely associated with those who were suspected to be subversive. A number of artists on this list credited this publication for preventing them from making a living in their chosen profession. They were blacklisted. While Dixon acknowledges that he was labeled a communist by this publication and others, he

never blamed this unfounded accusation as a reason for his inability to pro-
cure a permanent post with a professional orchestra. From Dixon's perspective, race trumped all other explanations.

Clearly, the federal government did not find the claims of Dixon's communist leanings to be valid, because in September of 1941, the National
Youth Administration (NYA) administrator for New York City and Long
Island, Helen M. Harris, announced that Dixon would take over as conductor
of the NYA Symphony Orchestra. The NYA was implemented in 1935 as a
New Deal program designed to provide work and education opportunities for
youth ages sixteen to twenty-five in a Depression-era environment. In the
beginning, Helen Harris was very happy to have Dixon on staff with the
NYA:

> The appointment of Dean Dixon to conduct the orchestra is in accord with the
> constructive policy of the NYA in giving its talented young musicians the best
> possible training and experience under the most talented conductors. Mr. Dix-
> on has been guest conductor twice with our orchestras and has been enthusias-
> tically received by the players, the critics, and the music loving public. We are
> happy to have Mr. Dixon on our staff and feel that he will make a real contri-
> bution to the advancement of our program of orchestral training for young
> people.[3]

Having heard the news about Dixon's new post, Chotzinoff wrote Harris,
praising her decision:

> I was very happy to hear that Mr. Dean Dixon, the young [N]egro conductor, is
> in charge of the National Youth Administration Orchestra. I can think of no
> better man for the job of training orchestral players and keeping them on the
> highest artistic level. . . . Aside from the racial angle, which I think is highly
> important at this moment, it seems to me that the National Youth Administra-
> tion is fortunate in having the services of a thoroughly equipped young
> American conductor.[4]

Dixon was especially excited about this position, because it represented
the first conducting post of his career that he did not have to create. He
wasted no time taking the young orchestra in a different, more ambitious
direction. With a limited number of rehearsals allotted to him, Dixon implemented a Friday night Beethoven concert series, which included one of the
eight symphonies (the ninth symphony was not considered in this series), a
recognized solo artist from the city, and the premiere of a new composition.
On Saturday mornings, he presented a music appreciation series, which was
broadcast on WNYC. He also planned three Sunday afternoon performances.
Because Dixon had to deal with a high level of disciplinary issues, it made
his accomplishments with this youth orchestra even more impressive. Ella
Davis, who was a freelance writer for various local papers in New York,

witnessed firsthand Dixon's remarkable display of poise, dignity, and focus. She remarked,

> Working with a group of inexperienced youngsters whose natural boisterous-
> ness was not always under control, [Dixon] was confronted with a special
> disciplinary problem. . . . He solved it with patience. . . . Once when a player
> persisted in talking while other instruments were rehearsing, Dixon stopped
> and asked the offender to play his own part, which he did, from beginning to
> end. When the solo was finished—and others had remained perfectly still
> throughout—Dixon said quietly, "All right. Now you can talk while we play."
> He literally never raises his voice. When he does get impatient or angry, which
> isn't often, he resorts to withering sarcasm. . . . His authority stems, not from a
> sense of personal power, but from his knowledge of the music. [5]

Davis went on to say that Dixon's intimate knowledge of each instrument made him appear, for the untrained ear, to allow a number of "sour notes" or lack of rhythmic integrity to go without mention. Dixon simply had the maturity to know when to stop and address those musical issues that could be quickly resolved while at the same time understanding that more challenging musical passages could wait until a later date.

The success of the NYA Orchestra with Dixon at the helm was evident with each performance. But it was not long after his tenure began that Harris wanted him out. Dixon and Harris had disagreements on the direction of the orchestra. Harris believed that the repertoire was too ambitious for these young, inexperienced musicians and as a result, produced performances that were mediocre at best. While none of the reviews of Dixon's performances with the NYA Orchestra supported this assertion, it was enough to abruptly end Dixon's tenure with the fledgling ensemble. Believing that there was something else afoot, Dixon sought the advice of Walter White, secretary of the National Association for the Advancement of Colored People. He explained to White that the decision to relieve him of his conducting duties with the NYA had more to do with Harris's music adviser than her. Dixon recalled that when the position with the NYA Orchestra became available, he and a number of young conductors applied. They were met by a panel of musicians, which was organized by Harris's music adviser. According to Dixon the music adviser was the nephew of a very famous composer who had aspirations to be a world-class conductor, but no talent to back it up. It was clear to Dixon that the music adviser wanted this position for himself. The auditions were a sham. The candidates were put through a barrage of questions, which had nothing to do with leading an orchestra but designed to confuse and purge the masses. Dixon was able to survive the ridiculous interrogation fraught with esoteric music references. Proving to be well versed in all areas of music, he avoided being taken in by the obvious efforts of Harris's music adviser and his panel. In the end, Dixon's newly acquired national reputation and previous successes with the youth orchestra as a guest conductor secured him the position. But he knew that given this experience he would have to fight to keep his job.

White was a dear friend of the Dixon family and supported Dixon's career from the very beginning. He agreed to look into the matter. He wrote Harris to inquire why Dixon, who just a few months ago conducted two of the leading orchestras in the country, with favorable reviews, was not allowed to continue his work with the NYA Orchestra. Harris's response was unsatisfactory to White so he quickly escalated the matter by writing the mayor of New York City, the Honorable Fiorello Henry La Guardia:

> I have just concluded a lengthy and quite unsatisfactory conversation with Miss Helen Harris of the New York NYA. She told me that she was telephoning at your suggestion regarding my letter of December 16th in which I raised the question of the reasons why Dean Dixon is not being continued as Director of the NYA Orchestra. Miss Harris tells me that the reason for this is because she feels that Mr. Dixon tries to do too much and that therefore the performance of the orchestra is not as good as she and her musical advisers think it should be because the orchestra does not have as many rehearsals and does not become as well acquainted with the music before performing it as it should. Miss Harris manifestly knows more about music that I do, though she modestly disclaims being an expert. She, therefore, is entitled to her opinion. But so am I entitled to mine. Based upon Mrs. White's and my hearing the orchestra, and even more upon the opinion of musicians who have spoken in glowing terms of Mr. Dixon's ability as a conductor and in his taking young people without orchestral experience and weaving them into as good an orchestra as the NYA, I am frankly disappointed at the failure of the NYA to continue the work with the orchestra of Mr. Dixon. [6]

When Dixon received a copy of this letter, he was impressed with White's tenacious advocacy for him. Unfortunately, the letter did not produce a reversal in the decision made by Harris. White, understanding that there were no other avenues of recourse for Dixon in this matter and that he desperately needed steady work, contacted Howard University in Washington, D.C. White discovered that they were looking to fill a position of dean of the School of Music and immediately began a writing campaign to get Dixon in that position. His letter to Dr. Mordecai Wyatt Johnson, the first Black president of Howard University, is evidence of White's unwavering advocacy of Dixon's talent:

> I learned from Mr. Dixon yesterday that there was not the opportunity for you and him to discuss the matter of his considering the post of Dean of the School of Music at Howard. As I said to you Saturday, it would be a 10-strike, in my opinion, for Howard if you could get Mr. Dixon. . . . If Mr. Dixon could be persuaded to come to Howard I would like to see some sort of an arrangement worked out which would not interfere with his amazing progress towards ever

greater distinction. This would, of course, mean much to Howard as well as to
Mr. Dixon and to the Negro. May I suggest, therefore, that you invite Mr.
Dixon to come to Washington to survey the field and to talk with you? If you
and he think there would be any value in my sitting in on the conference I
would do my utmost to be present. [7]

While Dixon was aware that White was inquiring about the position at Howard University on his behalf, he had no idea that the discussions had gone
up the ladder to the president of the university. Dixon never revealed whether
the position was officially offered to him. Had it been offered, Dixon would
have likely turned it down, because he never forgot the insincere advice
given to him by Judson about going to a Black college to teach his own
people. In Dixon's mind, Judson and others like him would have won in their
campaign to keep him away from a world-class orchestra on a permanent
basis.

Dixon took the unfortunate decision made by Harris in stride. Waiting in
the wings was Chotzinoff and the NBC Symphony. Dixon was engaged to
guest conduct the NBC Symphony on January 20 and 27 in 1942. The music
by Weber, Arnell, Prokofiev, Enesco, Creston, and Sibelius was well received by radio listeners and music critics alike. Of special note was Sibelius's Second Symphony performed at the second NBC concert on January
27. Noted photographer and music critic, Carl Van Vechten, relayed to Dixon in a letter,

> I couldn't come to the hall tonight, I heard every note and I can assure you that
> never has Sibelius' Second sounded so tremendous. As you know, all the
> conductors play this symphony and I have heard it three times this season, but
> YOU gave the work a new thrill. The special problem in this case is the
> adjustment of tempi to the range of dynamics, a problem you succeeded bril-
> liantly in solving. Those tempi in the last movement, faster than anybody else
> takes them (AND SO RIGHT!) had me breathless! You seem to be a conduc-
> tor of the first rank even before you have an orchestra. [8]

On May 11, 1942, Dixon continued his work with the New York Chamber
Orchestra by showcasing four American artists: Maurice Wilk, violinist; Virginia Lewis, mezzo-soprano; Emmanuel Vardi, violist; and Vivian Rivkin,
pianist. The concert took place at Town Hall and featured Mrs. Roosevelt as
the guest of honor. Unlike at the first Dixon concert she attended the previous
year, Mrs. Roosevelt spoke. After Walter White introduced the first lady to
the enthusiastic audience, Mrs. Roosevelt focused her remarks on how music
is ever so important given the current international crisis: "I think that in
times like these in a troubled world music is a universal language that all of
us need." [9] The concert was well received and "Dixon conducted with his
customary authority and economy of gesture, and the orchestra in its support

of the soloists was mellow and pure in sound, as well as admirably balanced and transparent."[10] Mrs. Roosevelt commented on the concert in her syndicated column, saying, "I heard from young American artists last night . . . arranged and conducted by Mr. Dean Dixon with the New York Chamber Orchestra. All the artists were excellent and the program was delightful. We should be thankful that, in our country, we can still give young artists an opportunity to be heard. The arts are the one avenue not blocked by the hate which comes with war. I think we should give every art expression our support whenever we possibly can."[11]

Dixon continued to have a very productive summer as a guest conductor. On July 11, 1942, he appeared with New York Philharmonic at Lewisohn Stadium for the second time in his career. Originally, there were to be two performances but the first scheduled concert was canceled due to inclement weather. Howard Taubman of the *New York Times* reported that given the circumstances, "He made the most of this chance last night, conducting with the energy and decisiveness of a young musician who knows what he is driving at. The salient quality of his conducting is its vigor, if one may judge from one concert. And that is a useful quality for a young conductor to own."[12] Dixon opened the concert with Mozart's *Marriage of Figaro* Overture and ended with Schubert's *Unfinished* Symphony. In between were two obscure works that the music critics characterized as novelties. Aram Khachaturian's First Symphony was performed to mixed reviews while the reviews of Jean Stor's Suite for Strings fared better for its brevity and solid construction. The tepid reviews Dixon received for programming these two contemporary works resulted in a response that although revised throughout his life, represented his unwavering support for new music: "[The conductor] should have a depth of personality that has something to say in both traditional and new music. Outside of that, I value most sincerity—sincerity in the matter of preparing a performance on a high artistic level and sincerity to the composer, achieving as much as possible of what the composer himself did, and what he had to do it with (his cultivation and knowledge of musical materials)."[13] Dixon believed that it was the responsibility of the twentieth-century conductor to vigorously advocate for living composers of extraordinary talent. He continued this tradition throughout his career.

Later that year, the Von Grona American Negro Ballet invited Dixon to conduct the pit orchestra in a performance to take place at the Lafayette Theatre in Harlem. Eugene Von Grona, a German-born dancer and choreographer, was fascinated by all things Harlem and wanted to incorporate the dance styles of this community with the European classical style. It was not unusual for Von Grona to program Stravinsky's *Firebird Suite* juxtaposed with W. C. Handy's *St. Louis Blues*. For Dixon, working with the ballet company helped to change an important aspect of his conducting. For years prior to this experience, Dixon had always conducted with a baton. An encounter with one of the ballet dancers opened his mind to the expressive powers of the hands.

As Dixon positioned himself in the pit, patiently awaiting a signal from stage that the dancers were in place and ready to begin, he noticed the ballet master placed himself on the outskirts of the stage. The curtains were drawn and you could tell that he positioned himself in such a way that he could easily view the dancers behind stage and the orchestra and Dixon in the pit. As the ballet master quickly reminded the dancers of things he'd like to see differently for this run-through, Dixon noticed how expressive and informative his hands were. "I had never seen a hand being so expressive in my life. So it struck me. If the hand is that expressive and the stick of wood is forever a stick of wood, then there is no point in using a baton."[14] Dixon did not use a baton for several years after this experience. He was not interested in sharing this epiphany with his students, nor was he interested in defending his decision to go without a baton. His goal was simply to emulate the ballet master and mold music with his hands.

On January 27, 1943, Dixon made his operatic conducing debut with a newly formed company called the Shoestring Opera Company. This was an unexpected move for those who knew Dixon well. He never minced his words when asked about opera and his participation in it. "I remember one class in Columbia University. I think I was speaking about why I didn't like opera, citing such things as one character, becoming angry, and raising his knife to kill another, and then holding it there for three minutes while he sings his aria! That just didn't work out for me. I felt that there must be some way of making opera more realistic."[15] It seemed that Leopold Sasche, who was president of the company as well as stage director of the Metropolitan Opera, convinced Dixon that opera did, indeed, have some redeeming qualities. Sasche enlisted Dixon to conduct the pit orchestra for their debut performance of Offenbach's *The Tales of Hoffmann* at Hunter College. The production was modestly conceived and presented. This was an experiment by all accounts. It was designed "to demonstrate that artistic dramatic music can be presented without the prohibitive cost of present-day grand opera."[16] It was also important to Dixon and Sasche that American singers and musicians were given an opportunity to perform in English to an American audience. The production cost was around $1,500. Dixon had a very small but efficient orchestra to work with. The ensemble was made up of a few string players, organ, and piano. Vivian Rivkin played the piano, which meant that the woodwind and brass parts were her responsibility. From the costumes to the chorus, everything was done with the least number of personnel and the highest level of artistry. Irvin Dillon (tenor) sang the role of Hoffman; Paul King (lyric baritone) sang the roles of Lindorf, Coppelius, Dapertutto, and Mirakel. And Stella Andreva, a soprano, who was on the roster of the Metropolitan Opera, sang the roles of Olympia and Antonia. While the critics pointed out the frugality of the production, they also remarked that the Shoe-string Opera Company's small budget did not take away from a quality performance. Dixon learned a great deal from Sasche. His own experience working with singers did not compare to Sasche's vast knowledge of the operatic repertoire and the voice. "It was the first time I had had particularly that kind of operatic experience with a man who was from the European opera school. It was a pleasure to work with him."[17] After the three sched-uled performances, there was no public record of the fledgling opera compa-ny continuing to provide quality performances on a modest budget.

Dixon saw a pattern developing in his career. For the previous two years he was associated with organizations with a mission he admired, but because of limited resources they folded. He was once again left with his Harlem orchestra, occasional concerts with his ad hoc professional chamber orches-tra, and his lectures. He no longer had time to teach privately, even though it was a main source of income. His lectures were beginning to yield more financially than his private teaching ever could. Dixon carried around his own record player and records from place to place, giving basic music appre-ciation talks and very specific talks like "Expectant Mothers and Music" or "Music and its Relation to Digestion."[18] His lectures were so popular that a couple of top-tier agencies approached him about how best to market his talent. "I earned my main money in America by teaching and lecturing."[19] Dixon enjoyed talking about all aspects of music, but he had no interest in doing these lectures for the rest of his career. He was still optimistic that his successes with the New York Philharmonic and NBC Symphony in 1941 and 1942 meant something and would result in a permanent conducting post with a professional orchestra somewhere. As he waited for that dream to become a reality, his patriotic sensibility was brought to the forefront. When the United States declared war on Japan after the deadly bombing of Pearl Harbor, Dixon tried to enlist. After his physical, it was concluded that because of his severe asthma, he was unfit to serve in the armed services and given the classification of 4-F. Dixon didn't waste any time looking for other ways to serve his country. He used his Harlem orchestra and chorus to raise aware-ness of the effects of the war by giving concerts in VA hospitals, schools, and civic centers throughout the city and surrounding areas. Performing in these nontraditional venues sparked an idea in Dixon that would require a different kind of ensemble. He was losing interest in his Harlem ensembles. Both orchestra and chorus continued to struggle financially and the level of perfor-mance seemed to remain stagnant. Dixon knew that it was only a matter of time before he would have to dissolve both groups. He never forgot his experience with the NYA Orchestra, which by now had ceased to exist. He enjoyed working with the young musicians and the innovative programming that resulted. A new youth orchestra would move in the same innovative direction as the NYA Orchestra. A few months later, Dixon began the process of creating his most popular orchestra, the American Youth Orchestra.

Chapter Seven

Search for Democracy

The American Youth Orchestra was founded in May 1944, upon the request of a small group of college student musicians. Initially, twenty-two students were invited by Dixon to audition. Seventeen showed for the audition. As the idea of a youth orchestra developed in Dixon's mind, he began to share to prospective sponsors the purpose of this group. He wanted to do something revolutionary. He wanted this orchestra to serve the people in an entirely new way. He wanted his group of young players to perform in all the venues that the traditional ensembles were not. He wanted to cater to those people who found going to a traditional concert cost prohibitive. Depending on where they performed and the cause they were supporting, the price for admission would either be free or set at a very nominal amount. He wanted to reach the next generation of concertgoers. Dixon always believed that those who were avid lovers of classical music were converted at a very young age. Dixon wanted this orchestra to forever remain relevant to the community that they served. Seeing the merit in Dixon's mission, the American Youth for Democracy, an organization that championed the rights of young people, agreed to sponsor the youth orchestra's debut concert. Other, more recognized admirers of Dixon quickly joined the cause. These supporters were the "Who's Who" in classical music and some of the most influential people within the social circles of New York City: "Bruno Walter, Yehudi Menuhin, Gregor Piatigorsky, Wilfred Pelletier, Paul Robeson, Aaron Copland, Mrs. Charles Guggenheimer, Oscar Hammerstein 2d, Henry Simon, M. Lincoln Schuster, Leonard Bernstein, Fannie Hurst, and Magistrate Anna M. Kross."[1]

The audition took place at the Chatham Square Music School on the lower east side. To ensure a "true democratic procedure," Dixon sat behind an ad hoc screen made up of two grand pianos with the lids raised to their highest point, which prevented him from seeing the musicians who came to audition. This exercise was to demonstrate the need to make decisions of acceptance based on one's ability and not on the basis of race, creed, color, or sex. From the seventeen musicians that auditioned, Dixon settled on thirteen promising young string players. He was pleased with this modest beginning, not concerned that the audition failed to recruit a complete instrumentation. The orchestra had its first rehearsal on June 13, 1944. The young ensemble quickly grew as word spread on what Dixon was creating. Dixon had this uncanny ability to attract young people of various persuasions whether they were musically inclined or not. His philosophy was not just to produce music at the highest artistic level but "to get the musicians to realize that the true worth and happiness in life comes from giving rather than receiving; and that they, as potential artists, are in a uniquely advantageous position to do such giving, and too, the giving of something very wonderful and beautiful— namely, great music."[2] As the ensemble continued to grow, it became painfully obvious that outside distractions were becoming more noticeable during their rehearsals.

> Soon the conditions under which we were trying to rehearse became quite impossible, due both to our own rapid numerical growth, which made the quarters cramped, and the complete uncooperativeness of the neighbors who insisted upon punctuating our music with the crash of falling bottles and cans in the adjoining areaway. Added to these noises were the loud, strident, bellowing voices emanating from the throats of family squabbles occupying the apartments whose windows were adjacent to the windows we had to use for ventilation. It was too much competition for us, thus we had to move from the Chatham Square School and seek other rehearsal quarters.[3]

In the midst of trying to settle in with his new youth orchestra, Dixon had to prepare for his guest conducting engagement with the Philadelphia Orchestra. Under the leadership of Maestro Eugene Ormandy, the Philadelphia Orchestra was considered by many as one of the premier orchestras in the country. It was announced in the local newspapers that Dixon, along with other leading conductors like Dmitri Mitropoulos, George Szell, Vladimir Golschmann, and Sigmund Romberg, were slated to lead the Philadelphia Orchestra during their summer residency at Robin Hood Dell. Celebrating fifteen years of world-class performances, the Robin Hood Dell concert series ran from June 19 to August 4, with concerts taking place every Monday, Tuesday, Thursday, and Friday evenings. Dixon was scheduled to conduct on July 17, performing the music of Gershwin, featuring excerpts from his opera *Porgy and Bess*, with soloists Anne Brown and Todd Duncan. Both Duncan and Brown made history in 1935 when they were handpicked by Gershwin to sing the lead roles in his revolutionary opera comprised of an all-Negro cast of classically trained singers.

With a successful performance conducting the Philadelphia Orchestra behind him, Dixon focused his attention back to New York and relocating his youth orchestra. They moved to the Greenwich House Music School in Greenwich Village, located on the lower west side. The school allowed Dixon's ensemble to rehearse in their main hall. This lasted until August, when the painters came to redecorate the school. Dixon called for a brief vacation with the hopes and full expectation that once the paint dried things would pick back up in September. The paint did finally dry, but when Dixon presented his rehearsal schedule for the orchestra to the school for their approval, he was informed that it conflicted with a program that was already in place. The schedule conflict could not be resolved, so a search for another rehearsal venue ensued. The best Dixon could come up with was the foyer of a birth control clinic located within a large office building on lower 5th Street. With the resumption of rehearsals in September, Dixon's string orchestra grew exponentially and the sudden influx of wind and percussion instrumentalists made the foyer more cramped, not to mention that there were not enough chairs. "Due to the lack of sufficient chairs to go around, the boys and girls were using office and waiting-room arm chairs to seat the string players, and the ends of tables and inverted waste paper baskets, some dangerously close to the floor, to seat woodwind and brass players."[4] This situation could not continue and Dixon looked for yet another venue. He found a gymnasium located in a large private school on Broadway in mid-Manhattan. The "echo-like" acoustics were challenging for rehearsal purposes but the best that could be acquired at the time. He eventually increased the number of rehearsals from two to three a week in preparation for their debut concert.

Dixon created an unusual but effective way to develop the orchestra's understanding of the sounds around them. Taking on the philosophy that all music is chamber music, Dixon wanted to make sure his young players had a keen appreciation for the music being played by other instruments in the ensemble. It was not uncommon to have a flute sitting next to a cello, or a violin hearing the horns up close and personal for the first time.

Dixon was able to grow the ensemble to such an artistic level that it was ready for its first concert. On December 16, 1944, the American Youth Orchestra made its debut performance at Carnegie Hall. On the program was Beethoven's Symphony No. 7, op. 91 in A Major, Nicholas Rakov's *Suite Dansante*, op. 8, Mozart's Piano Concerto in E flat Major, K. 482, performed by Vivian Rivkin, and Richard Mohaupt's *Townpiper Music*.

Olin Downes, music critic for the *New York Times*, was enthusiastic with praise for Dixon and his young orchestra:

> The stuff of a real conductor was manifested when Dean Dixon, the Negro
> batonist, appeared with the American Youth Orchestra. . . . If Mr. Dixon

fulfills the promise of this concert, he is going to be one of the leading talents among our young conductors of the present day. His performance of Beethoven's Seventh Symphony could occasion a few minor reservations, but none of these would condition importantly the fact that he is a musician of temperament and sensibility to his fingertips, of high intelligence, and with the qualities of leadership and control which make an orchestra play. [5]

Dixon began to implement his unique community programs that set the youth orchestra apart from other musical groups in the city. Dixon made sure that his youth orchestra was publicly supportive of all those servicemen and women who risked their lives to protect the core values of America: "This being an important area for the artist during the war—that is, the artist's place in a war effort, and after the war it's an important job to let those who have fought and sacrificed and are now incapacitated know that they have not been forgotten, nor has their sacrifice diminished in importance in the turmoil of re-conversion to pre-war normalcy. It's just a matter of how I felt personally about what could be done by a 4F artist during the war."[6]

The Servicemen's Hospital Concerts were given at Halloran General Hospital and St. Albans Naval Hospital on a regular basis. The Army Camp Concerts took place at two ports of embarkation, Camp Shanks and Camp Kilmer. And the Rehabilitation Center Concerts had their debut in Long Island at Camp Upton.

We had been giving concerts in the servicemen's hospitals and camps and I was taking soloists primarily from the orchestra again, [and] the vocal soloists were people who were willing to give their services to the war effort. . . . It had been set up for a heterogeneous audience. Many times we came in, we started our concert and it was in the recreation hall and I walked out on stage and I saw maybe 400 people sitting normally and maybe 50 sitting with just the bottoms of the shoes looking at me. So I developed a technique altogether of selling the music on folksy lines. [7]

Dixon quickly developed a reputation for fostering young American soloists and composers. By 1945, he had already featured twelve young American soloists in his performances with the American Youth Orchestra and five new works were premiered; three of which were by American composers.

But by far the most successful programs with his youth orchestra were his concerts for young people. Dixon was finally able to put into practice his philosophy on music education for young people that he developed while a student at Columbia University Teachers College. He created two age specific programs for youth. The Dramatized Concerts were designed for age groups from seven to ten. The Touch Concerts were designed for age groups from three to four.

It was based on the fact that the three and four year olds are in the touch or kinesthetic stage. A color or a quality attracts them to the degree that they go and touch it. Touching is an important thing. How could I get the orchestra touchable by three and four year olds? I put the children in the middle on small chairs and built the orchestra around them. We played real music, but when they became restive we turned to some other music—Shostakovich, Beethoven, Strauss, Brahms or whatever. Then in the middle of the concert we demonstrate each instrument. Then the children were invited to take their chairs and sit next to whichever instrument they felt like. . . . We played the final number with them sitting this way. [8]

All of Dixon's programs with his youth orchestra were very successful, but there was one lingering problem that seemed to plague him with all of the ensembles he created—money.

It was clear that the impressive list of supporters touted in all of the local newspapers did not translate into financial stability. The orchestra struggled financially throughout its existence. Like his Harlem orchestra, Dixon found himself spending a great deal of his own money, made primarily from his lectures and guest conducting appearances, to sustain the needs of his youth orchestra. It had gotten to a point where Dixon had to curtail many of his successful programs because of lack of funding. He spent a great deal of his time soliciting anyone who would listen to financially support his youth orchestra. In his letter to prospective donors, Dixon said, "Without substantial aid it will be impossible for us to continue with our program. The Servicemen's and the New Artists' Concerts, the Teen-Age and Music For Millions Concerts, all these universally admired programs will have to cease. And a vital force in American culture will be removed."[9]

Benefit concerts to raise money for the orchestra quickly followed. It seemed that the letters and concerts worked. Dixon was pleasantly surprised at the financial help he received from those he least expected. One in particular was Arthur Judson. This was the same Arthur Judson who represented most of the major orchestras and conductors in America, but declined Dixon's request to represent him. A letter dated June 9, 1945, written by Judson to the president of the New York Philharmonic, Harry Harkness Flagler, served as an overwhelming endorsement of Dixon's altruistic endeavors as director of the American Youth Orchestra.

The other day I had a visit from Dean Dixon, the negro conductor. I had known of him as an excellent conductor, who has appeared at the Stadium and with the NBC Orchestra, but I did not know of his fine personality and of his extraordinary efforts not only to further his own career but to help others. Every thing he makes goes into the Youth Orchestra, of which I enclose a circular. I do not know of any more worthwhile enterprise in the United States. Dixon needs some contributions to help him in what he is doing, which is literally lifting himself and his people up by their bootstraps. I have not a great deal of money but I am going to make him a modest contribution. I am not asking you to contribute but only telling you that I think this is something really worth while.[10]

As money began to trickle in from various sources, the American Youth Orchestra averted having to disband and continued their community programs throughout the city and beyond.

The summer of 1945 turned out to be as fruitful as the previous summer. On June 25, 1945, Dixon became the first Black conductor to perform with the Boston Symphony Orchestra. It was the "Colored American Night" concert series presented by the Boston Pops. Arthur Fiedler was only eight years into his iconic tenure, when he met Dixon on June 27, 1938, after his "Afro-American Night" concert with the Boston Pops. Dixon made a lasting impression on Fiedler that night and Fiedler knew that when it was the right time, he would invite Dixon as a guest conductor of the Boston Pops. Dixon shared the stage that evening with soprano Hattie Barber and pianist Donald Shirley. The concert was a resounding success. According to one reporter from the *Boston Guardian,* "The magnetism of Dean Dixon was easily the outstanding feature. . . . I have never heard better music from the Boston Symphony than I heard Monday night. . . . The way I see it history was made this night."[11]

Dixon returned to New York with another world-class orchestra under his belt. The funds that he raised over the summer for his youth orchestra allowed him to book Assembly Hall at Hunter College for the 1945–1946 season. This would be the venue for most of his concerts with the AYO. The plan this season was to perform all nine Beethoven symphonies. Each symphony would be accompanied by a new work and feature a young soloist. Dixon believed that Beethoven was the ideal composer to present to young listeners. But to pull this ambitious program off, he needed to reinforce his strings. He held auditions at Central High School of Needle Trade on West 24th Street. Each candidate performed a prepared piece and was given music at the audition to sight-read. The results of the audition were positive and Dixon was able to move forward with his Beethoven cycle.

As his popularity grew with every glowing review in the local newspapers, Dixon was given an opportunity to expand his music appreciation session from the libraries to the radio. The show was called "Music for You." Dixon said about the radio series, "What we plan to do in these sessions is to learn a whole lot about music and musical performance, and have heaps of fun and mental stimulation while doing this."[12] The series was aired several consecutive Saturdays in the afternoon on radio station WMCA. The radio show was successful. Around this time, a representative from the Office of Inter-American Affairs approached Dixon to ask if he would record an American work for radio distribution throughout Latin America. Dixon, of course, agreed, and he and the American Youth Orchestra recorded George Kleinsinger's *Overture on American Folk Themes*. Kleinsinger was an eccentric musician/composer most known for his popular 1945 children's song "Tubby the Tuba." Dixon knew Kleinsinger from his association with Camp Unity and was confident his overture would have great appeal to a Latin American audience.

Dixon (an "on advice" graduate) stayed closely connected with his former colleagues and teachers at Juilliard. On October 17, 1945, he was elected president of the Juilliard Graduate School Alumni Association. To accompany this honor, he was invited that same year to guest conduct the Juilliard Orchestra for three weeks. He was paid $400 for his services, which was much needed at the time. While this was not the first time Dixon appeared with the Juilliard Orchestra as an alumnus, this was the first time he conducted his alma mater without Albert Stoessel. The orchestra and opera program at the Juilliard Graduate School was still struggling with the untimely death of Stoessel. He died suddenly of a heart attack on May 12, 1943, during a performance at the American Academy of Arts and Writers. Stoessel was only forty-eight. Dixon, who had problems with Stoessel while a student a Juilliard, found comfort in the fact that Stoessel invited him back to Juilliard after he graduated to conduct a number of concerts with his former orchestra. Their relationship was in a much better place as evidenced by Stoessel, who wrote Dixon a very kind letter of support in 1941: "Your appearance at the 'home diamond' with our orchestra gave us all complete satisfaction. You have grown greatly since leaving the school and I have every confidence in your artistic future. Please count on me for every little boost I can give you in the difficult beginning years." [13] Dixon even recalls an earlier almost prophetic utterance from Stoessel when Dixon met him backstage at Carnegie Hall to congratulate him after his first appearance with the New York Philharmonic in 1940: "I [Dixon] went back stage to congratulate him. I don't remember what I said, something about being happy for him. But I remember what he said. There publicly, in the backstage room in Carnegie Hall, just after the New York Philharmonic concert, he said, 'Yes, Dixon, but it took me until I was 44. It won't take you that long.'" [14] A year later at the age of twenty-six, it was Dixon's turn. This and other correspondences between the two reveal a mutual respect for one another. It was clear that Stoessel believed in Dixon's talent, but did not know how to help him beyond the borders of Juilliard. Edgar Schenkman took over Stoessel's responsibilities as head of the opera and orchestra program from 1943 to 1947. Dixon would continue to guest conduct the Juilliard Orchestra until 1949.

Dixon's romantic life took a back seat to his aspirations to become a professional conductor. He was too busy to fall in love. But when Stoessel assigned Dixon to conduct a concert that featured one of Juilliard's most promising pianists, his life changed. Her name was Vivian Rivkin. Their relationship was made known to very few people. Vivian was White.

Chapter Eight

Black and White

Dixon and Vivian met while students at the Juilliard Graduate School. They began performing together in 1938, when Dixon featured Vivian as the solo pianist for his professional debut concert with the League of Music Lovers Chamber Orchestra. The majority of his concerts that called for a solo pianist featured Vivian. She was lauded as a pianist of the highest caliber. Her technique was commendable, her energy was contagious, and her musicality was always on display whether performing a concerto with an orchestra or collaborating with a chamber ensemble. She was a great conversationalist and had very clear views on everything from music to politics.

And she loved Dixon. She entered into this relationship fully aware that not everyone would accept it. Having a relationship with someone outside of your race was not something you did in the 1940s without some serious weighing of pros and cons. During this time there were some states that still had anti-miscegenation laws on the books. While New York was one of the states that did not have any laws against interracial marriages/relationships, it was still very difficult to live your life as a couple. Dixon experienced this firsthand. One evening, he needed to meet with Vivian at her home on 2017 Broadway to discuss their upcoming concert. They were very much a couple during this time. He pulled up to her apartment building driving his new Hudson and dressed in a fine suit, not looking at all like a threat to anyone. Before he could get out of his car, he was approached by two police officers. Because of his experience with the police during his teenage years, Dixon had built up hatred for the "men in blue." He knew when they called him over, that this would not be a pleasant experience. They wanted to know what he was doing in this part of town. Although Dixon tried to explain his reason for being in a White neighborhood at 9 o'clock at night, the officers were not really interested in his answer. They told him to "come over by the wall, turn around, and put your hands up on the wall. [Then] they frisked me [and said afterward], 'Don't let us catch you around here again.'"[1] At hearing that, Dixon tried to explain again his reason for being in this neighborhood.

"'I work here. I am working with my pianist over there . . . ' 'You heard what we said,'"[2] warned one of the officers. Dixon knew when to speak out in protest to an injustice and when to remain silent. The tone of the officer's warning was resolute, and Dixon knew that further discussion of the matter would precipitate a physical altercation that would not end well for him. Needless to say, he did not get to meet with Vivian that night. Dixon believed that if those officers knew of his romantic relationship with Vivian, he would not have been left untouched. Aside from the danger of being physically hurt from those who vehemently opposed interracial relationships, you faced rejection from your friends and family, both Black and White. Your means of making a living could be in jeopardy if someone on your job found out. If you were someone with any type of name recognition, the chance of a major backlash, if found out, rose exponentially. Dixon had enough going against him as a Black man trying to succeed in the world of classical music. He didn't need the discovery of his personal life to compound the situation. So he made sure only those closest to him and Vivian knew about their relationship.

Not many of Dixon's friends suspected anything beyond a respectful friendship between him and Vivian until his 1941 appearance with the New York Philharmonic. The rumors began when a local newspaper reported that along with McClara, Sylvanus Hart III, Walter White, and a few others, Vivian was among family and friends invited by Dixon as his special guests. On June 28, 1947, Dixon and Vivian were married. The ceremony took place in Milford, Connecticut, at a palatial country estate owned by a longtime friend and supporter of Dixon, Dr. Godfrey Nurse. Along with hosting the intimate affair, Dr. Nurse also served as Dixon's best man. Dr. Nurse made sure that the room where the ceremony took place was decorated with freshly cut garden flowers and dressed up with white satin ribbons. Only a small number of family and friends were invited to the ceremony. McClara was there, but noticeably missing were Vivian's parents. Vivian was very close to her parents. Sam and Becky Rivkin lived in Canton, Ohio, where Vivian was raised. They were very progressive-thinking people and in general did not have any objections to the idea of interracial marriage. Their major objection to Vivian's marriage to Dixon was not solely because Dixon was Black. Their concern was more of how others would react to their marriage. For as long as they could remember, Vivian wanted to be a professional pianist and travel around the world performing the masterworks. She had the confidence, and her success at Juilliard proved she had the talent. They believed her marriage to Dixon would prevent her from fulfilling her dream. Sam and Becky believed that Vivian and Dixon's quality of life would be dramatically impacted. What would happen if they decided to have a family? How would their children be treated? Would their children be fully accepted in either racial community? These were important questions that they were concerned about and wanted Vivian to seriously consider before making this life-changing decision. But the more immediate concern was their daughter's physical well-being. Vivian could be putting her life in danger by marrying Dixon. Vivian's parents heard enough vicious stories about lynchings throughout the South and to a lesser extent in their home state of Ohio. It meant nothing to some in the South during this time to hang a Black man if he were suspected of looking at a White woman in a suggestive manner. Vivian's parents didn't want to imagine what would happen to their daughter if someone with a "lynching mentality" knew that her association with Dixon was consensual. While Sam and Becky's views toward the marriage were not of a supportive nature, it's only speculative that this was the reason they did not attend the ceremony.

After the ceremony, Dr. Nurse invited everyone to the formal dining room where a feast was prepared. As dinner was coming to a close, the host requested that expensive French champagne be released from its bottle into the glasses of the assembled guests in order to toast the newlyweds. Dixon and Vivian honeymooned in Wellfleet, Cape Cod. But a job would interrupt their getaway, albeit for a short period. With the responsibility of supporting both his new wife and his mother, Dixon couldn't turn down any offer to work, even for the sake of his honeymoon. He was invited to lecture and conduct the symphony orchestra at the University of Wisconsin for their summer session. Vivian took advantage of the time alone to prepare for her annual recital in December at Town Hall in New York City. This recital would serve as the "kick-off" of her international tour, starting with several concerts in the States and then continuing in Europe. Dixon rejoined Vivian at Cape Cod after his engagement at the university ended. He and Vivian stayed there until September. Dixon had to get back to New York to start his fourth season with the American Youth Orchestra. His youth orchestra would be in residence for the 1947–1948 season at the Brooklyn Academy of Music. When Dixon and Vivian returned to New York, friends and colleagues were stunned to find they were husband and wife. The two major papers in the city, the *New York Times* and the *New York Herald Tribune*, did not report the marriage. The only city paper that reported the marriage was the *New York Amsterdam News*. It was not an editorial for or against interracial marriage. It was a matter-of-fact reporting of the ceremony, with a picture of both Dixon and Vivian prominently displayed. It's likely that Olin Downes, music critic for the *New York Times*, and Virgil Thomson, music critic for the *New York Herald Tribune*, both staunch supporters of Dixon, wielded a bit of their influence to keep this story quiet. The general consensus was that if this were common knowledge, it would cripple Dixon's chances for any permanent conducting post in America.

The newlyweds took up residence at the Hotel Ansonia on 2109 Broadway between 73rd and West 74th streets. Once known for its luxurious accommodations where the wealthy and famous resided, the Ansonia was a shadow of its former self. The hotel was in desperate need of basic repair and updating. The only source of steady income the building was producing was through its rental apartments. A large portion of the impressive edifice was turned into studio apartments, with a small kitchen and bath. There were also some suites that were available for rent. The suites were ideal for those in the performing arts, because the size allowed for grand pianos to be placed in any room without hindering one's ability to maneuver throughout the apartment. Another benefit of the suites was the thick walls, which allowed for occupants to practice their craft without disturbing the neighbors.

As Dixon settled into his new life as husband and soon-to-be father, he grew more and more disenchanted with the prospects of making a career for himself in America. His groundbreaking accomplishments in the early 1940s seemed so long ago and he began to question their significance. Given that no major orchestra, much less a regional orchestra, sought out his services as a permanent conductor, he often pondered if he were simply being placated or used as a gimmick for those entities who believed that these orchestra societies were not practicing the true democracy that they preached. He concluded each time those discouraging thoughts came to mind that his guest conducting appearances with the New York Philharmonic, NBC Symphony, Boston Symphony, and so on were legitimate.

> If I felt back in the 40s, when I was invited to conduct the New York Philharmonic and Philadelphia Orchestras, albeit the summer concert season, and the Boston Symphony, albeit "Colored America Night," [that] I felt this was all just patronization so I could wave my arms around on the podium, I might have accepted that. But I didn't feel that way. I had good audiences . . . they were enthusiastic and they were White. And the reviews, in all the papers were good ones. [3]

Dixon began seriously contemplating his future as a conductor in America. He could no longer wait on the sidelines while other young conductors were elevated to permanent posts around the country and he remained the guest conductor. Dixon was further persuaded to make a change after Vivian returned from Europe with wonderful notices for her performances. He knew that the first opportunity that presented itself would be his sign to make a go of it in Europe.

As Dixon continued his work with the American Youth Orchestra, he received news that put him back in the spotlight. On May 8, 1948, it was announced that Dixon was awarded the Alice M. Ditson Award. The Ditson

Conductor's Award was established in 1945 to recognize a conductor who demonstrated through performances his unwavering support for American music. Dixon was the fourth conductor to receive this coveted award. Howard Hanson, noted American composer/conductor and longtime director of the Eastman School of Music, was the first recipient in 1945; Leon Barzin, director of the New York City Ballet and the National Orchestral Association, was the recipient in 1946; and in 1947 Alfred Wallenstein was music director of the Los Angeles Philharmonic when he received the award. As a recipient of the Alice M. Ditson Award, Dixon received $1,000 and a guest conducting invitation with the Columbia Broadcasting System Symphony in conjunction with the Festival of Contemporary American Music at Columbia University. He appeared with the orchestra for their final performance on May 16 at the McMillan Theater. The nationwide radio broadcast featured the premiere performance of Wallingford Riegger's Symphony No. 3, which was commissioned by the Ditson Fund. Violist Paul Docktor appeared on stage with Dixon to give the premiere performance of Quincy Porter's Viola Concerto. And Robert Ward's Symphony No. 2 was the first work on the program.

It didn't go unnoticed to Dixon that he was the only recipient of the Ditson Conductor's Award without a permanent post either with a professional orchestra or music conservatory. He created an amateur ensemble from nothing, and four years later his youth orchestra was respected for its ambitious and successful performances and admired for its altruistic mission. Those who were able to attend their concerts found Dixon to be a compelling figure, destined for greatness. Dixon's reputation as a talented musician and consummate professional was solidified when he won the Ditson Conductor's Award. He was no gimmick used to appease those groups who were fighting for equality in all areas of the workplace. He knew his craft as a conductor. He understood the psychology of an orchestra. He mastered the art of building an orchestra and making it relevant to its community. These characteristics were usually attributable to those who were much older than Dixon. At age thirty-three, Dixon continued to work tirelessly to prove he was ready to take the helm of a professional orchestra of the highest artistic caliber. But at the same time, he came to the realization that his window of opportunity to achieve the dream of becoming a maestro in America was closing in front of his eyes.

In 1945, William Schuman, a noted American composer, took over as president of the Juilliard School. Schuman separated the orchestra and opera program, which was developed as one division by the late Albert Stoessel. The Juilliard Orchestra was divided into two sections. Section I Orchestra devoted its time to the symphonic repertoire. Section II Orchestra served as the orchestra for operas and concertos concerts. There was also a training orchestra formed to serve as an introduction to the orchestral repertoire as well as the feeder orchestra for both Section I and II orchestras. Schuman wanted a dynamic figure to take over the orchestra program. Someone with vision that was as comfortable programming new music as he was the standard repertoire. So for the first time in the history of the Juilliard School, three young guest conductors were invited to share the conducting duties of the two orchestras: Eleazar de Carvalho, Jean Paul Morel, and Dean Dixon. It was expected that one of these conductors would become head of the Orchestra Department. But even before the three guest conductors had a chance to prove themselves worthy of the coveted position, Schuman had already made up his mind to submit Dixon's name to the Juilliard School's Board of Directors to become the next head of the Orchestra Department. There was no mention in the official minutes of that meeting as to what happened when the board was presented with this request, but it was clear that by the time that meeting concluded, Schuman knew that Dixon would not become the head of the Orchestra Department. The position was offered instead to Jean Paul Morel. Schuman either had a change of heart in his support of Dixon or the board simply favored Jean Paul Morel.

To make matters worse, Dixon was not invited to return as a guest conductor for the 1949–1950 year. He was well liked by faculty and students at Juilliard, and his performances were well attended and received with enthusiastic approval from audiences. This wasn't a case where there was no longer a need for guest conductors once the permanent conductor was announced. They still needed guest conductors. The students at Juilliard, who respected and admired the work of Dixon, were not pleased by this decision. On February 10, 1949, a large number of students signed a petition protesting the decision made by the administration not to bring Dixon back. In the petition they characterized Dixon as an irreplaceable teacher, musician, and human being. The petition did not persuade Schuman to change his mind. This was a major financial blow for Dixon and his family, which now included an eight-month-old daughter, Diane. Dixon received a $5,000 salary as a Juilliard faculty member. This was steady income that his family very much needed. Unless Dixon was able to find another teaching position in the city, he would have to once again depend solely on his lectures and guest conducting invitations to support the family. Shortly after his departure from Juilliard, Dixon was hired to teach at the Manhattan School of Music. But it was also around this time that Dixon received an invitation from the French government to travel to Paris to conduct two performances with the Radiodiffusion Francaise Orchestra. The opportunity of a lifetime had finally been presented to him. Dixon, Vivian, and Diane were on their way to Paris.

Henry Charles Dixon and McClara Dean Dixon on a rooftop in New York City. *Photo and permission provided by Ritha Dixon (widow of Dean Dixon)*

Dean Dixon, seated fifth from left, in a group portrait with the symphony orchestra that he organized, at the Harlem Y.M.C.A., New York City, June 1933. *The Dean Dixon Collection, Photographs and Prints Division, Schomburg Center for Research in Black Culture, the New York Public Library, Astor, Lenox, and Tilden Foundations. Used with the permission of Ritha Dixon*

Dean Dixon in New York City, circa 1933. *Photo and permission provided by Ritha Dixon*

Dean Dixon with his mother in their home in Harlem, circa 1944. Marian Palfi Archive/Gift of the Menniger Foundation and Martin Magner. *Used with the permission of the Center for Creative Photography/University of Arizona*

Dean Dixon as guest conductor at the Juilliard School, circa 1944. Marion Palfi Archive/Gift of the Menniger Foundation and Martin Magner. *Used with the permission of the Center for Creative Photography/University of Arizona*

Dean Dixon giving a lecture on the music of Beethoven at a local New York City public school. *Photo by E. Morris Engel. Permission provided by Mary Engel*

Dean Dixon, Vivian (Dixon's first wife), and Diane in Paris, France. *Photo and permission provided by Lavi Daniel*

Dean Dixon, Vivian, and Gordon Parks in a Venice, Italy, hotel listening to a rehearsal of Park's concerto, Symphonic Set, circa July 1, 1952. *Photograph by James Whitmore. Used with the permission of Getty Images*

Conductor Dean Dixon, contralto Marian Anderson, and classical pianist Abbey Simon in Stockholm, Sweden, September 17, 1952. *Photo and permission provided by Ritha Dixon (widow of Dean Dixon)*

Dean Dixon conducting in Australia, circa March 15, 1963. *Photograph by Erich Auerbach. Used with permission of Getty Images*

The queen chatting to Dean Dixon, conductor of the Sydney Symphony Orchestra, during an interval in the concert given by the orchestra at the Royal Festival Hall, London, in connection with the Commonwealth Arts Festival, September 18, 1965. *Photograph by PA Photos. Used with permission of Landov Media*

Dean Dixon and the Frankfurt Radio Orchestra recording for a television broadcast, 1970. Photograph by HR/Kurt Bethke. *Used with the permission of Andreas Maul/Hessischer Rundfunk (Frankfurt, Germany)*

Dean Dixon with soprano Jessye Norman and the Frankfurt Radio Symphony Orchestra, 1970. Photograph by HR/Kurt Bethke. *Used with the permission of Andreas Maul/Hessischer Rundfunk (Frankfurt, Germany)*

Dean Dixon with the New York Philharmonic during a rehearsal at Central Park in New York City, 1970. *Rogers Photo Archives*

Dean Dixon performing with violinist James Oliver Buswell IV with the New York Philharmonic in Central Park, 1970. *Rogers Photo Archives*

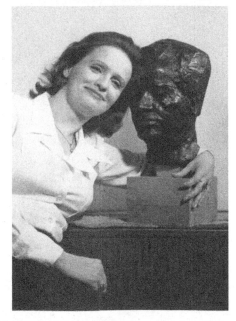

Ritha Dixon (Dixon's third wife) pictured here with a bust of her husband, 1974. *Photographs and Prints Division, Schomburg Center for Research in Black Culture, the New York Public Library, Astor, Lenox, and Tilden Foundations. Used with the permission of Ritha Dixon*

Diane Dixon (daughter of Dean Dixon from his first marriage to Vivian Rivkin) in Frankfurt. *Photograph by Ritha Dixon. Photo and permission provided by Ritha Dixon*

Nina Dixon (daughter of Dean Dixon from his second marriage to Mary Mandelin) in Zug, Switzerland. *Photograph by Ritha Dixon. Photo and permission provided by Ritha Dixon*

Dean Dixon rehearsing the Frankfurt Radio Symphony Orchestra for his final concert with them, 1974. *Photograph by Hartmut Blume. Photo and permission provided by Ritha Dixon*

Portrait of Dean Dixon in Brussels, Belgium, following his very last concert. *Photograph by Ritha Dixon. Photo and permission provided by Ritha Dixon*

Chapter Nine

Exodus

The opportunity that Dixon was waiting for had finally arrived, but with conditions. The French government provided the invitation but no financial assistance to get him and his family to Paris. Once again, Dixon found himself having to finance his own opportunities for advancement in the field of conducting. Not the least bit discouraged, he created a consortium of musicians that would travel to Paris with him and perform. Everyone in the consortium had to either contribute their own money and/or solicit family and friends to contribute to the cause. Dixon was able to convince three musicians to join him: Maurice Bialkin, cellist; Charles Holland, tenor; and Mildred Waldman, pianist. Each musician was asked to contribute $2,000 to the consortium for the trip abroad. All but one were able to raise the requested amount. Dixon didn't want to leave Charles Holland behind, because he believed in his talent and knew the proper exposure in Europe would benefit his career. Dixon found two sisters who lived in Pennsylvania that were open to supporting his enterprise, but they needed convincing. Dixon hopped in his Hudson and drove to Pennsylvania. He met with the sisters and gave a formal presentation of why he and his colleagues were planning the trip to Paris and why Holland's participation was essential. He ended his presentation with a recording of Holland in concert. Dixon was able to convince the sisters to sponsor Holland. It was done! They had raised the money needed to get to Paris. The hope was that they would be able to survive once they got there. Dixon had one major performance remaining with the New York Philharmonic before he, his family, and his musician friends made the long journey across the Atlantic.

Dixon was invited to conduct the New York Philharmonic's Young People's Concert on November 19 at Carnegie Hall. He was the ideal choice for this series because he had become known throughout the city as a specialist

in music education for youth of all ages due to his successful concerts with
the American Youth Orchestra. Aside from the racial bias, Dixon believed
the "baby specialist" label was a death sentence for his professional career in
America. Dixon believed this "label" made it easier for professional orchestras not to feel obliged to invite him for their regular subscriptions as long as
they had some type of youth concert series available.

Dixon, his family, and the members of his consortium arrived in Paris in
late November. He was set to conduct the Radiodiffusion Francaise Orchestra on December 5 and 8. During most of their stay in Paris, Dixon, Vivian,
and Diane called the Hotel Madison their home away from home. This traditional townhouse hotel, located in the heart of the intellectual district of
Paris, was an ideal place for this interracial family. The overt racial bias that
plagued him throughout his career in the States was less obvious in Europe.
Later in his career, having spent several years in Europe, he said about his
experience with racial bias: "To keep the record absolutely straight I must
inform you that in my personal history I have found no existing place where I
am not at some time, by some one, in some way reminded that I am a Black
man. I feel this is very important for all Blacks to know; namely, that there is
prejudice throughout Europe, even as in America. The great difference being
that it is less large, less all encompassing, less obvious, less violent, but
nevertheless there."[1]

Dixon began rehearsals with the radio orchestra shortly after their arrival
to Paris. His calm and assuring demeanor served him well, at least with the
musicians that immediately saw the talent that garnered so much attention in
the States. Parisians, who had not yet witnessed Dixon's gifts on the podium,
viewed his first appearance in their homeland as not only a spectacle of the
highest order but an audition as well. Because Dixon was promoted in Paris
as a specialist in American music, it was a surprise and a concern for many to
have Brahms's First Symphony programmed in his first concert in Europe.
Along with Brahms, Gershwin's *American in Paris* was also on the program.
Now Gershwin, they understood. But how could a Black man from Harlem
truly understand the European nuances of one of the finest symphonists to
ever live? Despite their concerns, Dixon was determined not to become the
"American specialist" in Europe in the same unfortunate way he was labeled
a "baby specialist" in the States. If Dixon allowed this to happen it would
make it increasingly difficult for him to negotiate his repertoire preferences
for future concerts. He needed to prove from the outset that he could perform
the European repertoire with the same kind of sophistication, passion, and
understanding as the music of his homeland. It paid off. His debut in Europe
was a tremendous success. His performance had a number of critics singing
his praises. One critic in particular stated that all that was remaining for
Dixon to become "the most complete conductor of our times" was a thorough
indoctrination in the European culture. Dixon's success made it possible for

him to eventually abandon the American component to his programming as an unspoken contingency to guest conducting prospects. That is not to say that Dixon wasn't a proponent for American music. By 1952, Dixon had presented the first European performances of more than fifty contemporary works by American composers like Henry Cowell, Howard Hanson, Ulysses Kay, Edward MacDowell, Walter Piston, Wallingford Riegger, Howard Swanson, and Robert Ward. Dixon wanted Europeans to know that American composers were not caricatures but well-trained, sophisticated, innovative musicians worthy of serious consideration.

His initial success in Paris did not translate to financial stability. For his work with the Radiodiffusion Francaise, Dixon received 10,000 francs, which was $28 in U.S. currency. His first year in Paris produced only five conducting engagements that paid him a total of $100. The 1949–1950 season left Dixon and Vivian concerned as to how they were going to make ends meet. Vivian was able to perform and teach a few students while in Paris, but her main responsibility was taking care of Diane. Dixon started a few ad hoc orchestras in Paris designed to bring in additional funds, but they didn't last very long. With their savings quickly depleting, and the consortium funds almost gone, Dixon had no choice but to travel back to the States to raise money. His first trip back was in early April of 1950. His goal to raise money during his brief stay in America was accomplished through a combination of lectures, guest conducting, and soliciting funds from wealthy businessmen who were interested to see Dixon's career flourish in Europe. His friends, who had deep pockets and connections throughout the city, set up a number of gatherings to allow Dixon to present his case for supporting "one of their own." This entire ordeal was very stressful on Dixon.

That stress had taken a serious physical toll on him during his third and last summer visit to the States in 1952. Unlike the first two visits in 1950 and 1951, his last visit did not include lectures or guest conducting as a way to raise money. This time around it was all about securing short-term and long-term loans. One morning, as he prepared to leave his mother's home to give a pitch for sponsorship, he experienced a serious asthma attack.

> The last time I was back in '52, I found that when I got up in the morning, I got up with asthma. No dog, no horse, no nothing. . . . I showered, and after I showered I had to stand in front of the window for roughly ten minutes, breathing deeply, before I could move. . . . This went on—ten minutes activity—ten minutes stop—while I had breakfast and picked up my briefcase and went out to raise money. When I got downstairs and got as far as from the house to the corner, maybe 40 or 50 meters, I had to stop and put my bag down. I always stood against the wall of the house wherever I stopped, put the bag down, and just looked up at the sky, the buildings, till I caught my breath. I couldn't go farther. I couldn't cross the street, the asthma was so heavy. [2]

Once the attack subsided, Dixon made his way to the designated place where he would give his presentation.

He began his pitch by presenting newspaper clippings of his reviews in Paris. He then talked extensively about the need for Americans to adopt the philosophy that Europeans demonstrated with their native musicians that showed great promise. Dixon saw firsthand in Europe that if you exhibited extraordinary talent in music, there was a system (both private and public) in place to support that talent. He then touted the fact that he had procured representation in France and Scandinavia. This was a very important part of the presentation to the prospective donors, because here was yet another demonstration of his talent and potential being acknowledged in Europe while ignored in the States. In less than two years, Dixon was offered a number of permanent conducting posts that he turned down on the advice of his management team. Accepting at least one of these positions would have surely brought in much needed revenue, so he felt obliged to explain to the prospective donors the rationale behind his managers' decision.

> A word as to my not having accepted the permanent conducting offers. Whereas they have certain prestige value and offer some financial return, Mr. Enwall, my Scandinavian manager, in grooming me for a place as one of the internationally known and accepted conductors, most strongly states that I should not accept any such permanent post at this stage of my career since it can only serve to bury rather than build me. He does suggest in its stead, however, that I endeavor to make time available for further study to enlarge my symphonic repertoire, and to also prepare myself to enter the field of opera in Europe. [3]

The last part of Dixon's presentation was an itemized listing of his income and expenses. Dixon's income for twenty-three concert engagements for the 1951–1952 concert season was $2,287.20. His expenses, which included transportation, food, hotel stay, management dues, and so on, were $7,062.86, which left a deficit of $4,775.66.

While Dixon put his best effort forward for every presentation, the response was tepid at best. He was expecting the wealthy donors to write huge checks as an investment in a worthy American musician. While there were a few donations that were in the thousands, most were in the range of ten to twenty dollars. Dixon was disappointed by the measly pittance donated and loaned to him. He knew these gentlemen could have easily covered his entire expenses in Europe and not felt any financial discomfort doing so.

While his efforts in the States to raise money were a bust, his management team in Europe was working hard to secure guest conducting engagements. He received his first extended guest conducting invitation with the Israel Philharmonic in 1950. He was there for the months of July and August. By the end of the year Italy opened its doors to Dixon, with an invitation to conduct the Alessandro Scarlatti Orchestra in Naples. While Dixon and Vivian were still struggling financially, they began to see some signs of movement in the right direction. They were halfway through their second year in Europe and Dixon's guest conducting engagements had already equaled the entire 1949–1950 concert season. To cut expenses wherever he could, Dixon was making plans to move his family out of the Hotel Madison and into a more affordable dwelling.

On October 6, 1950, Vivian penned a letter expressing her excitement about a unique proposal presented to Dixon by a young American architect.

> I am very excited at this moment. Dean met a young American chap, an architect, who has a fantastic idea for us. . . . He spent a whole week discussing this with all sorts of people. This morning we brought an engineer over to this chap's place. He too is excited about it. Well, the idea is that he wants to build us a houseboat. It will be docked on the Seine River within the city limits. The cost is ridiculously cheap, about five hundred dollars. I will get Dean to draw you a detailed picture of it, but really, the plans look terrific. It will be very modern. The wall that faces the river will be all glass. The beds, desks, tables will all be built in. There will be a small room for Diane with a double decker bed, a small bath, kitchen, and storage space. The living room will be about 22 by 15 feet. We will be able to connect with the city water supply and electricity and use bottled gas for heating and cooking. Bottled gas is very inexpensive here and lasts a long time. [4]

Vivian continued in her letter that after their engineer friend spoke with the architect, asking various technical questions about things she and Dixon knew nothing about (like water proofing, insulation, etc.), he was impressed with the proposal and if it were approved by the city he would be the young architect's next customer. Dixon was so excited by the prospect of a unique home being custom-built for his family that he couldn't sleep that entire night. The architect's fee for building the houseboat was 10 percent of the cost, which came to fifty dollars. The next day, Dixon made it his priority to visit the local port authority to get more information on rules and regulations for building a domicile of this type. No correspondence exists to indicate what transpired at the port authority office, but the excitement that was clearly evident in both Vivian and Dixon did not result in a houseboat being built on the Seine River. Instead, they settled in a small apartment a few miles from the Hotel Madison.

As Dixon became more recognized in Europe as an exceptional interpreter of Beethoven and Brahms, he was asked to give his views of the two composers and what they meant to him from a conductor's point of view. He said,

> I find that there is more to do with the orchestra in Brahms than with Beethoven, whereas on the other hand Beethoven gives me personally more intellectual satisfaction. But in the mixing of Brahms' orchestral colors, in getting the

feeling of the classic-romantic, near romantic, this cross juxtaposition of the
rubati, of things that Brahms didn't write down where the music has to move a
little, where he writes for example a diminuendo and within that diminuendo
are crescendo diminuendo—these subtleties are not part of the cloth of Beethoven, so for a conductor building and molding and shaping and coloring
there is more to do along these lines in Brahms. [5]

This very clear distinction of composers was not only evident in his performances but in his criticism of conductors that felt the need to romanticize
Beethoven. Statements like this not only cemented to many Europeans his
understanding of "their" music, but his reputation as an intellectual with
common sense was growing.

In mid-December of 1951 Dixon and Vivian were preparing to leave
Paris for an engagement in Vienna with the Vienna Symphony Orchestra.
Both were performing on the same concert. When possible, Dixon always
tried to negotiate a piano concerto on his programs that would feature Vivian.
This was a win-win situation for the Dixon household, because, of course,
two paychecks were better than one. This duo engagement also allowed them
to travel to different cities as a family—with Diane and their housekeeper,
Germaine, always close by.

Before their departure to Vienna they met with noted American photographer Gordon Parks. Parks was working for *Life* magazine and was stationed
in Paris for two years to cover the French collection. He was also a novice
composer struggling to complete his first piano concerto. He asked if Dixon
and Vivian would listen to a recording of what he had completed. They
agreed. Parks was thrilled that after the hearing both Dixon and Vivian were
impressed at what he had written thus far. They were even more impressed
that Parks had no formal training in composition. Parks had developed "an
intricate mathematical system for using numbers that corresponded to
notes."[6] This unorthodox system provided Parks the means to create themes
and harmonic structures. Dixon encouraged Parks to contact him once the
concerto was completed because he wanted to program the work at an upcoming concert. A week later Parks received a letter from Dixon with very
detailed instructions on ways to develop a better understanding of musical
form. Dixon advised Parks to find two or three good recordings of any
symphony and/or concerto he desired and to listen to them numerous times,
until it became second nature. He wanted Parks to be able to detect the
nuances of musical form for each work. Dixon would follow up with Parks
through correspondence, asking specific questions, as a way to guide his
creative process in the right direction. A few months later, after receiving
much needed encouragement from Dixon and Vivian, Parks enlisted the help
of Henry Brant (a composer and respected orchestrator based in New York
City) to help him with putting his ideas on paper. Dixon knew Brant and

recommended that Parks seek his help. Parks sent Brant a piano recording of all the main themes for each of the four movements that were to be used in the concerto. When Parks returned to the States, he worked arduously with Brant to complete his concerto. After several months of revisions, the composition was orchestrated and ready to be performed. He gave the concerto the title Symphonic Set for Piano and Orchestra. Parks received a cable from Dixon in the summer of 1952 simply stating, "Your work is programmed for Venice concert on the 10th of July. Send score quickest. We expect you to follow it. Dean." Parks was finally able to dust off the score that had been lying in wait in his hall closet for some months. He made plans to have the score shipped out in June, and Parks arrived a few days before the concert. When he arrived he was finally able to listen to his composition with full orchestration for the first time. A recording was made of one of the rehearsals. Parks, Vivian, and Dixon reconvened in a hotel room and listened to the recording for any last-minute changes. The concert took place in the picturesque five-hundred-year-old courtyard palace of the Doges. Parks's work, which was third on the program, was given a prolonged ovation. Vivian would record the concerto in New York several years later.

Dixon's major break in Europe occurred in Helsinki, Finland, on December 14, 1951. He was invited to replace an ailing Igor Markevitch as guest conductor of the Helsinki Stadsorkester. He had already conducted in Helsinki in April, so the natives were already aware of Dixon's ability. But replacing Igor Markevitch, someone who was already established in Europe, at the last moment with Dixon, who was just starting to build his reputation in Europe, made for a dramatic spectacle. On the concert program was Beethoven's *Coriolan* Overture, Brahms's Second Symphony, and Sibelius's Fifth Symphony. It was a success. One critic stated, "Dean Dixon . . . is an excellent interpreter of European symphonic music, and it is indeed a pleasure to note that Sibelius' music is in good hands—in the long, dark-skinned hands of a musician, hands that despise the baton but give a remarkably living rhythm."[7] The concert was also heard on the radio. There was one particular person listening to the radio that night whose praise of Dixon's performance would elevate his reputation like no other could. It was Jean Sibelius, the renowned Finnish composer, who heard the concert and phoned the intendant the next day inquiring about Dixon: "This is a man I want to see. He has understood what I meant." Word of Sibelius's praiseworthy comments of Dixon's performance spread throughout Europe. Arrangements were made for Dixon to meet the Finnish composer at his home, "an honor given few Americans during the last years of the composer's life."[8]

Dixon was the only American invited to Sibelius's home that afternoon. Dignitaries from France, Germany, and Italy were in attendance. Dixon, initially, had some difficulty communicating, because at that time he was only fluent in English. As he did for all of his conducting engagements in

Europe, where English was not generally spoken, Dixon prepared notecards with salutations, questions, and so forth.

At the moment Dixon met Sibelius, he was instantly impressed at the octogenarian's physical appearance.

> Though 87, Sibelius stood straight as a soldier. . . . His tremendous bald head was by then a trademark, as were his remarkably large ears. His penetrating deep blue eyes and every movement radiated energy; his skin, despite his age, appeared youthful. . . . [When] offered coffee, I chose to drink it black. The composer suddenly looked up, an amused look in his eyes, since this was also his preference. Later, we were offered six or seven different types of liquor and I chose cognac—as did Sibelius; now studying me, for cognac was his choice. We were offered cigarettes and I declined because I was at the time a heavy cigar smoker. At that moment his eyes lit up, he raised his glass toward me and shouted, Skol! From then on we were in the world of music. He congratulated me on my performance which he had heard on the radio. [9]

Dixon followed up his successful performance with two concerts for young people. The event was sponsored by the Mannerheim League and the Modern Music Society. Dixon opened up the event with a speech to the children hoping that each of them would experience pleasant and spontaneous moments throughout the concert. Dixon brought to the Helsinki community an innovative and entertaining way to introduce young people to the orchestra without watering down the music or its meaning. He prepared "fairy tale" stories that would allow for various instruments in the orchestra to demonstrate a musical term. After a brief introduction, Dixon began his presentation by saying,

> Once upon a time there was a little boy who was born BRIDGE (cue the Brass, Violin, Woodwinds). Outstanding about this little boy was the fact that he has a father whose main interest in life was AUGMENTATION (cue the Trombone). That is, except when he was occupied with his DIMINUTION (cue the Flute). Well, one rainy day this little boy opened his closet door and to his great surprise saw, standing there looking at him, a big frightening TRILL (cue the Piccolo). You can imagine his shock! His breath did a large FERMATA (cue the Tuba). His feet made rapid COL LEGNO (cue the Strings). His heart went PIZZICATO (cue the Strings). His eyes went down in GLISSANDO (cue the Trombone). He then screamed, turned around, ran out of the room and up the stairs in one long SCALE (cue the Oboe). At the top step he tripped and fell down the stairs in a big ARPEGGIO (cue the Clarinet). Out of breath he picked himself up and tried the stairs again, but found that he was so nervous that the stairs seemed to be moving and he could only go up stairs in a BROKEN SCALE (cue the Bassoon). Finally, arriving at the top he started to run again, but this time in ACCELERANDO (cue the Strings: do re mi fa sol fa mi re do etc.). After 5 or 6 kilometers he began to get a little tired and we find him running in RALLENTANDO (cue the Woodwinds: sol fa mi re do re

mi fa sol etc.). But then he began to ask himself, "What am I afraid of?" and taking a big sigh in PONTICELLO (cue the Strings) he stopped and started to converse with the TRILL in animated ANTIPHOCATION (cue the Trumpet and Piccolo). And that, dear friends, is where we leave our hero till next time.[10]

Dixon used this and other methods he developed in the States with the American Youth Orchestra throughout his time in Europe when presenting concerts for young people.

All in all, Helsinki was the beginning of Dixon's career in Europe. Thanks in part to Jean Sibelius's stamp of approval, orchestras throughout Europe were lining up to get a chance to book Dixon as their next guest conductor. Reporters of all nationalities were also lining up to get a chance to interview Europe's newest sensation. Within two years, Dixon went from six guest-conducting engagements in Paris to more than sixty throughout Europe and beyond. His management team began negotiations for his first guest conducting engagement in England. They also began contract negotiations with the Westminster Recording Company to record three concertos in Vienna with Vivian as the piano soloist.

As his professional life seemed to be heading in the right direction, his personal life was something different altogether. It began in Helsinki when he was introduced to the Finnish journalist/playwright Mary Mandelin.

Chapter Ten

Mary

Mary Mandelin was born in Finland, a descendant of Finnish nobility. She was raised on the Arrajoki Estates in the Nastola Province. At the time, this massive property was made up of more than ten lakes and untouched backwoods. Mary was a sheltered child, who was raised to appreciate the finer things in life. Her education as a youth was one of privilege and prestige attending the Svenska Flickskolan (a private school for girls in Sweden). Her university life was spent in France's Sorbonne. Her father was president of the Scandinavian Red Cross and worked for the Finnish government. "He belonged to the Swedish-speaking minority of Finland, who owned the big estates and ran the Government and the universities."[1] Her mother was a member of the famous Wrede af Elima family. They were the epitome of nobility, wealth, and influence.

After her formal education in France, Mary moved back to her homeland in 1939, where she actively participated in the Winter War.[2] Mary was a member of the Lotta Svärd during this period. This all-woman organization was an auxiliary to the army and helped in all areas as needed, especially in the hospitals and air raid warning positions. Mary became ill during her service with the Lotta Svärd and was sent to Denmark for treatment. It was very likely that her illness was quite serious to be sent to a place that at the time was under occupation by the Nazi regime.[3] Once Mary recovered she remained in Denmark and worked as a guardian to Finnish children. She also fell in love with a marine officer by the name of Reims. Mary and the captain were married a short time later. Their marriage produced two children, Daniela and Marina. Captain Reims spent a great deal of his time away at sea, so Mary focused her attention on raising her children and writing. Feeling uncomfortable with the stiffness of her aristocratic life, after the war she moved to Helsinki, where she made a life for herself as a journalist for the local paper.

It was in 1951 that Mary was sent to cover the Red Cross benefit concert that featured Dixon as the guest conductor. Like most in her country that had not seen Dixon in action, she was skeptical. Everyone was talking about the brilliance of this Negro conductor from Harlem, but Mary was not convinced. It wasn't until she saw Dixon handling the music of Brahms and Sibelius with such grace and authority that she fell in with the rest of Europe who had already experienced this high level of artistry on display. However, Mary's reaction to Dixon's presence on stage was likely different than most. As Dixon entered the stage to mount the podium, Mary was surprised to find herself physically attracted to him, having never met the man before her visit. This unexpected reaction was so disturbing to Mary that she began to tremble. She was very comfortable in her marriage with Captain Reims, raising her children, working as a journalist, and honing her skills as a playwright. Moreover, Mary made it clear that while growing up in Paris, she associated with Negroes at social events and disliked every moment she spent in their sight: "I was frightened of them."[4] Mary clearly understood her current status as a married woman, that Dixon was a married man, that they both had children, and he was Black. But in her mind, she could not shake the thought of Dixon being in her life. She believed they were destined to be together.

While her initial assignment was to write a story on the conductor and the Red Cross benefit concert, she was compelled to meet Dixon in person. She knew the concertmaster of the orchestra performing that night, so she phoned him to request an interview with Dixon for the newspaper. The concertmaster was giving a cocktail party and Dixon was going to be in attendance, so he arranged for the two to meet. Mary recalled getting to the cocktail party very early. Dixon had not yet arrived. Mary was nervous to meet the man who had ignited such feelings in her from just one indirect meeting. She was pacing near a window, talking to herself, trying to muster up the courage to do an interview, in the usual way she had done many times before. Mary recognized that there would be one major difference with this interview. She had fallen in love with Dixon at first sight! Finally, it happened. Dixon arrived. The concertmaster introduced the two and then went about his business of hosting. When Mary saw him face to face, she knew that "this is the man I must marry! I was so shocked and embarrassed by the force of my feeling that I turned and walked quickly out of the room. He was furious, thinking I had snubbed him. He followed me and we talked and that was that!"[5]

Initially, Dixon was oblivious to Mary's feelings until the interview commenced. It seems she was able to get at least one official question in before things turned personal. Mary remembered from the interview that Dixon was always fascinated by the music of Sibelius, with particular interest in his fifth symphony. "When I interviewed him, Dean told me how he had walked the streets of Harlem analyzing the score [of the fifth symphony] in his mind."[6] They met again in 1952, when Dixon was invited by Sibelius to Helsinki to conduct his music. From that point on, they began seeing each other whenever they could. They also traveled together, occasionally, when Dixon had conducting engagements outside of Paris. One trip together nearly cost them their lives. Dixon and Mary traveled to the Saari Estates in Finland to meet with the director of Mary's plays, Vivica Bandler. At that time, they were returning from a conducting engagement in Sicily. Against the advice of Mary, Dixon decided to drive his new car from Sicily to Finland. Dixon referred to his pride and joy as a "new dollar smile." The roads in Finland during this time of the year were treacherously slick, covered with a blanket of snow and ice. Mary's fear was realized. Dixon lost control of the car and ran into another vehicle coming in the opposite direction. Dixon's "new dollar smile" was no more. What made the situation worse was that on impact Mary hit her head on the console and blacked out. Dixon spoke not a word of Finnish and everyone he encountered during this ordeal spoke not a word of English. Three hours passed before help arrived. While Mary would make a full recovery, she required bed rest for ten days. Dixon was there during her recovery. There was no denying it. They were a couple. There was only one problem. They both were still married to different people.

Dixon recalled that around this time he and Vivian began the serious discussion of separation and eventually divorce. The unpleasantness of knowing that a marriage was over was made even more awkward when contracts that had been negotiated and signed long before the dissolution of said marriage still had to be honored. This was the case for Dixon and Vivian. The contract that was negotiated in 1951 with Westminster Recording Company was signed in April of 1952, with scheduled recording dates a few months later on October 21 and 26. They were slated to record Edward MacDowell's two concertos for piano and orchestra with the Vienna State Opera Orchestra. Their personal difficulties did not interfere with their professional obligations. The recording sessions in October finished on time. The album was released the following year, receiving favorable reviews. Shortly after their recording session in Vienna, arrangements were made for Vivian and Diane to move back to America. Their divorce was final on December 17, 1953, in Copenhagen. In the decree, the Danish courts ordered Dixon to pay child support and alimony totaling $60 a week. To this Dixon stated, "This was an IMPOSSIBLE amount for me to realize."[7] He was unable to keep up with the payments and Vivian had no choice but to seek legal remedies.

By all accounts Vivian was devastated by the dissolution of her marriage. It was clear that she didn't want many people in the States to know about the divorce. When asked by a reporter with *Jet* magazine (a publication covering various topics in the Black community) to confirm their divorce, she claimed that she and Dixon were still married. Her career, which was on a major upward trajectory, became stagnant when she moved back to New York. She still performed (primarily solo and chamber) and recorded occasionally, but nothing major came of it. She opened up a piano studio, teaching from her apartment at the Hotel Ansonia, where Dixon and Vivian first resided as husband and wife. Teaching privately became her main source of income. And she was very successful. Gordon Parks was one of many notables of New York who took their children to study with Vivian. The dream of being an internationally recognized pianist that she embraced while matriculating at Juilliard was not to be. While there was no record of Vivian ever corresponding with Dixon again, she did make sure that Diane maintained contact with her grandmother, McClara. Dixon would not see Diane again for nearly twenty years.

News of Mary's impending divorce from Captain Reims was a major scandal in Scandinavia. No one in Mary's family and within her social circle fully understood why she could even consider marrying a Black man. His fame, his charm, and his intellect did not matter. It was the color of Dixon's skin that should have brought Mary to her senses. During the year that divorce papers were being filed, many of Mary's friends and family disowned her because of her decision to openly live with Dixon before the divorce was final. This for many was like pouring salt on an already festering wound. She was no longer welcomed in the social circles and family gatherings that she had grown accustomed to. While this treatment hurt Mary, she was more concerned about how her daughters would react to the divorce and Dixon becoming a permanent fixture in their family. According to Mary, Daniela and Marina did not have a close relationship with their father and Captain Reims was not interested in separating his daughters from their mother. Moreover, there is no record of Captain Reims expressing concerns with his children being in residence with Dixon.

Mary was surprised at how quickly Daniela and Marina embraced Dixon as their father figure. On January 25, 1954, Dixon and Mary were married. Six months later in Helsinki on July 28, Mary gave birth to a healthy girl, Nina Dixon. After the birth of Nina and as Dixon's reputation grew, Mary was able to mend some relationships with friends and family, but others would never be able to forgive her for what she had done.

Dixon's first appearance in Sweden with the Gothenburg Symphony Orchestra was on January 27, 1952. He was engaged for four concerts. The main work on the program was Beethoven's iconic Fifth Symphony. The success of this concert was so profound and so well received by the Swedish natives that later that year Dixon was offered additional guest conducting dates with the orchestra. The hope in Gothenburg was that he would accept the invitation to become one of three principal conductors of the orchestra the following year. Dixon accepted the offer because he and his manager,

Mr. Enwall, believed that the prestige of the orchestra and its central location (the second largest city in Sweden) provided the right place to further his career. He shared the position with outgoing principal conductor Issay Dobrowen (1941–1953) and current principal conductor of the Gothenburg Radio Orchestra, Sixten Eckerberg (1937–1970). While contractually, Dixon was the sole principal conductor for the Gothenburg Symphony Orchestra, it was decided to keep Dobrowen and Eckerberg on, temporarily, as a shared position for those who had issues with a foreigner taking the helm. It was a precaution that proved to be unnecessary. A few years later, without any preamble, the concert programs listed Dixon as the "Forst dirigent." He brought to the city of Gothenburg a quiet but self-assured personality that was well received by the Swedish natives. The orchestra appreciated his bold ideas for programming, making sure that he promoted the contemporary works of Swedish composers like Hilding Rosenberg, Lars-Erik Larsson, and Gunnar de Frumerie. His interpretation of Brahms, Beethoven, and Mozart were highly lauded. Dixon moved his new family to Sweden where they settled in a small flat in Gothenburg.

Mary's role in the Dixon household became a crucial one. While Dixon was an exceptional musician, it was Mary who helped him understand better than anyone at the time the European culture. She spoke several languages, which made it easy for Dixon to correspond with other countries about guest conducting engagements. Dixon was a quick study and was well on his way to becoming fluent in German, Swedish, and Italian. But Mary was with him at most of his engagements to translate when necessary. Although Mary's background had no remote connection to Dixon's life in the States, she clearly understood his plight as a Black man in America and the American-influenced cities of Europe. "It is no good for him being just as good as someone else. Because he is Dean Dixon, with a different colored skin, he must be twice as good. It is very wearing on him. I am strong and I take some of the blows for him."[8] She also felt it was important to play the role of the dutiful wife when they were together in public. "When he is present I must consciously check my personality. He is the star, and all I can be is a little twinkling light somewhere in the corner."[9] The submissive role that Mary publicly demonstrated slowly but surely birthed resentment in their marriage because she began to lose her identity. She was no longer Mary Mandelin, the journalist and playwright. She became Mrs. Dixon, the constant companion.

With the acquisition of his first permanent post in Europe, Dixon found that not only did the number of guest conducting engagements increase, but the artistic level of the soloists that were engaged to appear with him went up exponentially. Walter Gieseking, who, according to Dixon, was at the apex of his artistic powers, was slated to perform the Brahms B-flat Piano Concerto with him in Turin, Italy. Dixon was aware of Gieseking's larger than life personality as an artist, but was not completely prepared to deal with the ego that accompanied it. It all started during one of Dixon's rehearsals when a messenger sprinted into the auditorium to inform Dixon that the "maestro is here!" The assumption was that Dixon would stop everything he was doing to welcome Geiseking personally. Dixon was never one to stop a rehearsal for anyone, barring some type of an emergency. Since this was clearly not an emergency, Dixon replied to the messenger that he would see the maestro at the end of the rehearsal. When they met, Dixon noticed immediately this very tall, imposing figure of a man looking down at him. According to Dixon, Gieseking had an air of superiority about him that could cause some uncomfortable moments. Once they were introduced, Dixon asked Gieseking if he would play for him so as to have a better understanding of how to handle the orchestra. Gieseking refused, stating that he never played more than once a day. Instead he proceeded to make a fuss about where the piano and microphones were positioned. He had everything moved to his specifications. He also felt the need to personally greet members of the orchestra right before the rehearsal started. Dixon believed Gieseking thought very little of him as a conductor and was trying to take control of the entire affair, essentially usurping his authority. As the rehearsal commenced, there were ensemble problems throughout. As they reached the climax of the first cadenza of this massive concerto, Dixon somehow missed a beat and there was a momentary gap between piano and orchestra. Dixon turned to Gieseking and asked, "Do you plan to play it this way?" To which Gieseking replied, "Just listen to the left hand. I will play it the way I played it [before]."[10] As the rehearsal continued more problems occurred, but Gieseking seemed impressed with how the young conductor was handling the situation. Clearly recognizing that something had to give for this performance to go well, Gieseking said to Dixon, "You conduct. I will follow you." From there it all seemed to flow beautifully. The concert was a success and Dixon found in Gieseking a true friend. Sadly, in 1955 Gieseking and his wife were passengers on a bus that was involved in a serious accident. Gieseking survived, sustaining severe head injuries, but his wife died from her injuries. Gieseking eventually recovered and was performing and recording again. Dixon was stunned to discover that a year after the accident, the larger than life pianist from Germany who was one of the great interpreters of Debussy and Ravel, and the friend who gave him such a difficult time on their first meeting, suddenly died.

Having a permanent post with steady guest conducting engagements made for a comfortable lifestyle. The steady income made it possible for Dixon to purchase a small villa in Lago di Como. Situated a few miles from Milan, Italy, Lago di Como, or Lake Como, is shaped like an inverted Y and surrounded by hills and mountains with beautiful villas and resorts interspersed throughout. Dixon loved it when he was able to make it to his second home in Italy. He recounts, "How wonderful it is to be able to pick my restaurant and know that I am served as well and as best as they can manage. And never have an empty taxi that I need pass me by."[11] "The places, which we found prejudice or racism in Italy, were where their clientele had been or still was primarily American. In order to keep the American dollars, since they had heard so much of 'if you let a Negro into this place, then I won't come back,' it was much easier to keep Negroes out."[12] On many occasions in Europe, Dixon experienced subtle and not so subtle forms of discrimination. In most cases Dixon took it in stride, appreciating the different levels of bias when comparing America to Europe. However, he had very little tolerance for this type of treatment when he was with his family. He recalls a tense moment in Malmo, Sweden, when he was with his family that tested his tolerance to its limits.

> Once we got on a ferry between Copenhagen and Malmo and we came in a party; the two of us [Mary and I], our three children, and a maid. We walked up to the first-class restaurant (we had first class tickets) and my wife asked for a table of six. The waiter takes a quick look and says, "We have no place." So I said, "How come?" because we were very early. "I don't serve Negroes," says he. I said, "You wait," and I dashed up to the captain. The captain was enraged. The ferry was delayed for half an hour, there was a big scene, and the fellow was kicked off.[13]

Dixon never heard the phrase "we don't serve Negroes" anywhere else but in the States and those places in Europe where there was a very strong connection with American tourists and businesses.

Being associated with Dixon, Mary endured the same bewildered looks and treatment that Dean received. It eventually took a toll on her. When asked her views on interracial marriages she said, "[I] would always advise others against a mixed marriage. I believe the chances of it succeeding are slim in spite of my own marriage being extremely happy."[14] Moreover, she often worried about Nina's fate as a child of mixed race. As a way of coping with the realities of her daughter's future, she would make the comment that Nina was better off than most children of mixed race because she had fair skin and looked more Italian than Black.

News of Dixon's life in Europe was featured in a December 1957 article in *Ebony* magazine entitled, "World's Foremost Negro Conductor Dean Dixon becomes permanent director of symphony orchestra in Gothenburg, Sweden." It featured a number of pictures of Dixon's villa in Italy and his new family. Aside from the racial aspect, which was ever-present no matter where he resided, the article gave the impression that Dixon was "living the good life." Vivian was aware of Dixon's new life in Europe, because it was around this time that *Jet* magazine reported that she filed a suit against him in New York Municipal Court for unpaid alimony. According to Vivian, in the four years since their divorce was final, Dixon only paid $120 in alimony. Vivian claimed that Dixon owed more than $10,000. The court ordered that Dixon's royalties from Westminster Records, which at the time were $3,000, be given to Vivian for alimony arrears. The assumption was that if he could afford two homes, he could afford to take care of his first daughter.

Dixon appeared with the Hessischer Rundfunk Symphony Orchestra in Frankfurt, Germany, on January 9, 1959, performing Beethoven's Symphony No. 6, Hindemith's Concert Music for piano, brass, and harp, with pianist Monique Hass, and Ravel's *Rhapsodie Espagnole*. It was during this time that Dixon and Mary began making plans to leave the Gothenburg Symphony for Germany. For Dixon, Germany was the epicenter of great music making and the place to be in order to move upward in his career. Moreover, his reputation as an excellent interpreter of Brahms, Beethoven, and Mozart in the "Germanic tradition" did not go unnoticed. So when the decision was officially announced to leave Sweden, Dixon had been offered and was seriously considering three permanent posts in Germany: the Hannover Radio Symphony Orchestra; the Bavarian Radio Symphony Orchestra in Munich; and the Frankfurt Radio Symphony Orchestra. Dixon chose Frankfurt.

Chapter Eleven

Drama, Down Under

In October of 1962, Dixon was invited to conduct the major orchestras of the Australian Broadcasting Commission (ABC). The tour was scheduled to last for ten weeks. Dixon started his tour in Melbourne for six days; Brisbane for three days; Adelaide for three days; Perth for two days; five subscription concerts with the Sydney Symphony Orchestra; back in Melbourne for one day; and he ended his tour with a Mozart festival in Sydney Town Hall.

Dixon's debut in Melbourne, where he performed Mahler's Ninth Symphony, set the tone for the remainder of his concerts in Australia. One critic said that "from the tension he radiated from the very first bars onward it was quite clear: Dixon is a giant of music."[1]

But it was the performance on November 21, 1962, when Dixon made his debut with the Sydney Symphony Orchestra, that made a lasting impression on all those in attendance, especially the ABC general manager, Sir Charles Moses. He performed Sibelius's Symphony No. 4, Strauss's *Till Eulenspiegel's Merry Pranks*, Prokofiev's Piano Concerto No. 3, and Falla's *Three Cornered Hat*. Even before his appearance in Sydney, Sir Charles had already heard great things about Dixon from his previous performances in Australia and wanted to meet with him personally: "I feel it is about time we met—you've been here too long already without me seeing you! Can you have lunch with me at Broadcast House, on Monday, 26th of November? Please try to make it."[2] Dixon was able to meet with Sir Charles at Broadcast House to discuss the current vacancy in Sydney. He left Australia knowing that he was a serious candidate to replace the Ukrainian conductor Nicolai Malko, who was the orchestra's director until his death on June 23, 1961. Sir Charles said of Dixon that he made a fine impression in Australia and that he would like to see him back again.

Dixon jetted back to Frankfurt with a sense of accomplishment in Australia. But he quickly had to turn his attention to his responsibilities in Frankfurt and prepare for his next major guest conducting engagement in London. The BBC Symphony Orchestra invited Dixon to guest conduct on March 20, 1963, at the Royal Festival Hall. He performed Mahler's First Symphony. After a successful debut with the BBC, he was quickly invited to return next season for two guest conducting engagements. His appearance on October 30, 1963, featured Bruckner's Ninth Symphony, and his appearance on February 19, 1964, featured Mahler's Seventh Symphony. It was after these well-received performances that Dixon was lauded as an exceptional interpreter of the symphonies of Mahler and Bruckner. Along with Brahms and Beethoven, he would count Mahler and Bruckner among his favorites and programmed them often throughout his career.

By the time the decision was announced by the ABC that Dixon was taking the helm of the Sydney Symphony Orchestra (SSO), he and Mary had to quickly figure out the logistics of how this new position would fit into his already hectic schedule. He was already spending close to 110 working days of each year with his orchestra in Frankfurt, leaving the remaining time for his guest conducting engagements. Mary felt that Dixon was spreading himself too thin already and that taking on another permanent position so far away from Europe was not wise. But Dixon believed he could make it work. First, it was paramount that he make sure that his new position did not interfere with his obligations in Frankfurt. Second, he and Mary had to work out their transportation and living arrangements in Frankfurt. They sold their home in Bergen-Enkheim (the city district in the eastern part of Frankfurt) and moved into an apartment in the heart of the city. This was done for mobility and easy access to and from the airport. Third, they enrolled Nina, who was nine at the time, in the Frankfurt Rudolf Steiner School. This particular school had a branch in Sydney, which made for the least amount of interruption in Nina's studies when she accompanied her mother and Dixon to Australia.

When asked by a reporter why Dixon would disrupt such an ideal European arrangement by taking the position in Sydney, he responded by saying that he believed the SSO had the potential to be one of the world's best orchestras; that the Australian audiences have achieved a high level of listening culture; and that Australia was the only place in the world where he had not experienced any racial bias.[3] Dixon's comment on his experience in Australia as it related to racial bias was used by many Australians writing on this historic appointment as an opportunity to deal with the realities of life for the Aborigines. It was just a year ago, in 1962, when Dixon was first introduced to the people of Australia, that the Aborigines were given the right to vote in the Commonwealth elections. Five years later, a 1967 landmark referendum that amended the constitution gave the Commonwealth authority to make decisions on the welfare of the Aborigines. This meant that they would be counted in the national census for the purposes of electoral representation.[4] Those who reacted to Dixon's comments on racial bias in Australia were not necessarily criticizing his statement. They simply wanted to emphasize that this was "his" experience in Australia, and that many Aborigines could not say the same.

On May 18, 1964, Dixon received a letter from Sir Charles, informing him of the possibility that the SSO would accept an invitation to appear in England next year for the Commonwealth Festival. It so happened that the festival director, Ian Hunter, was in Sydney and Adelaide to hear the SSO and was impressed with their performances. Sir Charles told Dixon that this was the first time that any orchestra in Australia was invited to perform at the Commonwealth Festival. Dixon responded the following month, saying that he was delighted to hear about the invitation but that it was imperative that the ABC confirm their participation sooner rather than later because his concert schedule with Frankfurt was already set. Moreover, the Hessischer Rundfunk was planning a tour throughout Europe that would take place around the same time as the Commonwealth Festival. Given the conflict, Dixon recommended that Sir Charles contact Intendant Hess of the Hessischer Rundfunk in Frankfurt requesting that Dixon be available for the trip to London. Sir Charles did exactly that. Once the dates of the festival were confirmed, he contacted Intendant Hess requesting if Dixon could be available the following year from the end of August to the third week of October to perform with the SSO in England. Dr. Wicht, the program director for the Hessischer Rundfunk, responded later that month that Dixon had to be in Frankfurt by September 1 and would not be available beyond that date. Dixon found out from Hess about the decision and immediately began devising an alternate plan so that he could fulfill his responsibilities in Frankfurt and still make an appearance with the SSO in England.

Dixon's first season with the SSO as its new music director was abbreviated, meaning that he was only available during the summer months of 1964. This was because Dixon had conducting engagements during the spring months of March, April, and May in Europe that were confirmed years in advance. He arrived at the Sydney Airport in June of 1964. He was met by an impressive number of reporters and photographers. Dixon's appointment as music director of the SSO was big news in Sydney. The reporters noticed Dixon's right hand was wrapped in a bandage and asked him what happened. Dixon explained that the injury was the result of striking his hand against a music stand during a rehearsal with the BBC Symphony a few months earlier. After the "paparazzi-like" welcome at the airport, Dixon and Mary were taken to their hotel. Waiting for Dixon at the lobby of their hotel were his music scores for his upcoming performance with the SSO. Because of his numerous conducting engagements, Dixon had very little time to review his scores while in transit to the next performance. He insisted for every conducting engagement outside of Frankfurt that the host orchestra have the scores waiting for him at his hotel and that they be meticulously marked to his specifications. Dixon always made sure that he had enough time in the hotel to review his scores before his rehearsals. For those instances where the host orchestra did not comply with his wishes, he had no problems expressing his displeasure to his management team.

> Greetings from Helsinki, Now 8:25am on the day of the first rehearsal and I still do not have my scores! I understand that they [representatives of the host orchestra] will pick me up at 9:30am. The rehearsal starts at 10:00am—no scores yet. I spent a hellish (personally) day yesterday for 13 hours here in Helsinki—ready to study and no scores. Is it my fault? Please tell me what we can do about it. It is the only thing that I ask of these orchestral societies before the first rehearsals: THAT ALL PARTITURES BE AT THE HOTEL! Packing until four in the morning—2 hours in bed—all to take the early flight to here, rest, and study—All Lost! Please advise me how to not let this happen again— thanks.[5]

After a much-needed rest from his long flight to Sydney, Dixon was ready for his first rehearsal with the SSO. But things didn't go as planned. Not yet fully recovered from the injury he received in London, a more serious injury occurred during his rehearsal. While conducting a movement from Tchaikovsky's Sixth Symphony, Dixon felt a pain began to run through his arm. He equated the pain to several spears piercing through him. After a local doctor looked him over, it was concluded that he had torn some fibers in his right shoulder. The doctor recommended that he not use the arm for six days. Dixon said to this, "I love doctors. They are very necessary for human progress. But I came to conduct."[6] Dixon offered a compromise. He would give his arm "half-rest" for twelve days and would receive injections and heat treatment to alleviate the pain and prevent the injury from getting worse. When news got out that Dixon was not canceling the concert due to his injury, the admiration already expressed for him throughout Australia was deepened. For the entire eight weeks, which consisted of thirty-four performances, he was able to conduct while keeping his right arm immobilized. Dixon quickly became aware of the smallest things that were taken for granted when he had the full use of both arms. Each rehearsal and performance had to be carefully choreographed so as to make sure he had enough time to turn the pages of the score; cue those instruments on his right side with his left hand; and know when to use the left hand for marking time or phrasing a musical line—all of this while trying not to re-aggravate his injury. The ABC could not have asked for a better marketing plan to promote the SSO and their new leader than seeing pictures of Dixon in all of the major newspapers, conducting with a sling on his right arm.

Dixon's first season with the SSO was a resounding success. He looked forward to coming back next year for a full season of concerts. Sir Charles, the critics, and the Australian people were unanimous in their excitement about the future of the SSO with Dixon at the helm.

On August 24, 1964, while Dixon was awaiting his flight to take him back to Frankfurt, he was approached by a number of reporters. He was asked about his first experience with the SSO as its music director. To which he responded with excitement, "I will conduct my last concert in Zurich on March 16 and I will be on the next available jet back to Australia—and to my orchestra." When Dixon was asked his opinion as to the health of the SSO and how they compare to their European counterparts, his response was that the SSO had the potential to be a "truly great international orchestra," but there were a number of issues that needed to be addressed. It was Dixon's view that the orchestra's two most immediate issues were that they were overworked due to a shortage of musicians and that the woodwind section needed to be developed to a higher artistic level. This response prompted a follow-up question from the reporter. It was asked if he felt the SSO was ready for an overseas tour. This was in reference to the invitation that the SSO received to appear at the Commonwealth Festival next year. Dixon responded that "the orchestra will tour overseas when it is ready. It is not ready now and no one can say when it will be ready."[7] Dixon went on to say that the SSO needed to be at the performance level of ensembles like the London Philharmonic and the orchestras of La Scala and Vienna to ensure a successful overseas tour.

The impromptu press conference was not well received by the ABC. Tal Duckmanton, deputy general manager of the ABC, heard about the comments while he was in Singapore. He contacted Dixon by cable to inform him that both he and Sir Charles were puzzled by his comments made at the Sydney airport. Dixon responded by saying that he didn't understand how his comments at the airport could have embarrassed Sir Charles and others with the ABC. He was shocked by the cable and requested clarification regarding their concerns. The following day Dixon received a cable from Charles Buttrose, director of publicity and concerts with the ABC, who had been given the responsibility of dealing with this matter quickly, before it turned into a publicity nightmare. He wrote,

> You should be safely home by now after your Australia adventure. I hope you found everything as you wished. Here, we are still feeling the repercussions of the Dixon explosion and I've fixed a meeting with Joseph Post on Friday to discuss a number of things you raised during your last few hours here. I had a long session with the GM yesterday afternoon about the European project. The Herald, Mirror, and Sun ran stories about our views on the orchestra's fitness to play in Europe at present, so your views are known to the players now if they were not previously.[8]

Dixon didn't understand why the ABC was so surprised by the comments he made at the airport. This was not the first time he had stated his concerns about the SSO performing at the Commonwealth Festival. It was back in July, at a formal gathering sponsored by the ABC, that Dixon informed Duckmanton of his concerns. While Duckmanton informed Sir Charles of his conversation with Dixon, Sir Charles did not contact Dixon until after the report hit the newsstands in August. He wrote Dixon expressing his disappointment about the comments to the press: "I cannot understand why you should have felt it necessary to delay making this comment until the eve of your departure and then to make it to Mr. Duckmanton, instead of coming direct to me weeks ago, if this is what was in your mind."[9] Sir Charles went on to say that he had to take special measures to quash Dixon's statements because the press began phoning his office. He read to the press the letter Dixon sent on June 10 expressing his excitement for the trip to the United Kingdom; spoke about their positive conversation on July 27; and read a quote from Ian Hunter, the Commonwealth Festival Director. "To have done otherwise would have been to deal the fine people of the SSO a blow which would have seriously affected their morale and would have done a great disservice to yourself."[10]

The ABC moved forward with plans to take the SSO to the Commonwealth Festival. The conflict created a rift between the ABC and Dixon that in the end could not be mended. But Dixon was determined to find a way to move beyond this incident and work out an arrangement to conduct the SSO in England. Dixon was able to arrange with the Hessischer Rundfunk to appear with the SSO in its opening concert in London, with the second concert to be led by an Australian conductor, to be named later.

During this difficult period, Dixon reached out to his newly acquired friends in Australia to make them aware of the first major conflict between him and the ABC and to seek their advice. One of his friends put him in contact with a freelance writer by the name of Richard O'Sullivan, who expressed support of Dixon's assessment that the SSO was not ready for an overseas tour. Unbeknown to Dixon, lines were already being drawn throughout Australia expressing their support for or against the overseas tour. O'Sullivan believed that Dixon's authority was already being questioned at the start of his tenure in Sydney, because (according to O'Sullivan) had this been a concern expressed by a "Bernstein" or a "von Karajan," the issue of any tour of this magnitude would be quashed. Dixon was in agreement with O'Sullivan's assessment but still was willing to move forward with the tour. It wasn't until Dixon received a phone call from O'Sullivan about a major announcement in Sydney that he began to question his future affiliation with the ABC. On September 24, 1964, it was announced that Ernest Llewellyn, concertmaster of the SSO, was resigning effective January 6, 1965. Dixon was stunned by this announcement because he "had no idea that anything like this was even being contemplated." When Duckmanton was made aware of Dixon's comment on the resignation announcement, he immediately made contact with Dixon to say there was a break in the line of communication. According to Duckmanton, he had instructed someone with the SSO to contact Dixon regarding Llewellyn's resignation, which obviously did not happen.

Frustrated and concerned about his future with the SSO, Dixon wrote Sir Charles on November 15, 1964, stating that in light of Llewellyn's resignation,

> I cannot undertake to conduct this orchestra in London without him (Llewellyn) as concertmaster from now until the end of the tour. It would be artistic suicide and would serve neither your, nor my cause. This, I fear, must be my final standpoint vis a vis the scheduled tour. I will naturally in every other sense fulfill my contract with the ABC. My earnest proposal is that if the tour still has to take place it should be conducted solely by Australian conductors. It would be the cleanest way, the least exposed, and the most discreet for all parties concerned. [11]

Dixon's major issue with this entire matter was that he was never consulted about the resignation of his concertmaster. He seriously considered resigning, because he believed that keeping him out of the loop of such an important decision undermined his authority as music director. This would never have happened in Frankfurt.

The New Year began with Sir Charles retiring as general manager of the ABC and Duckmanton taking his place. Plans for the overseas tour were being finalized. Dixon was back on the roster for the first London performance because they were able to work out an arrangement for Llewellyn to stay on long enough to complete the tour. Moreover, Sir Charles was able to increase the size of the orchestra from ninety-two to one hundred, which was a direct response to one of Dixon's initial requests. The tour itself was extended for several concert dates in Asia

Dixon and Mary returned to Sydney in March of 1965 for a full season with the SSO. For their last visit, Dixon and Mary had stayed in a hotel. But this was not an acceptable living arrangement on the occasion when Nina accompanied them to Sydney, so they immediately began looking for a permanent residence. Mary wanted a property that gave her a feeling of spaciousness. Their search ended when they happened upon what Dixon described as "a haven and retreat in a flat overlooking Pittwater on Broken Bay, north of Sydney." [12] To the Dixon family this flat exuded a sense of peace and tranquility. The view was spectacular. Beyond the jetty and expansive yachts, they could easily view the Tasman Sea from the main rooms of their new home away from home. The flat was modestly furnished and included two bedrooms, a dining room, one bathroom, a lounge room, and a kitchen.

The dining room was Dixon's favorite because of the wood-burning fire-place. Dixon's new home was ideal for entertaining. He was a connoisseur of wines and looked forward to those moments when he could share his knowledge and libations with his friends and family. He was also a wonderful cook and on occasion would take over the kitchen with gleeful abandon, using every pot and pan available to him to create his epicurean masterpieces.

Dixon settled into his position as music director in Sydney with a daily schedule that left very little time for anything else. Each day began at 6 a.m., when he was promptly picked up by his "chauffeur-driven government car" to take him to the ABC headquarters. His position entitled him to a business manager, office space, and a secretary. He conducted six to eight hours each day, with meetings and administrative responsibilities taking up the remainder of his day.

Dixon's second season with the SSO was a success. He returned to Frankfurt feeling that he had done all he could to prepare his orchestra for their London appearance. Dixon's rehearsals with the SSO were intense, perhaps more than usual, because they were selected to give a command performance for Her Majesty The Queen of England and her Consort Prince Philip.

Dixon and Mary arrived in London on the afternoon of September 17. They were two hours late because of inclement weather, which meant Dixon had less time to rest before his eight-hour rehearsal with the SSO later that day. They met the following morning to go over the protocol associated with a command performance. The concert took place in the Royal Festival Hall to a standing room only audience dressed in formal attire. When the Queen and Prince Philip entered the performance hall, everyone stood to their feet; the orchestra played the entire "God Save the Queen," and they bowed to Her Majesty. The featured pieces on this special program were Brahms's First Symphony and a contemporary piece from an Australian native: Richard Neale's *Homage to Garcia Lorca*. Neale's piece was performed before the intermission. Queen Elizabeth was familiar with Dixon from his performances with the BBC Symphony. She requested that Richard Neale's score be sent to the royal box. A reporter wrote that to have a score brought to the royal box was unprecedented. It turns out that Prince Philip wanted to speak with Dixon about the piece.

Mrs. Dixon and I were formally presented to the Queen of England and the Duke of Edinburgh. The royal couple conversed with us at quite some length and the Prince showed a keen interest in the mechanics of modern music, referring in this case to the piece we had just played. . . . The Prince wondered if this kind of music was more difficult to play than classical music, if it could be played wrongly, etc. After the pause we performed the Brahms First Symphony and, I am happy to state, the public responded with an almost riotous applause, which ended in shouting and stamping rhythmic clapping. The queen allowed us seven curtain calls, herself clapping all the time, before she left and the performance was over. [13]

Dixon returned to Frankfurt feeling very pleased with his performance with the SSO.

When Dixon arrived in Sydney the following year, he was hopeful that the tremendous success he experienced in London with the SSO had generated enough goodwill with the ABC to start the very difficult process of rebuilding the infrastructure of Australia's most promising orchestra. From the beginning of his tenure in Sydney, Dixon began hearing from musicians about how poorly they were being treated by the ABC. According to Dixon, many of the musicians didn't know how long they would be able to remain with the orchestra if conditions didn't get better. He began writing down the concerns expressed by members of the orchestra and created a list of reforms that he called his "23 Points." Dixon found out quickly that the ABC was not going to move fast enough on these much-needed reforms. Believing that the implementation of these reforms was essential to have any chance of building an orchestra of international repute, Dixon had made the very difficult decision that once his contract expired in 1968, he would resign as music director of the SSO as a form of protest.

On June 22, 1967, Dixon met with Duckmanton to inquire as to why the ABC was not making a serious effort to improve the working conditions of the SSO. Not satisfied with Duckmanton's response, Dixon presented the general manager his list of reforms and informed him that he was going to resign after his contract expired. He went on to say to Duckmanton that he would be giving a press conference detailing the reasons he could no longer remain in Sydney. This included providing copies of the 23 points to the press. Duckmanton understood very clearly that a press conference to announce Dixon's resignation and the dissemination of his 23 points would be an explosive indictment of the ABC. According to Dixon, Duckmanton knew he could not comply with many of the 23 points presented to him, so he tried to stall by asking Dixon to meet with a select group of officials from the ABC and the SSO to further discuss these reforms with the hope that a compromise could be found. Nothing was resolved at this meeting. On July 5, 1967, Duckmanton met with Dixon one last time in an attempt to persuade him to reconsider this press conference. Duckmanton suggested that instead of the press conference, Dixon should go back to Frankfurt and think about the issue for a few weeks, then write him directly stating his concerns. From there Duckmanton said he could address the issues behind the scenes. Dixon didn't like that idea. He was convinced that by having this press conference he could bring to the public's attention the pervasive issues that were keeping the SSO from becoming an internationally recognized orchestra with benefits comparable to their European counterparts. Realizing that no amount of cajoling was going to dissuade Dixon from his decision, Duckmanton asked if he could at least have a copy of his statement so as to know what to expect and be prepared to respond accordingly. Dixon saw no problem with this request and agreed to provide a copy of his statement.

On Sunday morning, Dixon called and left a message informing Duckmanton that a copy of his statement was available for pickup. An hour after the message was sent, Dixon began passing out copies of the 23 points to all interested parties. According to Dixon, Duckmanton was under the impression that he would be able to review his statement before presenting it to the press. He was mistaken. The statement made its way to the ABC's legal department and shortly thereafter Dixon received a call reminding him of the defamation of character clause in his contract. Dixon was not intimidated by the call, because he had been given assurances by his lawyer that there was no violation of the defamation of character clause in his statement.

Dixon met with the press on July 9, 1967, and gave a prepared statement.

> I have very much regret in announcing that I will resign from the musical directorship of the Sydney Symphony Orchestra as from the end of next season. In other words I shall not be available for the reappointment as Musical Director of the S.S.O. after the termination of my present contract, which terminates in 1968. I announce this with regret because my interest in the orchestra and its development is as great as ever. My decision to resign is not due to a lessening of involvement with the orchestra. On the contrary, I hope that my resignation will be accepted as it is meant, namely a gesture on behalf of the welfare of the orchestra. My decision arises out of a strong personal conviction that a gesture of this kind may help to secure benefits for the orchestra, which I feel, is long overdue. I have attached to this statement a list of urgent needs for the betterment of the conditions of the players. This list has been submitted in a series of discussions to high officials of the ABC. The items presented on this list I regard as not only necessary, but as requiring immediate implementation. I say this because it is my belief that no orchestra can continue to develop if its members are harried by personal anxieties and discomforts. These anxieties and discomforts have built up strong feelings among the orchestra over a period of many years and have certainly been influential in causing many players to seek employment elsewhere. I have been told that 18 players have left the orchestra in the last 3 years. This is a loss of an order, which no major orchestra can afford to sustain. I am convinced that the points I have listed need immediate action in order to cure this malaise of long standing. My discussions with high ABC officials have been cordial and my own attitude towards the Commission is one of sympathy and friendliness. I believe that the ABC genuinely intends to do something constructive about at least some of the points of reform I have listed. But the discussions have also convinced me that the ABC is not going to move far enough and fast enough in this direction. Therefore, I feel it is consistent with my deep concern for the welfare of the orchestra to make a gesture designed to draw urgent attention to the orchestra's needs. When I say this, I do not mean

that my resignation is a sham resignation. I do not feel I should defer it on the grounds that the ABC hopes to achieve certain things in the future. In order to mean anything a gesture of this kind must be firm and resolute. I shall not withdraw my resignation. But I add that I shall always be delighted to come back to see how the orchestra is progressing. And I add further that I should certainly feel honored to accept—if it is offered—the re-engagement of the Musical Directorship of the SSO at some time in the future, providing that the points of amelioration I have listed are fulfilled. I shall treasure the memory of the friendships I have formed among musicians and music-lovers in Sydney and in Australia generally. I hope I have been able to contribute something to musical life here. I am not resigning in a huff or without thought. It could certainly be said that my appreciation of the defects of the orchestral situation here has more in it of sorrow than of anger. [14]

After the press conference Dixon was given a three cheers farewell from members of the SSO who were made aware that he would be making this public stance and wanted to be there to support the man that brought national attention to a cause directly affecting them.

Once the press conference saturated the media, Duckmanton was put in a defensive position to protect the reputation of the ABC. When asked about the controversial statements of Dixon, Duckmanton said that during the June 22 meeting he actually suggested to Dixon that he wait on making a public statement regarding the "so-called 23 points" because many of those issues were subject to be negotiated with the musicians' union. He then said to the media that he told Dixon that it might be best to part amicably given that he knew he would not be able to remedy the concerns to Dixon's satisfaction. Moreover, Duckmanton stated that three months prior to this June 22 discussion with Dixon the ABC had no intentions of renewing Dixon's contract and were looking for his replacement, because Dixon was unable to spend more than three months of each season in Sydney due to his obligations in Europe.

It didn't take long for the ABC to announce that a young Israeli conductor, Moshe Atzmon, was appointed as the new music director of the SSO. In addition, Duckmanton made it clear to Dixon that he would not be returning in 1968, meaning that he would not be allowed to fulfill his contract. He wrote,

At a meeting of the ABC held in Sydney on July 20, 1967, the Commission resolved that the public statements made by you prior to your departure from Australia on July 10, 1967, constituted action on your part which, in the opinion of the Commission, brought discredit on it as an organization. The Commission therefore resolved that your engagement with the Commission, the terms of which are set out in a letter to you dated July 19, 1965, be terminated forthwith. I therefore, as directed by the Commission, give you notice that your engagement with the Commission is at an end. [15]

Chapter Twelve

Prague

Dixon first met with Dr. Joachim von Hecker, head of production at Bärenreiter-Verlag, in the fall of the 1966 to discuss the possibility of working together on a record. Dixon was impressed with the proposal and agreed to sign on. The original plan was to have Dixon record with his Frankfurt orchestra, so once he was on board, Dr. Hecker met with the representatives of the Hessischer Rundfunk to secure their participation. But in the end, they were not able to agree to the terms of the proposed contract. This was a major disappointment for Dixon because it was his hope that this recording opportunity would not only expose more listeners to the quality work he had done in Frankfurt since his tenure began in 1961, but also lead to future recordings with more reputable companies. Moreover, this was the opportunity Dixon believed he needed to define his legacy. He, like many in his profession, understood that his legacy was inextricably tied with his recordings. The applause given to him after an exhilarating performance was satisfying; the rave reviews of his music making with orchestras throughout Europe were appreciated; but it was the recordings that meant a great deal to Dixon. Here was an opportunity to show the world that his interpretations of the canon and the contemporary were as good as anyone else out there. The fact that none of the major recording companies were sending Dixon invitations to record for them made it even more paramount that any recording he did with his Frankfurt orchestra had to be of the highest quality.

On November 1, 1967, Dixon penned a letter to members of his orchestra and the Hessischer Rundfunk administration, which expressed his disappointment and explained the reason he would, yet again, not be recording with his Frankfurt orchestra.

With a sad, sad pen I write to say how sorry I am that we shall again not be able to go into serious record-making together. With Columbia Records we had our first real offer sometime back. We failed then to come to a point of agreement that would allow us to make records for them. Now when Bärenreiter asked me whether I would be interested in recording for them my first spontaneous answer was "Yes, gladly." However, my immediate question was put to them as to whether they would consider doing the records with me, and the Hessischer Rundfunk Symphonie Orchestra. After appropriate perusal their answer was yes. After that the wheels began to turn in Kassel at Bärenreiter and in Frankfurt on the part of Hessischer Rundfunk and on the part of Hessischer Rundfunk Symphonie Orchestra. Finally we were so far forward that only one major point remained—the aspect of who plays what in our recording work. As in the affair with Columbia Records my request again was to have the last responsibility and the last say in this area. At the time of my first discussion with Bärenreiter, my standpoint was that there were some twelve of our musicians that I felt were not in the "recording way" acceptable. At our last discussion—the orchestra, Vorstand and myself on October 31, 1967—I made the compromise offer of saying that there were no longer twelve names in question but that I am willing to try the first recording with the Hessischer Rundfunk Symphonie Orchestra as it now stands, as my basic Frankfurt recording orchestra, but that I, as Chefdirigent of this orchestra, must have the final right to say who is to play first, amongst the winds, for each composition to be recorded. More compromise I cannot make for this is for me an artistic problem: concerned with which color of tone, which nuance tendency, which sensitivity, which rhythmic softness, which rhythmic hardness, which matched-tone potential has which musician and would therefore play best with whom in which work, who naturally leans more to the classic; to the romantic, etc. Not being able to agree to my request for the above means that I am unable to take the final artistic responsibility for the outcome of the proposed recordings. Not being able to take this responsibility means that Bärenreiter has no one who can therefore take the artistic responsibility for our proposed work with them and this means that we have an untenable situation. I repeat: I am truly deeply sorry that we shall not be recording together. [1]

Now that the Hessischer Rundfunk was out of the picture, Dr. Hecker needed to find another orchestra to record. Later that year, he met with the representatives of the Prague Symphony Orchestra to secure their participation, with the understanding that Dixon had already been selected as the designated conductor for the recordings. Negotiations continued the following year between March and July, meeting at the Bärenreiter offices in Kassel and Prague. In July of 1968 a contract was signed between Bärenreiter and the Prague Symphony Orchestra to produce two recordings. The first would be Beethoven's Seventh Symphony and the second Brahms's First Symphony.

On August 16, 1968, Dixon and Mary arrived in Prague, Czechoslovakia, two days prior to the beginning of the first recording session. They stayed at the Esplanade Prague Hotel. Once they got settled in their room, they met for lunch with Dr. Hecker to discuss the recording schedule. Mrs. Kalcikova, a representative from Supraphon Records (a Czech-based recording company committed to quality recordings of Czech music), was there as well. She was interested in working with Dixon on a future project in Prague. It was during their lunch that Mrs. Kalcikova was able to give them a personal account of the political unrest that loomed over not only Prague, but all of Czechoslovakia.

It began in January of 1968, when Alexander Dubcek took over as First Secretary of the Communist Party in Czechoslovakia. In April of that same year, what was known as "Prague Spring," Dubcek established a number of programs, which were interpreted by many as too democratic in nature. First Secretary Leonid Brezhnev of the Soviet Union looked at these new reforms by the Czech leader as a threat to the stability of the Warsaw Pact. [2] While there was clearly concern expressed all around as to how this event would play out, no one could have predicted what would happen four days later.

Dixon began his recording session with the Prague Symphony Orchestra on the morning of August 18. Later that afternoon, the session ended with the completion of the fourth movement of Beethoven's Seventh Symphony. Dixon and Mary took advantage of the beautiful weather that Sunday afternoon to visit a family friend they had met some time ago. Ladislav Bohac, who was a famous Czech actor and a political activist, invited the Dixons to spend the day with him and his wife at their country villa, which was about forty kilometers east of Prague. It was there that Dixon and Mary learned more about the treatment of the Czech people by the Soviets and the demonstrations that were taking place in the city. It was clear that Ladislav was a proponent of all of the initiatives of Dubcek and skeptical of the motives of the Soviet-led Warsaw Pact. Dixon and Mary returned to their hotel more concerned by the ever-growing political unrest between Prague and the Soviet Union. But they had to stay focused on the task at hand.

The recording session resumed that Monday afternoon from 4 p.m. to 10 p.m. They completed the second movement of Beethoven and began rehearsing the introduction to the first movement. On August 20, Tuesday morning, Dixon recorded the first movement. Later that evening they listened to the second movement and the introduction of the first movement as they began the editing process. Dixon and Dr. Hecker were very pleased with the second movement. They believed this movement represented the highest level of artistry and emotion one could attain by this orchestra and were hopeful that the same level of performance would present itself in the other movements. That evening Dr. Hecker escorted Dixon and Mary back to their hotel. After saying goodnight to the Dixons, he went back out to take a look at a possible new venue to record in. It was an old theater located on the outskirts of the city. He returned to the hotel around 10:30 p.m. Dr. Hecker said, "There was hardly any traffic on the streets. I had a late dinner and went to bed at 11:30 p.m. During the night I was wakened by the sound of heavy air traffic, but dismissed it with a thought that passenger planes were unable to land and therefore had to go over the city. I went back to sleep."[3] What Dr. Hecker, Dixon, Mary, and many others sleeping that night in Prague were unaware of was that the city was being invaded.

On the evening of August 20, 1968, the Soviet Union led Warsaw Pact troops into Czechoslovakia to thwart all liberation reforms initiated by Alexander Dubcek. Dubcek had given Brezhnev assurances that these reforms would in no way jeopardize his government's commitment to the 1955 treaty. Brezhnev was not convinced.

On that following morning Dixon was scheduled to complete the Beethoven recording. But due to the invasion and gunfire that was heard throughout the Wenzelsplatz (one of the main public squares in Prague), everyone in the hotel was ordered not to leave the building. A curfew was imposed throughout the city. As a result of the curfew, the orchestra and recording crew could not meet and therefore the recording session was postponed until further notice. Later that morning, Dixon, Mary, Dr. Hecker, and the other hotel guests were asked to make their way to the basement where the bar was located. It was believed that if the hotel was fired on by Warsaw Pact tanks or troops, the basement was the safest place to be. That afternoon things begin to quiet down but the invasion was still going on. Dr. Hecker likened this "quieter situation" to Sartre's Geschlossene Gesellschaft.[4] The hotel guests remained in the basement for the rest of the day. Dixon, obviously, had no interest in staying in Prague any longer than necessary and very likely expressed it during his time in the basement. It was then that he met up with a salesman from Offenbach, Germany. After they were introduced, the salesman remembered Dixon from hearing his many performances with the Hessischer Rundfunk on the radio. After talking and becoming more acquainted with Dixon, Mary, and Dr. Hecker, the salesman offered to drive them out of Prague. This was a risky proposition, because no one in the hotel really knew the extent of the invasion and whether the Soviet-run occupancy was a full-out war or a military deterrence. After carefully weighing their options, Dixon, Mary, and Dr. Hecker agreed to travel with the salesman through occupied Czechoslovakia, with the hopes of returning home unharmed. They left in the salesman's car around noon on August 22. By that time, a state of emergency had been instituted in Prague. They were told that the Wenzelsplatz was strewn with demonstrators and tanks. So it was recommended that they travel the southern route by way of the city of Tabor. They passed a number of military convoys until they reached Freistadt—a small border town in Austria. There was no problem getting into Austria. The Czech military protecting the border allowed them to leave. But they later discovered that Warsaw Pact tanks had already taken up positions one hundred meters from the border, only allowing Western European vehicles to pass.

From Freistadt, they continued to Munich where they stayed the night, and on August 23 they made it safely back to Frankfurt.

Dixon continued his work in Frankfurt and his many guest conducting engagements, but stayed in contact with Dr. Hecker. They were making plans to return to Prague as soon as possible to complete the Beethoven recording. But the events there reached an international proportion when leaders, political activists, and musicians from around the world openly expressed their opposition to the occupation. Among the most ardent of those musicians was Czech conductor Rafael Kubelik. He left his homeland after the 1948 Communist coup, believing that the Communist Party would finish what the Nazi regime started. It was Kubelik who started an international boycott of his homeland and the nations of the Warsaw Pact that were willing participants in the occupation. He urged his musician colleagues from around the world not to perform there until the Soviet-led Warsaw Pact left and independent governance was restored. It was reported that more than one hundred internationally recognized artists signed the petition to boycott. Dixon was one of the signatories. On September 21, 1968, while at a guest conducting engagement in Buenos Aires, Dixon received an urgent letter from Dr. Hecker updating him on the situation in Prague:

> The situation in Prague seemed to become very bad last week, after the return of Dubcek from Moscow. Nobody was able to look forward on which way things there would develop. The people in our Verlag advised me to wait until the situation is more clear. Even to write a letter to Prague seemed to be too dangerous for the Prague people up to this moment. The secret service men from Moscow are seeking people there now, and each person who receives a letter from Western Germany may be in danger. In spite of these facts I will try to clear up the situation as soon as possible.[5]

The situation in Prague eventually calmed down enough for Dixon and Dr. Hecker to schedule a return trip to resume their recording. Mary did not accompany Dixon on his second trip to Prague. The plan was to be there from November 2 to November 11.

As scheduled, Dixon arrived in Prague to resume his work with the symphony on November 2. He rehearsed the third movement of the Beethoven, which lasted for six hours. This was an unusually long rehearsal for one movement. Dr. Hecker's explanation for the lengthy rehearsal was due to the fact that Dixon took all the repeats in this movement. It was also likely that Dixon had to deal with, perhaps, a lack of focus from the orchestra, who understandably had more pressing issues on their mind than playing a Beethoven symphony. They met on Sunday, November 3, and completed the recording of the third movement. On Wednesday, November 6, they successfully recorded the fourth movement, which completed the recording of the entire Seventh Symphony. Taking full advantage of their precious time together, Dixon began rehearsing the third movement of Brahms's First Symphony, which was originally scheduled for the November dates. Recording was canceled on November 7 and 8 because "noon and evening demonstrations were of a very aggressive character. At noon, very close to the hotel, Russian flags were burned, there was a noisy strike, traffic was completely blocked, and the Czech police made arrests."[6] Dixon took the brief respite as an opportunity to learn more about the history of the Czech people, who knew all too well the ravages of a tyrannical occupation. He visited the Jewish cemetery and museum where he was shown paintings done by children during their imprisonment at the Theresienstadt concentration camp located in the garrison city of Terezin. This "camp ghetto" mainly served as a transit facility for Czech Jews who were awaiting transport to either concentration camps or labor camps in German-occupied countries. Seeing these paintings was especially moving for Mrs. Bohacova, who served as Dixon's tour guide, for she was imprisoned at Theresienstadt and later transported to Auschwitz. The current occupation by the Soviets, albeit not as severe as the Nazi regime, nonetheless brought back memories of old for all those who lived through or had family or friends who were directly impacted by the occupation. Dixon's somber trip to the Jewish cemetery and museum made it clearer than any explanation given to him in the past as to the emotional strain this current occupation was having on the people of Czechoslovakia.

On November 9 and 10, Dixon recorded the third and second movement of the Brahms, feeling good with the end results. The following Monday, on November 11, he returned to Frankfurt with a third visit to Prague having been already scheduled for February 1, 1969, to complete the Brahms recording. A few days after Dixon returned to Frankfurt and after very careful consideration, he informed Kubelik that he would no longer be honoring his original commitment to boycott Czechoslovakia. On November 14, 1968, he wrote,

> On Aug. 22, 1968, you sent me a cable asking me not to give any concerts in the five countries whose armies occupied Czechoslovakia, and neither in Czechoslovakia, as long as foreign troops are present in Czechoslovakian territory, and the legal government will not be functioning. On Aug. 23, 1968, I answered you by cable that I agreed to the appeal and that I was joining it. During the last few days I visited Czechoslovakia—not to give concerts—but to finish a recording that had been interrupted by the August events. This trip was according to our conversation and agreement on October 2, 1968, when I stopped off in Munich to speak with you. Now I should like to inform you that I feel that I must change my decision and that I shall conduct concerts in Czechoslovakia. . . . The Czechoslovakian government and people are taking all possible and extraordinary steps to promote cultural activities with foreign countries. It would be incorrect to impose cultural isolation upon this country. While in Czechoslovakia now I received the deep and distinct impression— from a broad cross-section of the Czechoslovakian people—that now is the

time that they need still more help from their friends throughout the cultural world. And now is the time to come to their aid by not isolating but by demonstrating the friendship. Any cultural boycott of Czechoslovakia now seems the more unjust when just now a number of other international artists, bodies and cultural institutions of several western countries demonstrate their friendship to Czechoslovakia in a quite opposite way. . . . Please consider these entirely new circumstances as the reason for the present change of my original decision. [7]

There is no record of a response to Dixon's letter, but Kubelik would continue his boycott and not return to Czechoslovakia for another twenty-two years.

Dr. Hecker arrived in Prague on January 31 and Dixon arrived the day of the scheduled recording on February 1, giving him only a few hours to rest. The rehearsal of the fourth movement ended earlier than planned because Dixon was too exhausted to continue. For the following day they scheduled two sessions, one in the morning and one in the afternoon. The hope was to finish the Brahms recording that day, but Dixon was only able to record the allegro section of the fourth movement. He was too sick to continue. Suffering with a 104-degree temperature, Dixon was rushed back to his hotel to receive medical treatment from doctors of a nearby hospital designated for foreigners. Dixon believed he contracted the "Hong Kong flu" during his trip to Japan in 1968 and never got over it. He remained in his hotel room, under the watchful eye of Dr. Hecker, for several days. Dixon eventually returned to Frankfurt, but suffered four relapses due to the flu and, as a result of being hospitalized, had to cancel a number of his concerts. He provided evidence of his hospitalization for all of those missed engagements so as not to be found in breach of his contract to appear. He was finally able to adjust his hectic schedule to return to Prague in early July. Once the recording was complete, Dixon was able to listen to both the Beethoven and Brahms symphonies and was surprised at how unified everything sounded given the recording sequence of events. Dixon continued a long and fruitful relationship with Prague, making several more recordings with the Prague Symphony Orchestra and the Prague Chamber Orchestra.

As for the occupation, one year after the implementation of major reforms in Czechoslovakia, Dubcek was forced out of his position in favor of Gustav Husak, who was more willing to cooperate with the Soviets. The reforms that were put in place during Dubcek's tenure were eventually reversed. The Czechoslovakian government was once again a cooperative member of the Warsaw Pact.

Chapter Thirteen

Sojourn Home

On June 29, 1966, Dixon received his first legitimate inquiry from an orchestra in the States to appear as a guest conductor. It was Leopold Stokowski's American Symphony Orchestra. The invitation read, "On behalf of Maestro Stokowski and the Board of Directors of the American Symphony Orchestra may I extend an invitation to you to be a guest conductor for the 1967–68 season at Carnegie Hall."[1] Dixon was honored by the invitation but due to his hectic schedule was unable to accept. On April 1, 1968, Dixon received his second inquiry from the Detroit Symphony. They invited him to guest conduct on September 25–27, 1969. Again, Dixon responded that his schedule would not permit his participation. He further suggested "that we [should] try for a period in the 1972–73 season. I fear that prior to that season my promises and commitments will not allow our consideration."[2] Even if his schedule made it possible to consider these two invitations, in the end Dixon would have likely turned them down. This was mainly because there were legal issues in the States regarding his first marriage that had yet to be resolved. Vivian was still trying to collect on years of unpaid alimony and child support. There was a sense of urgency from Vivian to have this matter resolved sooner than later. She was diagnosed with cancer and knew there would come a time that she would no longer be able to perform and continue her piano studio, thereby eliminating the only source of income for her household. Vivian's last public performance was on May 7, 1967, at Carnegie Hall. She performed on an all-Mozart program with the New York Orchestral Society. Vivian Rivkin died on the evening of January 31, 1968, at Lennox Hill Hospital, leaving Diane, who was nineteen at the time, with no financial means. Dr. Stanley Bregman would serve as Diane's legal guardian. Not long after Vivian's death, Maxwell T. Cohen, the lawyer in New York that was handling Vivian's claim, retained legal representation in Frankfurt to petition the courts there to gain access to Dixon's bank account to resolve his financial obligation. Cohen claimed that Dixon owed over $27,000 in alimony arrears. Dixon retained lawyers of his own to fight the petition because the amount Vivian's representatives claimed was owed to her did not represent the amount of funds already taken from his bank account in Sweden in 1956 and 1959. Moreover, if Vivian's representative were successful in getting the full amount they petitioned for, it would literally bankrupt Dixon. His financial obligations in Europe tied up most of his current and future income. Dixon heard from Pervil Eastman (his lawyer in New York) that Cohen was so livid over the decision to vigorously fight the petition that he made it his personal mission to "break" Dixon's career and have him arrested if he ever stepped foot in the States. While it was true that the invitations to appear in the States were few and far between, it was the threat of imprisonment and a besmirched reputation that fueled Dixon's indifference to returning to his homeland. He knew this issue would have to be resolved before any invitation to return to the States could be seriously considered.

Meanwhile, Dixon was working with an agency in Berlin to help him achieve a very specific goal in his career. He had conducted all of the major orchestras in Germany on numerous occasions, with one exception—the Berlin Philharmonic. Dixon wanted to join the exclusive ranks of guest conductors like Karl Böhm and Eugen Jochum. He tried, through his association with the Hessischer Rundfunk and other agencies, to secure an invitation with the Berlin Philharmonic, but to no avail. Dixon's reputation in Europe, which he guarded very closely, was exceptional. Herbert von Karajan was the principal conductor of the Berlin Philharmonic during this time, and there was no reported animus between the two maestros. Moreover, there was no indication of overt racial bias from Karajan, given his eventual collaboration with soprano Jessye Norman, as well as his relationship with George Byrd, a young Negro conductor from North Carolina that developed a good reputation throughout Germany after his brief studies with Karajan. Dixon offered no personal insight for not having received an invitation from Germany's premier orchestra. But he was hopeful that his association with this agency in Berlin would prove fruitful. It did not. The invitations he did receive through this agency were not at the artistic level that he was accustomed to in Europe. It was Dixon's belief that appearing with any orchestra that did not equal his reputation could hurt his career. This was clearly expressed in a letter Dixon wrote on December 19, 1967:

> Through some mistake of reading your letter, in the heat of preparing for my Hessischer Rundfunk Symphony Orchestra's Scandinavian tour, I read Hamburger Philharmonic. Now that I have re-read and see that you are speaking about the Hamburger Symphoniker, I must say that they are so un-identical

that I can only express great surprise that I received such an offer from you. In the first and last aspects I am the Chefdirigent of the Hessischer Rundfunk Symphony Orchestra and, as such, can afford to only go to certain high level orchestras! As I wrote and mentioned to you before, the Berlin Philharmonic would be interesting for you to get for me! I am truly only interested in the major and first class orchestras.[3]

The relationship between Dixon and the agency in Berlin ended soon after this correspondence, along with any chance of ever appearing with the Berlin Philharmonic. It's likely that this incident prompted Dixon to make a very important decision on how he would be represented in the future. In the summer of 1968, he wrote to all of his contacts in Europe to inform them, "in order to centralize all my professional matter, I have handed my world-wide general management to Mr. Martin Taubman. This will considerably unburden me administratively and will thus serve to make things easier and more practical for all parts concerned."[4]

Around this time, Dixon began corresponding with an American agent who was interested in representing him in the United States and Canada. Sherman Pitluck worked for an Indiana-based agency that had offices in New York City. He was planning a trip to Frankfurt the following year to meet with the Hessischer Rundfunk and other European orchestras to discuss the possibility of representing them for future tours in America and Canada. Pitluck reminded Dixon that they previously met at an event he was hosting in New York in the 1940s. While Dixon did not recall their brief encounter in the States, he was nonetheless interested to hear more about how Pitluck would introduce him to a new generation of American concertgoers. Pitluck was not the only agent interested in representing Dixon in the United States and Canada. Arthur Judson also expressed an interest. Early in his career in the States, Dixon worked tirelessly to seek Judson's representation, succeeding in every task given to him by the influential impresario. But according to Dixon, Judson always found an excuse as to why he could not manage him. If Judson had represented Dixon during his time in the States, his exodus to Europe would have likely not been necessary. Dixon's experience with Judson was a great disappointment, but for some reason, he felt compelled to reconnect with Judson by sending him a brochure that listed all of his accomplishments since leaving the States. Judson was clearly impressed because not long after receipt of the brochure Dixon received a telegram from him on August 21, 1968, saying, "Thanks for sending me brochure covering recent achievements. May I represent you in the United States and Canada? There may be openings in the near future because of political situation."[5] Dixon responded the following week that Taubman was in New York City on business and "will most certainly be getting in touch with you concerning the contents of your telegram which sound most interesting."[6] There was no evidence that a meeting ever took place between the two, and no further correspondence from Judson.

Dixon had already become very comfortable with Pitluck over a period of months of corresponding. So after discussing the matter of representation with Taubman, Dixon confided with Pitluck that before a series of prestigious guest conducting engagements could be secured for him in the States, he needed help to resolve his ongoing legal problems. Pitluck, seemingly unaffected by this major obstacle, immediately began pitching the idea of a "Dean Dixon Return" to a few wealthy philanthropists that he felt would be willing to help. Pitluck came up with a solution and wanted to discuss the matter with Taubman in person when he arrived in Europe. He was able to secure a financial commitment from W. Clement Stone, who was a wealthy businessman and author, known for his philanthropic endeavors. In the summer of 1969, Taubman met with Pitluck in Milan, Italy, to discuss Dixon's possible return to the States. This was also an opportunity for Taubman to get a sense of Pitluck's trustworthiness, given that he and Dixon had never heard of him prior to his initial correspondence. Taubman cabled Dixon the following day and told him that "[the] multi-millionaire friend of his appears to be somebody who is not a benefactor of a philanthropist, but wants to make a few more millions by investing here and there. Sherman is of the opinion that his friend would definitely not give you the $30,000 as a token but might put the money at your disposal to be repaid later in stages. I personally think very little of the whole story, this between you and me. Anyway, Sherman told me that he will meet with you in Frankfurt on June 20, and then you can judge for yourself."[7]

Dixon's first meeting in Frankfurt with Pitluck went so well, that he cabled him the following month to say, "It looks and feels good for the possibility of our doing some real fine work together—fingers crossed and God willing."[8] Despite Taubman's skepticism, Dixon was convinced that there actually existed this "angel" who was going to provide the necessary funds to free him from his financial obligations in the States. Pitluck took Dixon's approval of their first face-to-face meeting as his sign to begin making inquiries with reputable orchestra societies for his return visit. He also began asking Dixon very specific questions about the claim against him in the States, to which Dixon responded that he would put him in contact with his lawyers in Frankfurt to provide all the details. After his conversation with Dixon's lawyers, Pitluck wasted no time contacting Eastman so that they could set up a meeting with Cohen to discuss a settlement. According to Pitluck, Cohen was less than cooperative when the discussion turned to money. But Pitluck made it very clear that while he was representing Dixon to try and resolve this matter with haste, the $27,000 amount that Cohen presented to the courts was a non-starter. Realizing this may be the only window of opportunity to settle this matter once and for all, Cohen agreed to bring the amount down to $15,000 with a third of that amount to be paid in advance to cover his legal expenses. Pitluck tried to negotiate a lower amount, but Cohen would not budge. While Pitluck was disappointed with the negotiated settlement, Dixon saw this as a clear victory, because this was less money he would have to repay his benefactor.

Dixon's excitement over the news of an impending settlement was restrained, because for the past two weeks he had been recovering in a hospital from a procedure to correct an eye condition. He described the procedure as "a prophylactic-electric-no-blood-affair." The operation was a success, but it was imperative that Dixon rest and remain calm that summer to ensure a full recovery. This was not the first time Dixon had issues with his eyes. Two years earlier, he was rushed to a hospital to receive treatment for a "left-eye thrombosis," which required several weeks of recovery. From this point on Dixon began having frequent hospital visits due to his poor health. Doctors believed that it was mainly due to high blood pressure and an overextended work schedule.

Pitluck had proven himself to be an invaluable resource and showed a total commitment to his prospective client's efforts to resolve the "Dixon vs. Dixon" matter. Pitluck earned Dixon's respect and his business. On August 21, 1969, Taubman cabled Pitluck informing him that Dixon wanted him to represent his professional interests in the United States and Canada, effective September 1. Taubman then requested of Pitluck that if he required a formal contract that he should provide him an AGMA (American Guild of Musical Artists) form, in triplicate, so that it could be reviewed and, if accepted, signed by Dixon. Shortly thereafter, Pitluck submitted a formal contract to Taubman that was subsequently agreed to by both parties, with the understanding that some minor revisions were still needed. Once the contract was signed by Dixon and returned to Pitluck, he continued his pursuit of engagements with reputable orchestras in the States.

In early September, Dixon received an unexpected letter from one of his Subud brothers who learned of his legal and financial dilemma.[9] It was an offer to pay Dixon's entire alimony settlement in cash, with a very flexible repayment schedule. Dixon informed Pitluck of the good news and within a few days Cohen, who was pleased with the new payment arrangement, lowered the settlement amount to $13,000 as long as it was received within thirty days. Once Eastman approved the paperwork presented to him from Cohen's office, it was finally done. Within a few weeks Cohen received the funds from Dixon and in return Cohen informed the lawyer he retained in Frankfurt that the case against Dixon was settled. Cohen also informed Eastman that the settlement monies would be divided into two accounts for Diane one would likely be used to settle her mother's estate and pay the bills, and the other account was likely designed for long-term savings. Dixon was now faced with an even more complicated dilemma—trying to mend his relationship with Diane.

Initially, Dixon made two attempts to re-establish contact with Diane; from a letter mailed directly to her in March of 1968, to a letter mailed to McClara in August of that same year to be hand-delivered to Diane, but none of these attempts were successful. Dixon reached out to Eastman after he heard that Cohen was impressed at his sincere desire to re-establish a relationship with Diane. Cohen also told Eastman that Diane was in desperate need of a father figure and hoped that she would be receptive to Dixon's attempt to reconnect. Cohen asked Eastman to provide him copies of the letters that Dixon wrote to Diane. The hope was that if Cohen presented the letters to Diane personally, essentially giving this reunion his stamp of approval, then Diane might be more open to Dixon's effort to try in some way to make recompense for abandoning his first daughter so many years ago. Dixon clearly knew that all efforts to reconcile his relationship with Diane were a long shot, at best, and that everything he did from this point on in his communications with Diane had to be done with great care. He understood that no words of affection could ever make up for his absence in her life. In December of 1969, Dixon received word from Eastman that Cohen phoned Diane to read the recently acquired letters to her. She was in Europe when she received Cohen's phone call. The response from Diane was tepid. She was still dealing with the newness of her mother's death and likely not interested in dealing with her father on any level at this point in her life. However, Cohen seemed to be somewhat persuasive in getting Diane to at least consider the idea of reconciliation, but he later cautioned Dixon that this "will require a great deal of sensitive approach."[10]

In late September, Pitluck informed Dixon that he made contact with the New York Philharmonic and that they might be interested in engaging him for the summer of 1970. Dixon was pleased at the prospect of an appearance with the New York Philharmonic, but was concerned about the implications of accepting a summer concert engagement: "One small thought crosses my mind about the summer concerts: when I was still in the States—up to 1949—the summer concerts were on a somewhat lower level than the winter concerts. Does that situation still exist today? If yes, would I be in any way doing myself a disservice in doing the summer spots?"[11] Pitluck assured Dixon that while there was a clear difference in prestige between a summer engagement and a winter engagement, this would in no way damage his reputation. Dixon had to be reminded that his name recognition in the States was virtually non-existent, given his twenty-one-year self-imposed exile. But these summer engagements would clearly illustrate, to the many American concertgoers that would see him for the first time, why he was so revered abroad.

By late December, Pitluck was finalizing Dixon's schedule for his return visit and sketching out possible dates for the fall of that same year when he received a message from Taubman regarding Dixon's availability. Taubman informed Pitluck that "Dean has now no more free periods during October or November 1970 and there is nothing open for booking until May of '71 and possibly not even the August time for Washington, D.C. unless I cable you."[12] Pitluck felt that this last-minute change by Taubman was unfair to his efforts at trying to get Dixon the best possible opportunities with top-ranked orchestras in America:

> A pattern of action is developing which causes me great concern and which, while it is very likely unintentional is nevertheless quite unfair. We first agreed in Zurich that I would have [the] November 1970 period and also the summer of 1970. Now under any workable policy, that should be my booking period and before any change is made I should be contacted, cabled if necessary, but certainly approached to see if my negotiations will permit your changing, before any such change is made. Also, it doesn't make sense for me to work hard to develop the American market and then have no time for proper booking. As a matter of principle I am deeply concerned over this pattern of development and feel we must settle this matter at once. [13]

While Taubman appreciated Pitluck's frustration in this matter, he also felt it was his primary duty as Dixon's general manager to make sure that his client did not have any available dates unused. Taubman believed he provided Pitluck with a generous amount of time to secure conducting engagements for those dates previously agreed to, but as time went by and Taubman saw that Pitluck had not confirmed those dates, he moved forward and booked invitations from his end in the interest of his client. This initial conflict over scheduling would not be their last.

At the start of a new year, Dixon's schedule was set for his return to the States. Pitluck had secured dates with the New York Philharmonic, the Pittsburgh Symphony, and the St. Louis Symphony. The next step was publicity. Pitluck convinced Dixon and Taubman to bring in a publicist to create a plan of action on how best to market Dixon's return to the States. Herbert Breslin was a young publicist who had already developed a reputation for being a savvy and brash promoter. His clients were impressive; he had successfully promoted the careers of vocalists like Elizabeth Schwarzkopf, Joan Sutherland, and Marilyn Horne. He was also a brilliant manager, helping to cultivate the careers of a gifted young Spanish pianist named Alicia de Larrocha and a young Italian tenor by the name of Luciano Pavarotti. His strategies for promoting his clients were very creative, using talk shows, variety shows, and commercials to expand his classical artists' name recognition beyond the concert halls. Breslin charged a fee of $750 for his services. Dixon found that reasonable, given his reputation, and gave Pitluck the go-ahead to bring Breslin on board.

Dixon arrived in New York City on July 15, 1970. He was scheduled to appear with the New York Philharmonic for its annual parks concert series. Many who knew Dixon was returning home forewarned him that the city he grew up in had changed dramatically since the last time he was there. But he was not prepared for what he saw. It was like driving through a foreign land for the very first time. Dixon was in awe at the number of impressive new buildings that had been erected in a span of twenty years. Harlem was also transformed, but not for the better. Depression set in as he entered his old neighborhood. The impromptu tour of the city he no longer knew ended when the driver stopped at 302 Convent Avenue. He was home. McClara was still living in the flat where Dixon had spent his young adult life. He had not seen McClara since he brought her to Sweden in 1958 to meet her second granddaughter, Nina. She was happy to see her son. McClara was ninety years old and while her body was frail her mind was still sharp. Despite her infirmity, McClara was determined to celebrate Dixon's return by preparing a Sunday dinner on a Wednesday night. Before McClara opened the door, Dixon could already smell the savory aromas of a feast in the making. Dixon said about McClara that "she still cooks beautifully." On the menu was roasted lamb that had "a beautiful crust on the outside" and was so tender "you could cut it with a fork," a simple salad, corn on the cob, pickled beets, and gelatin fruit for dessert. [14] Eastman was scheduled to meet with Dixon that evening at McClara's place to talk business and made it just in time to join them for dinner. Afterward, McClara made her way to her favorite chair to relax while Dixon and Eastman washed the dishes. Dixon noticed during their conversation that McClara's hearing and eyesight had deteriorated significantly since the last time he saw her. She needed both a hearing aid (which she did not use because she claimed it kept making this annoying buzzing sound) and eyeglasses (which she did not use because she claimed they were the wrong prescription). There were plans being made to place her in a nursing home, so that she could be properly cared for. McClara welcomed the change because she no longer felt safe in her neighborhood. Having heard about a number of muggings of elderly people where she lived, McClara feared she would be next. Dixon enlisted the help of a number of his close family friends to find a suitable place for McClara. Bob Kaufman was one of those friends. He and his wife, Dorothy, looked after McClara while Dixon was away. They wrote Dixon regularly to provide updates on McClara's health and overall well-being. One day Bob picked Dixon up to take a look at a prospective nursing home for McClara. When they arrived at the nursing home, they were met by the person in charge, who took them on a tour of the facility while discussing the cost and the logistics of moving in. The facility was very clean with high ceilings all around. McClara would get a private room, which would allow her to bring some of her things from home. She would have to share a bathroom with one other resident. She could have company anytime of the day. It seemed the ideal place. Dixon informed McClara that they may have found her next home and that it was only a matter of time before she would be able to move in. Dixon just had to work out the financial arrangements. Before he returned to Frankfurt, Dixon gave Pitluck permission to access his New York bank account so that McClara could be provided a monthly stipend until she was officially placed in the nursing home facility.

After a wonderful, albeit short stay with McClara, Dixon moved to the Hotel Meurice on 145 West 58th Street on July 19. The hotel was closer to where he would be performing, and it seemed a more appropriate place to conduct interviews and meet with Breslin and Pitluck as needed.

His interviews on television, radio, and print media were well received, but what surprised Dixon in the most pleasant way was how he was treated by all who met him. There was "the most wonderful homage and respect" given to him. Pitluck even noticed as he and Dixon sat in the office of Carlos Moseley, the managing director of the New York Philharmonic, that "people kept coming by and were introduced to him and all of them said, 'It is an honor.' And this was not just lip service, but you could tell that it was genuine."[15] When Dixon returned to his hotel he noticed that he was having problems seeing out of his left eye. He had experienced some blurriness a few days prior but thought nothing of it. He was now very concerned and immediately sought medical assistance. After an examination, the doctor informed Dixon that he was suffering from a hemorrhage of his left eye due to high blood pressure. "It got up to 220 over 140; they got the upper number down to 190 but the 140 doesn't move and that's the dangerous one."[16] He was given drops to take in the morning and at night to help relieve pressure on the left eye. He was told that because of his high blood pressure he would be prone to future hemorrhages. The doctor expressed to Dixon with the greatest urgency that he needed to be examined thoroughly by a specialist to find the cause of his high blood pressure and treat it immediately. Dixon was frightened by the news but decided to wait until he returned to Frankfurt to be examined by the specialists there. The reasons being that he was told Germany had more experience in cases like his and the cost for treatment in Europe was more manageable than in the States.

Dixon's rehearsals with the New York Philharmonic started on July 20. It was the usual affair of trying to get a highly regarded professional orchestra to listen to a guest conductor on issues of interpretation with repertoire they had performed on numerous occasions. Patience and cooperation on that level were reserved for more "recognized" conductors. But Dixon had enough experience in this area that he knew when to let something go and when to insist. "I can be a very nice fellow at rehearsals, be very sweet, or I can be a very pernickety bastard if I have to be. I didn't want to create enemies."[17] He simply made it very clear that he was only interested in hearing what the composer wrote and nothing more. Given the outdoor venue, getting the ensemble to listen in a more deliberate way was his biggest challenge.

Before Dixon gave his first performance at Central Park, he was invited to a reception in his honor in the Blue Room at City Hall. The mayor of New York City, John V. Lindsay, presented Dixon with the key to the city. In his remarks, Mayor Lindsay said, "I am pleased to welcome such a distinguished, sensitive musician on his return to his native city. Dean Dixon had sacrificed much in the pursuit of his career. America also sacrificed much because of intolerance and discrimination. I sincerely hope that this series of three guest appearances with the New York Philharmonic will be the beginning of new recognition for him in his own country to add to his illustrious achievements in Europe."[18]

On July 21, he was in Manhattan at Central Park; on July 23 he was in Brooklyn at Prospect Park; and on July 25 he was in Queens at Crocheron Park. For all three concerts Dixon conducted Hans Werner Henze's *Trois pas des Triton*, Sibelius's Violin Concerto with James Oliver Buswell, and Brahms's Second Symphony. The park concerts were a resounding success. So much so that Moseley immediately began negotiating with Pitluck for Dixon to appear later that year during their subscription season. Moseley offered him the dates from November 23 to 30. Dixon was to be one of three guest conductors to replace Maestro George Szell, who passed away on July 30, 1970 (the other two conductors were Robert Shaw and Milton Katmis). At the time of his death, Szell was the music director of the Cleveland Orchestra and music advisor for the New York Philharmonic. The latter was a position designed to provide continuity during the time between Leonard Bernstein's departure in 1969 and Pierre Boulez's arrival in 1971. Pitluck successfully negotiated Dixon's fee and transportation and all that was remaining for everything to be in place was for Dixon to postpone a recording session in Frankfurt, which was scheduled at the same time. Before Dixon left New York for Philadelphia, Pitluck arranged a meeting with Ben Barkin, director of publicity for Schlitz Brewery. Pitluck pitched the idea to Barkin to have the beer company underwrite "a series of ten appearances with major orchestras in major cities of the country, and make it a salute from Schlitz."[19] As they did with the New York Philharmonic's parks concert series, Schlitz would jointly sponsor each concert with each host orchestra. While there were more details to be worked out, Dixon was very pleased with Pitluck's proposal and looked forward to seeing a final itinerary.

Dixon traveled to Philadelphia to conduct the Pittsburgh Symphony Orchestra in two performances at Temple University. His first performance took place on July 31 and featured Beethoven's *Egmont* Overture; Brahms's

Fourth Symphony; and Purcell's *Dido's Lament* and Mahler's *Rückert Lieder* with soprano Jessye Norman.

This was Dixon's first performance with Jessye Norman. "In 1968 Norman won the German Radio Stations' International Music Competition (ARD Wettbewerb) in Munich. As Music Director of the Frankfurt Radio Symphony Orchestra, Dean was involved either as one of the jurors or he conducted; anyway, that is how he knew Jessye Norman. The prize winners (this competition has several categories and therefore several First Prize Winners) were granted concert performances with the Orchestras of the participating Radio Stations—and Frankfurt was one of them."[20] He made contact with Norman after her successful opera debut as Elizabeth in Wagner's *Tannhauser* with the Deutsche Oper Berlin in 1969. He inquired if she would be available in the States for his performance in Philadelphia the following year. Norman responded that the last week in July was open and that she would be delighted to perform with him. She inquired how much time she would be given and provided a list of possible repertoire. Dixon chose two selections from her list. The performance was well received by all who attended. Although they did not perform together often, their concert in Philadelphia produced a mutual respect and admiration for one another. The second performance in Philadelphia took place on August 1 and featured Schumann's Piano Concerto in A minor with Dubravka Tomsic and Beethoven's Seventh Symphony. A week later on August 7 and 8, he concluded his summer guest conducting engagements with the St. Louis Symphony.

Dixon returned to Frankfurt in "high spirits" and ready to speak of his wonderful experience in his homeland to anyone who would listen. He talked to Taubman a few days after his return and gave him a full report, with special recognition being given to Pitluck for a job well done. Dixon was especially pleased that he would be returning to New York in November to conduct an all-Beethoven concert with the Philharmonic. But the most pressing issue at the time was his health. Dixon was still having problems with his left eye from the hemorrhage he experienced in the States. Taubman had to cancel several conducting engagements in the fall so that a specialist could see him. After a guest conducting engagement in London, Dixon spent a week at a sanatorium in Baden-Baden to treat his high blood pressure. He said, "It did me the world of good . . . the blood-pressure is down to 185/100—impossibly good for me."[21]

As Dixon was continuing his recovery at his home in Frankfurt, he began to reminisce on his wonderful summer excursion to the States. Out of everything he experienced from his trip home, perhaps the one thing that was etched in his memory was the generous remarks given by Mayor Lindsay at the ceremony where he was presented the key to the city. He was so touched by the honor that he penned this letter to Mayor Lindsay on October 5, 1970.

Dear Mayor Lindsay,

    Greetings from Frankfurt, and please, if you can, forgive the lateness of this letter. An impossibly retarded schedule, on all fronts, due to these new airplane checks and therefore delays, plus some necessary medical check and control sessions made life quite impossible for the days since we met. All things, however, are now beginning to take their rightful timing place and one of the first on my list is to speak with you through the mail. I would take this opportunity to say a deep thanks to you for your welcoming me "home" with our official meeting and your presenting me with the key to the city of New York. Too, for the thoughtful and profoundly impressive words you used in the presentation itself. I have performed before and been presented to royalty and heads of State in many parts of the world—Sweden's King, Norway's King, England's Queen, Belgium's Queen, Germany's Chancellor, Australia's Prime Minister—but never in any case has the presentation to or the meeting with had the impact that being presented to you has upon me. To finally be welcomed in such a warm way to one's city of birth by a man whose moral strength, courage and actions have for so long been admired by one is such a blessing and gives one such a lift both spiritually and physically, that I can only be humbly grateful and thankful to our Almighty God; and I say to you a personal and sincere "thank you."[22]

Dixon's return to the States represented, more than anything else, a need to be accepted by a country that he felt abandoned him so many years ago. The remarks from Mayor Lindsay, the wonderful treatment by all he encountered in the States, and Dixon's heartfelt response brought closure to one of his most cherished desires. His need for unconditional acceptance by his fellow Americans was finally fulfilled during his sojourn home.

Chapter Fourteen

I'm Not Tired Yet

Dixon returned to New York in November of 1970 to prepare for his guest appearance with the New York Philharmonic. He was tired. The trip from Europe to the States was exhausting. It reminded him of his not so pleasant trips from Frankfurt to Sydney. Dixon's week with the Philharmonic was the only engagement for his second return to the States. But it was a subscription season engagement, so it was worth the trip. Dixon was in high demand while he was in New York. His days were filled with meetings with his manager to try to schedule additional guest conducting dates, interviews with both radio and television, cultural societies organizing luncheons in his honor, fittings with the tailors, meeting with old and new friends. It was too much. There was no time to rest. But Dixon was determined that no matter the physical cost, as long as he was able to move, he was going to fulfill his engagements.

One of the first things that Dixon did upon his return to the States was to officially end his relationship with his publicist, Herbert Breslin. "I was never comfortable with him. The wild ties all of the time; the multicolored costumes. Basically I feel he was too interested in Breslin and not that much interested in the client."[1] Dixon's assessment of Breslin was confirmed after being told by Pitluck about a conversation he had with Breslin. The story was that when Dixon was scheduled to appear on the *Today Show*, Pitluck suggested to Breslin that he should try to get Dixon on the *Dick Cavett Show*. According to Pitluck, Breslin responded that "Dixon is not that big yet. That will have to wait."[2] Dave Kleger, a publicist and longtime friend of Dixon, was not of the same opinion as Breslin and took it upon himself to contact the producers of the *Dick Cavett Show*. It didn't take Kleger long to secure an appearance for Dixon on the show that Breslin believed he was not ready for. Dixon was so impressed with Kleger's work that he hired him to take over his publicity. While it was likely that Pitluck was in agreement with ending their relationship with Breslin, he did not agree with Dixon's decision to replace Breslin with Kleger. Pitluck believed that Kleger lacked the experience needed to manage Dixon's publicity. Pitluck's assessment was proven right on a number of projects entrusted to Kleger. So with Dixon's reluctant approval, Pitluck terminated Kleger's services and hired Audrey Michaels, who was highly regarded in the field. Even Taubman knew of Michaels's reputation and encouraged Dixon to give her a chance.

Dixon returned to the States in January of 1971 to begin his nationwide tour sponsored by the Schlitz Brewing Company. His first stop was with the Kansas City Philharmonic on January 19–21. "Robert A. Uihlein, Jr., chairman and president said, 'Schlitz is pleased to be able to bring the outstanding talent of Dean Dixon to Kansas City. His appearance last summer with the New York Philharmonic confirmed that he is among the world's leading conductors. We believe that Dean Dixon's national tour will be another example of the unique contributions to the culture of the world our country is making. We at Schlitz are most proud to play a part in it.'"[3] The Schlitz-sponsored tour would take Dixon to Minnesota, Milwaukee, Detroit, District of Columbia, Chicago, Philadelphia, and San Francisco, with several appearances with the New York Philharmonic to round out the 1971–1972 season.

The tug of war between Taubman and Pitluck was becoming more pronounced. Pitluck continued to express his concerns that Taubman was not providing enough dates for him to properly manage Dixon's career in the States. The latest incident was a cable to Pitluck from Taubman saying that Dixon would not be available for any engagements in the States for the fall of 1972 and the first two months of 1973. Taubman believed that "it would just impose too much physical and nervous strain on [Dixon] to commute between the States and Europe."[4] While Pitluck shared Taubman's concern for Dixon's health, recognizing the strain the commute could have on him, he nevertheless thought it disingenuous that Taubman booked Dixon in Italy and France for the entire period in question, instead of taking the opportunity to allow him to rest. To deny Pitluck any of this time put in serious jeopardy Dixon's chance of making a lasting impression on the American public: "We must realize that the public should not be allowed to 'cool off' too long."[5] Dixon had no desire to get in the middle of the back and forth between Pitluck and Taubman. He could see both sides of each argument and believed they both had his best interest at heart. So for the time being, Dixon's communication with Pitluck was on matters that had nothing to do with scheduling conflicts. For days, Dixon had been thinking about ways he could showcase the advancement of Black classical instrumentalists. He reminisced with sadness when growing up in Harlem as a budding young violinist how alone he felt not seeing anyone who looked like him playing the classics in the orchestras throughout the city. This was, of course, the impetus behind the creation of the Dean Dixon Symphony Orchestra. Even with his successes abroad, Dixon recognized that negative perceptions about Blacks in classical music still existed. His idea was to create a chamber orchestra made up of the very best Black classical instrumentalists, believing that with every success-ful concert a racial barrier would be brought down. He would call the thirty-member ensemble the Dean Dixon Chamber Orchestra, "or even by another [name] with me as conductor."[6] And they would tour throughout the States and Canada. Dixon believed there could also be a major financial windfall if the recordings for each of these concerts could be sold to one of the big recording companies. Pitluck's response did not focus on the racial angle but rather the consequences of creating a chamber orchestra. He said, "The mar-ket for chamber orchestras is different than for a full orchestra and it would almost look like you were giving up making the grade with the big orchestras as a conductor and were going to settle for a chamber orchestra slot. To go around with a fine chamber orchestra for one season as a guest would be one thing but to start your own group and realize that that is it for you."[7] The idea was permanently shelved. In the end Dixon saw the wisdom in Pitluck's comments. Moreover, he also saw too many similarities with the many or-chestras he started in the States that led to nowhere.

The frustration of Pitluck, which was by now being clearly expressed in his correspondence to Taubman, had officially reached a point of no return:

> I hope you realize, Martin, that you really make it difficult for me by giving me such poor availabilities. I really don't know how I can develop a career for Dean at all in this country since I have practically no reasonable availability for him until the 1973 time. We will have to take this into consideration, frankly, when we begin to re-evaluate the renewal of the contract because it is really impossible to plan anything of importance with no availability.[8]

Taubman responded by saying,

> While I fully concur with your point of view regarding the somewhat short periods which we were able to give you for the USA, I want you to understand the reasons for this. Firstly, we had to consider Dean's commitments in Frank-furt and also invitations and offers which Dean received from various Euro-pean concert organizations to which we simply had to give priority over the US due to lack of time on Dean's part during the past couple of seasons. Secondly, I felt it my duty to consider Dean's somewhat delicate state of health and the strains which professional activities in the US involve plus long travel, change in climate, environments, rehearsal schedules, etc., which are considerably heavier than similar factors here in Europe.[9]

Pitluck could see the writing on the wall. He was keenly aware that if he could not continue to deliver top-tier orchestras for his client that the renewal of his contract with Dixon would be in jeopardy. After hearing about this latest exchange of words, Dixon once again tried to calm the waters by writing Pitluck:

> Greetings from Frankfurt. Nothing truly new happening here except for work, work and more work. Said work is going very, very well. The health is fine. I just received permission to be able to live in Zurich—thank God—all in all life is quite positive in its many crooked aspects now. I believe that your and Martin's letters are rather constantly crossing each other during these times— especially those concerning my availability and date-periods. I hope that that particularly rough river has by now been crossed by you two. [10]

One of the highlights of Dixon's return to the States in 1972 was his guest conducting engagement with the National Symphony in the District of Columbia. On March 3, 1972, Nancy Hanks, who was the director of the National Endowment for the Arts, gave a small party for Dixon in Georgetown. He was deeply moved at the number of old pupils and new admirers who expressed their excitement at his return and their respect for his accomplishments in Europe. Barbara Watson of the State Department was there, along with her sister, Grace. They both knew Dixon very well. They grew up in the same neighborhood and Dixon taught Grace the violin. Cultural Affairs Adviser Leonard Garment and Ray Satchell, executive vice president of Schlitz, were also there expressing appreciation and support. Dixon was originally scheduled to meet with President Richard Nixon at a reception in his honor, but Nixon had not returned from his historic trip to China and was unable to attend. Instead, a letter from President Nixon was delivered by an official and read that evening.

> Dear Mr. Dixon:
>
> It gives me great pleasure to join in welcoming you to the Nation's Capital and in expressing my personal congratulations to you on your first American tour after twenty-one successful years as a leading conductor in Europe. May your sojourn in Washington be as rewarding for you personally as it is certain to be for those who attend your outstanding performances.
>
> Sincerely,
> Richard Nixon [11]

Dixon made his Washington, D.C., debut with the National Symphony that Tuesday night at the Kennedy Center.

As Dixon was completing his last guest conducting engagement in the States for the 1971–1972 season with the San Francisco Symphony, Pitluck made contact with Maestro Eugene Ormandy with the hopes of securing a guest conducting spot for the 1974–1975 season with the Philadelphia Orchestra.

I met with Dean Dixon this morning and told him of your promise to recommend him as guest conductor in Philadelphia for the season '74–'75. As you advised, I am also sending a copy of this letter to Boris (last name is Sokoloff—manager of Philadelphia Orchestra). My relationship with Dean has frankly reached a point where I will have to secure such prestigious engagements as this one with your orchestra to continue to hold him. This in spite of the fact of my having secured for him engagements this current season with the New York Philharmonic, Chicago Symphony, National Symphony in Washington, D.C., San Francisco, Detroit, Minneapolis and Milwaukee at excellent fees. When we had lunch in Saratoga a couple of years ago and then talked further in your hotel suite there, you may recall that I was then on my way to Europe and expected to sign a managerial contract with Dixon and you indicated that you would be happy to help me, personally, and that you had very favorable recollections of Dixon's work. [12]

Dixon was back in Europe preparing for a full roster of engagements for the 1972–1973 season that included appearances in Frankfurt, Gothenburg, Malmo, Norrkoping, Paris, Lausanne, Bern, Basel, Zurich. There were also extensive performances in Holland and Belgium. But no guest conducting engagements were on the books in the States. After his discussion with Dixon in San Francisco and his encouraging dialogue with Maestro Ormandy, Pitluck believed his relationship with Dixon was on solid ground. It was not. What Pitluck did not know was that four months prior to his correspondence with Maestro Ormandy, Taubman, with the help of Dixon's publicist, Audrey Michaels, reached out to another representative to take over Dixon's management in the States and Canada. The decision to terminate their relationship with Pitluck had been in the works for some time. It was believed that there had to be someone out there who could work around Dixon's schedule in Europe and still maintain regular guest conducting engagements with first-tier orchestras in the States. Oblivious to what was going on behind the scenes, Pitluck cabled Dixon on April 6, 1972, informing him that he would be exercising his option to renew his contract with Dixon for an additional three years, which would go in effect in September of 1972. Dixon conveyed this cable to Taubman. It was clear that they had to act immediately. On April 7, 1972, Pitluck received a phone call from Dixon's lawyer in New York. Dixon's lawyer wrote him, giving the details of that phone conversation.

I telephoned Sherman Pitluck. Mr. Pitluck is unhappy, of course, and sounded bitter. He advised me that he had sent out that very day a notice that he was exercising his option to renew the agreement. I was at pains to make it clear to him, without going into details as to the reasons, that you believe that your North American career can be better enhanced through other management; and that we believe that a termination of the agreement can be effected on terms which both protect his reputation and which would provide adequate compen-

sation for the engagements scheduled or anticipated for the renewal term. . . .
At the conclusion of our discussion, in which I urged that a meeting take place
of ourselves with him and his counsel, he agreed to turn the matter over at
once to his lawyers, and to ask them to telephone me. [13]

It was done. The man who made it possible for Dixon to return to America
after a two decade self-imposed exile, helped him resolve his ongoing legal
problems with Vivian, and successfully negotiated top dollar for guest conducting engagements with top-tier orchestras in the States was no longer
Dixon's manager. Bill Judd took over Dixon's management. On November
9, 1972, Pitluck received a letter from Boris Sokoloff, general manager of the
Philadelphia Orchestra, inquiring about Dixon's schedule for the 1974–1975
season. His letter to Ormandy and follow up with Sokoloff paid off in the
end. But it was too little too late for Pitluck. He referred Sokoloff to Judd.
However, the Philadelphia engagement was nearly lost, because Judd never
confirmed the dates with Sokoloff. Taubman had to step in to confirm the
dates but insisted that Judd handle the contract negotiations and other matters
to close the deal. Moreover, if Taubman had not been involved in negotiating
Dixon's second appearance with the Chicago Symphony, he would have had
no guest conducting engagements in the States for the 1973–1974 season.
Audrey was very disappointed at Dixon's modest itinerary in preparation for
his third return to America. Dixon shared her disappointment, questioning
why Judd was unsuccessful in securing more conducting engagements. Audrey, acting on behalf of Dixon, met with Judd to have a frank conversation
about Dixon's itinerary to see if something could be worked out. After six
months and numerous failed attempts to make contact with Judd to discuss
Dixon's future in the States, both frustrated and dismayed, Taubman wrote
Judd to say,

> It is with my most sincere sorrow and regret that I am writing these lines to
> you which I felt I was prompt to do after a long and comprehensive talk I had
> with Dean the other day when we met the day after a concert of his in Munich.
> Both Dean and I voiced to each other our unhappiness and profound discontent
> over the whole managerial situation with you. As you know, Bill, there has
> been precious little contact between the two of you ever since you had ex-
> pressed your desire to take him "under your wings" for the U.S. and Canada
> after Dean had decided to sever his unsatisfactory professional relationship
> with Sherman Pitluck. Both Dean and I—and also Audrey Michaels who, as
> you will recall, was instrumental in getting you together so-to-speak—were
> under the justified impression that the new relationship between you and him
> would be a very harmonious and fruitful one for all parties concerned. The
> almost complete lack of contact on your part with Dean since the earlier part of
> this year we just failed to comprehend. . . . If you felt you were too overloaded
> with work for your other artists or that you could not "cope" with Dean for
> whatever other reasons, why did you not find the time and/or the courage to

say so quite frankly? In consideration of all of the above mentioned, don't you think it would be fair to both Dean and yourself to annul, that "marriage" between the two of you which, in fact, was never "consummated"? PLEASE let me have your soonest reaction to the above and without any inhibition. [14]

Judd responded, "Dear Martin, I have your letter of July 12th and of course will accede to your request on behalf of Dean Dixon. Therefore, please consider our arrangement annulled." [15]

Audrey Michaels immediately put Dixon in contact with Harry Beall, president of Arthur Judson Management. Although Beall was associated with the legendary impresario, he was unable to secure a string of guest engagements with top-tier orchestras because of the same problems that Pitluck dealt with during his tenure as Dixon's manager.

In 1972, Dixon was hospitalized for several weeks. This hospital stay put Dixon in a very difficult financial position. He expressed to Audrey in a letter, dated June 27, 1972, that he would be unable to pay her usual fee because his illness would keep him out of commission for five months. He asked if he could play $50 a month to just "keep our professional relationship from grinding to a full stop." He was also concerned about hospital costs, because he was unable to secure health insurance in Germany; Nina's tuition for school; and guest conducting cancellations.

Dixon's hospital stays were becoming more frequent. By all accounts from his doctors his health was slowly deteriorating. Dixon relied more and more on Ritha Blume, Taubman's assistant, to help him manage his professional and personal responsibilities.

Chapter Fifteen

Ritha

Roswitha Blume was born in Erfurt/Thuringia on November 18, 1939, shortly after the war broke out. The war left its stamp on the Blume family, especially after they moved to Königsberg in East Prussia, now known as Kaliningrad. Her father was a journalist for the Deutsche Nachrichtenbüro (German News Office, comparable to the Associated Press), and this was the reason for frequent moves from one city to another. When Russia entered the war, the constant bombing and the fear of a Russian invasion forced the family to flee from East Prussia to Berlin and then to Dresden in February 1945. The city was full of refugees from the east, and somehow Roswitha, her two sisters, and her mother survived the inferno that cost the lives of approximately thirty thousand when the Allied forces bombed the city and practically erased it. They lost their home and their belongings but they were together and alive. After days of travel by train, on foot, or some odd vehicle, they arrived in Deggendorf in Bavaria where they lived in a construction container for more than five years, while their father was imprisoned by the Russians. But even during these hard times, Roswitha's mother insisted that her children should take piano lessons with another refugee who taught them for practically nothing. When her father returned from Russia in 1950, he found employment as a journalist again, which meant moving once more, this time from Bavaria to Detmold/Lippe in Westphalia. With his new income, Roswitha's father saw to it that all his children would continue their music lessons, and it seemed that music had a healing effect after all that had happened to the family. Roswitha loved playing her cello but realized early on that she did not have enough talent or the endurance necessary for a successful career. Instead she chose a vocation that followed in the tradition of her father's family and started as an apprentice at the local Detmold newspaper. Her next stop in the newspaper business was Hanover, Germany.

But it was the untimely death of her beloved mother that prompted Roswitha to make the decision to go back to school. She first moved to Rome to study Italian and later to London to get her degree in English. With her background of war and loss of a place called home, she longed for some safety in her life. Switzerland seemed to be both destiny and the right destination. She moved in 1965 to the city of Zug and found employment first at an American company and later at Martin Taubman's Impresariat, where she started working as his assistant in 1967. She attended concerts and performances of most of Taubman's clients, handling their administrative arrangements, publicity, and any other issues that might come up at a given moment. During that time Roswitha became Ritha at the request of Taubman. He claimed that Roswitha was "impossible" to pronounce, "like one of the Walkyries," especially for his American clients, and after some discussions it was decided to take the "R" from the beginning of the name and "itha" from her family nickname, Witha.

It was at that time that Ritha was asked to meet with one of Taubman's clients in Zurich: it was Dixon. "I met Dean when he conducted the Zurich Tonhalle Orchestra, and I remember that we talked for hours afterwards. He was a unique and charismatic person and to this day I have never met anyone like him. We became friends and this was the basis for a deep and everlasting love."[1]

Dixon's marriage to Mary was ending. He had already moved out of their Frankfurt home in 1970, which officially began the three-year waiting period, as mandated by German law, before a divorce could be granted. Dixon endured the waiting time because he knew there was someone special waiting for him on the other side. "This woman of mine, Ritha Blume, is one of the finest specimens of human being that the Good Lord has ever put on this earth. I consider myself extraordinarily fortunate in having met her."[2]

Ritha traveled with Dixon to New York in 1971 and was introduced to McClara, who took an instant liking to her. She returned to New York with Dixon the following year along with Nina, who by this time was aware of her father's new relationship. Dixon commented about the interaction between Ritha, Nina, and McClara saying, "There is now a three-way, new found love affair going on between my mother and Ritha and Nina."[3]

When Dixon and Ritha started talking about living together as husband and wife, Dixon made appointments for Ritha to meet all of his doctors so that she could get a comprehensive report on his current health condition. Ritha knew that Dixon's eyes were giving him great difficulties, but it was his heart and blood pressure that were the main issues of concern. There seemed to be an unspoken truth about Dixon's overall health. They understood that each day was to be lived as if it was their last one together.

Dixon started receiving letters from a number of his colleagues in Australia, letting him know that the new opera house in Sydney was almost finished and how much they would like to see him there as a guest conductor. There was only one problem. Dixon was suing the ABC for breach of contract during his time with the Sydney Symphony and the matter had yet to be resolved. There was no way an invitation would be forthcoming given the current situation. Audrey, Dixon's publicist, made it possible for any real discussion to be had in this matter. She knew a high-ranking ABC official and invited him to a dinner party to get a better sense of the Dixon vs. ABC situation. The official was able to explain the situation in great detail. He also offered suggestions on how to resolve this issue in such a way that Dixon could be once again welcomed in Sydney with open arms. Dixon dropped the lawsuit and an invitation soon followed.

On September 20, 1973, Dixon's divorce from Mary was official. He, Mary, and Ritha met afterward for a meal in a relaxed atmosphere in order to seal their friendship, which lasted until Mary's death in January of 1985.

That same year, Dixon and Ritha were planning to get married in Zurich, but due to the seemingly endless paperwork, Australia seemed the better option. Dixon was scheduled to appear in Sydney for seven concerts (with four different programs) and a fourteen-day stay. Upon arrival at Sydney airport on October 29, Dixon was met by an impressive number of representatives of the press with questions abounding. Of particular interest to them was the dropping of the lawsuit, to which Dixon answered in a "good flower-power style 'Love conquers all.'" He was then asked, "Maestro, what are your next plans?" To which he responded that he was getting married. This was unexpected but welcome news and the papers covered the event with every detail they could find. The marriage took place at Sydney's Town Hall on November 8. But Dixon and Ritha couldn't sit back, relax, and enjoy the newness of their marriage. Later that evening Dixon conducted the Sydney Symphony Orchestra. On the program were Britten's Violin Concerto with Wanda Wilkomirska as soloist and Sibelius's First Symphony. Roger Covell of the *Sydney Morning Herald* wrote in his "Master of the Hall" review: "Dixon, the SSO and the Opera House Concert Hall, in other words, are likely to put the listener in love all over again with the sheer impact and sensuous freshness of orchestral sound. . . . Summing up the return to Australia, a newspaper called it homecoming; the welcome from press and public was overwhelming."[4] Dixon was quickly re-engaged to return in 1975 for a four-state tour: New South Wales, Victoria, South Australia, and Western Australia.

As Dixon's tenure was coming to a close with the Hessischer Rundfunk, he wanted to make sure that there were enough guest conducting opportunities lined up to keep him busy. So he contacted Taubman and asked him to start putting the word out in Berlin and throughout that he was available to work, no longer burdened with the responsibility of a music director.

On May 10, 1974, Dixon celebrated the end of his fourteen-year tenure with the Hessischer Rundfunk with the same large-scale work that he began his tenure with: Beethoven's Ninth Symphony. Soloists were Gundula Janowitz (soprano), Marie-Louise Gilles (alto), Werner Hollweg (tenor), Hans Sotin (bass).

Later that month, Dixon returned to the States for a two-week engagement in Chicago. According to the critics, the concerts were less than impressive, which was the opposite result of his first visit to Chicago in 1972. Karen Monson of the *Chicago Daily News* wrote, "The problem was right out front. Dean Dixon, back on the podium for a two week engagement, proved himself equipped to deal with neither the Chicago Symphony, Bruckner nor Schumann."[5] Robert C. Marsh of the *Chicago Sun-Times* said, "Part of Dixon's problem is that he gives his musicians long, sweeping beats that end below the music stand where no one can see them. This is very strange, indeed. A conductor of Dixon's experience surely need not be told to keep the essential movements of the baton up where they can be read clearly from the back of the stage."[6]

On August 15, 1974, Dixon wrote the Frankfurt Radio Symphony Orchestra for the last time as its chief director.

> Dear friends, colleagues and fellow artists,
>
> On May 10 last I begged off from talking too seriously with you and asked your permission to put such deep and important thoughts in a letter to you which I would deliver later—this is that letter. There has been time now since my last concert with you as head conductor—time to think, time to reflect, time to evaluate; and I do feel that I can now, with a better perspective, say my official "Auf Wiedersehen" to you as head conductor. From the many emotions connected with our official parting the main one—high above all others—is one of "THANKS!" Thanks from me to you for your practically 100 percent cooperation, for your fine sense of self-discipline, for your constant extending of yourselves musically and artistically, for your comradely collaboration even when we had areas of disagreements; for your controlled patience, for your sharing of my artistic visions when we were deeply involved in the music, for your hard work and personal sacrifice, for your partnership in our growing together, for your so-oft superior expenditure of energy, for your unceasing goodwill, for your understanding of my invented Deutsch when I spoke of "magen (stomach) rhythms, spazieren rhythms, pianissimo von Hinten, etc."; thanks also for your beautifully developed concept of orchestral tone colors, for your finely developed sensitivity to infinite dynamic possibilities, for your lightning-fast response to my musical-emotional changes, as dictated in and between the printed page, for your excellent ability to rise to the demands of the occasion, for your sensitive and excellent musicality, etc. I could go on for hours, but better I don't. To have received all of the aspects from everyone constantly was impossible—but to have received so much of so many of these things from each individual so often lets me leave you with peace in my heart. We shall meet again each year I hope, and we plan, and

meantime I wish you all God's help in constant growth spiritually, musically, artistically, and emotionally. Again—Thanks! Dean Dixon[7]

On September 3, 1974, McClara had a letter dictated to Dixon and Ritha from the Morningside House in the Bronx.

> Dearest Dean and Ritha,
> I am dictating this letter to Ms. Murphy here at the new home, since you know that my writing has become very poor. I want you to know that I am settling quite well at Morningside House. I also want you to know that you should take all those belongings that you would still want from the old place, if you can arrange for it. I have put the lamps and one small cupboard as well as one table in store with Dave Kleger at his office. Your books and important papers, dear Dean, are with Bob and Dorothy Kaufman at their apartment. So, if you can arrange for shipping these things to your new home in Switzerland, you know that everything belongs to you anyway as you paid for it to start with. I hope that you can take these things to Europe without problem and wish you happiness with them since I have to part with everything here anyway.
>
> With love for both of you, I am, your Mother,
> McClara Dean Dixon[8]

This was the last letter Dixon would receive from McClara.

Dixon was back in America to conduct the Philadelphia Orchestra on April 3–8, 1975. The reviews were much different compared to his two-week engagement in Chicago the previous year. In Philadelphia he was filled with excitement and fire, despite the fact he was using a cane after a foot operation. James Felton of the *Evening Bulletin* in a review titled "Dixon's Belated Debut Is Brilliant, Exciting," ended by saying, "Dean Dixon is still very much a conductor to reckon with. A permanent major post should be open to him somewhere in his own country."[9] Felton and many others who hoped that Dixon's return would result in a permanent post in America were sorely disappointed in the end. Philadelphia was to be the last time Dixon conducted an American orchestra.

After his successful engagement in Philadelphia, Dixon and Ritha traveled back to New York to see McClara and for Dixon to receive an honor from his alma mater. On May 14, 1975, at Teachers College, Columbia University, Dixon was awarded the Medal for Distinguished Service. The citation read:

> Distinguished musician and teacher of music, whose brilliant international career as a conductor has for a quarter century instructed his countrymen in the virtues of creative collaboration, and whose role as teaching exemplar has demonstrated to youth of every race and creed that talent, artistic devotion, personal commitment, and social courage can render society more open and just and therefore give new meaning to the goal of full and equal citizenship.

In recognition of these gifts and accomplishments, Teachers College takes
pride in awarding you its Medal for Distinguished Service. [10]

It was reported by the *Sydney Morning Herald*, on September 30, 1975, that
Dixon had to cancel his Australian tour due to suspected heart trouble. He
was only able to complete seven of his scheduled twenty-four concerts between September 8 and November 1. His illness was initially thought to be
the flu, given that it was accompanied by a fever. After two days of rest, he
resumed his conducting schedule but his symptoms got worse. Dixon was
taken to St. Vincent's Hospital hours before he was to take the podium to
conduct the Melbourne Symphony. He was seen by a heart specialist and was
informed that he had a leaking aortic valve. It was recommended that he
forgo his remaining concerts and travel back to Zurich to consult with his
physicians there. Dixon and Ritha flew back to Switzerland at the end of the
week to meet with his physician. After a battery of tests were done, it was
concluded that Dixon needed open-heart surgery.

Given the seriousness of this procedure, Dixon felt the need to write his
last will and testament. It read, "I Charles Rolston Dean Dixon, do hereby
declare that in the event of my death my wife Roswitha Dagmar Dixon shall
be my only heir. I leave it to her discretion to distribute— as she sees fit—a
part of my personal belongings to my two daughters Diane and Nina Dixon.
Everything else is in her hands to keep or dispense with. I do not wish to be
cremated." [11]

On November 8, 1975, Dixon entered the Zug Kantonsspital and was
scheduled for his surgery at Zurich University Hospital five days later. Ritha
described the situation in a letter to a family friend.

> Dean has been operated on Thursday. Everything went so far better than
> expected, that is, the complications are under control. He is still in the inten-
> sive ward with artificial respirator, tubes everywhere, and kidney and lung
> trouble. They will keep him there for another 3 days maybe, if all goes well.
> No visitors are allowed, but they let me see him for 5 minutes today. I don't
> know whether he recognized me, but I can't do anything for him anyway. Just
> wait and pray and try to stay calm and optimistic. This suffering is so terrible;
> when you really have to give up and leave it in a higher force's hands, that is
> the only help we have. [12]

On December 24, 1975, at 5:20 a.m., McClara died of cancer of the
pancreas, at the age of ninety-five. Dixon was unable to attend her funeral
because of his fragile health after the open-heart surgery. His closest New
York friends from way back, Robert and Dorothy Kaufman, supported his
mother to the very end and made all the arrangements for her funeral.

As Dixon began his long road to recovery, he was optimistic that he would be able to resume his conducting engagements, albeit a more modest schedule. He said to a friend,

> Life and death hung in the balance for five days but I was lucky and now on the long road to recovery. It goes beautifully, but awfully slowly does the strength come back. Depression over the "langsam" tempo keeps trying to come in but so far I have been successful at keeping them out. Hoping the doctor will let me go back into the conducting-ring by May—fingers crossed. Meantime to the hospital everyday for massage or gymnastics—in and out of water—and home exercises everyday. Lots of sleep and as much relaxation as is possible—with my nicely complicated personality . . . I definitely will not work or allow myself to be worked as hard as in the past. Basically one or two concerts a month will be my new line, and in between REST and LIVING! [13]

In May of 1976, Dixon returned to the podium after five months of rehabilitation from open-heart surgery. He was excited about being back on his feet and wasted no time communicating with old friends about guest conducting opportunities.

> This is just a note to let you know that I am "back in life" again and have started conducting this month in Vienna. Everything went very, very well, and I am this week leaving for a concert at the "Prager Frühling." So you see, I can continue making conducting plans instead of looking for another profession. . . . Coming back to our talks and various letters of last year, I would very much like to discuss a date for a guest concert with Museumsgesellschaft, especially as my next pair of concerts with the Frankfurt Radio Orchestra is fixed for January 1977. This would leave a good possibility in either October 1977 or the second half of December 1977. Please let me know how this would look for you, because I would like to finalize my schedule for that season. [14]

Along with Dixon, everyone seemed to be optimistic about his health and overall recovery.

Dixon and Ritha had just returned from a successful conducting engagement in Brussels and were settling back in at their home in Oberaegeri, Switzerland. The plan was for Ritha to go to Zurich with a friend and for Dean to cook the meal for when they returned in the afternoon. Dean felt really good that day. And when he embraced Ritha before she left, his last words were "I believe I have come full-circle. Living with you here in peace and quiet has priority over all else." On her way back home, Ritha suddenly felt uneasy and found a telephone to call her husband. He sounded blurred and told her three times, "I am very, very dizzy."

She rushed home to find him stretched out on the bed, complaining of not being able to see. She first thought it might be a blood clot behind the eye, when he remarked that there are colleagues who conduct with closed eyes, but quickly changed her mind and took him by car to the Zug hospital, approximately a thirty-minute drive. After waiting in the emergency room for some time, Dixon lost consciousness and the doctors concluded that he had suffered a stroke. They were fighting for his life, but in vain. Ritha asked for a quiet room to be by his side in silent prayer when Dixon breathed his last breath. At midnight the fight was over. He could let go peacefully.

Dean Dixon died at 12:05 a.m. on November 4, 1976. The cause of death was apoplexy, which is more commonly known as a stroke. He was laid to rest at the cemetery in the village of Oberaegeri/Kanton of Zug, Switzerland.

Epilogue: On My Shoulders

As news of Dixon's unprecedented accomplishments in Europe made its way back to America, both his contemporaries and a new generation of Black conductors were given hope as they saw before their eyes a narrow path being paved for their inclusion into this last bastion of elitism. Dixon was keenly aware of what his accomplishments meant to all who were destined to follow in his footsteps: "By virtue of my being what I am here [in Germany] and in Australia, at least these places have been opened to black conductors and Germany means all of Europe. Because when any Negro announces himself as a candidate for a position or a job or a guest conductor's spot in Europe today, he does it against the background of the reputation that I have established. That reputation is good, so his chances of being accepted now are that much greater."[1] This was no boasting on Dixon's part. At the apex of his career, he was inundated with letters, telegrams, and even telephone calls from Black singers, composers, instrumentalists, and conductors desperately seeking advice on how best to navigate their careers in America and Europe. On his shoulders stood every Black conductor who dared to dream the impossible; whether their careers were based in the States or Europe; whether they had direct contact with him or not. It was the symbolism of a Dean Dixon that spoke to the possibilities of something greater. On his shoulders stood:

Everett Lee (1919–) was born in Wheeling, West Virginia. He began his violin studies at age nine and went on to attend the Cleveland Institute of Music as a violin major. Lee moved to New York as a freelance musician. He landed a job as concertmaster on the Broadway show *Carmen Jones*. He received his first major conducting break when he was asked to replace the ailing conductor of that same Broadway musical, becoming the first Black conductor to do so. This success led to Leonard Bernstein enlisting Lee to conduct his musical, *On The Town*. But like Dixon, Lee would find his biggest success in Europe. In 1952, he traveled to Rome on a Fulbright grant. Somewhere along his travels throughout Europe he met and became close friends with Dixon. Dixon believed in his talent and was influential in helping Lee secure the position of chief conductor of the Norrkoping Symphony Orchestra in Sweden. His tenure with the Swedish orchestra lasted from 1962 to 1972. "Lee considered the most significant milestones in his conducting career to be his performances at the Bordeaux Festival, the Royal Opera in Stockholm, a 'Marriage of Figaro' performance with the Opera Ebony, and appearances with the Munich and New York Philharmonics. He also valued greatly his four-year tenure as music director of the Symphony of the New World."[2]

Denis de Coteau (1929–1999) was born in Brooklyn, New York. He started his musical training on the piano and later added the viola. He decided early in life that he was destined to be a musician or a diplomat. That decision was later amended when he attended a performance of the New York Philharmonic, with Dean Dixon as the guest conductor. The young de Coteau said about the experience, "It just overwhelmed me. At that point I decided that [conducting was] what I wanted to do, and I did later study with [Dixon]. I studied score reading, counterpoint, and harmony in New York for three years at his home on Convent Avenue. . . . Dixon was very important in that he got me started and gave me the discipline that is required to be a conductor. He was a difficult taskmaster. He never let up the pressure even though I was only ten or eleven when I started study with him."[3] In 1968, de Coteau was appointed assistant conductor of the San Francisco Ballet. In 1974 he was promoted to music director and held that position until 1998.

Henry Lewis (1932–1996) was born in Los Angeles, California. He began playing the piano at age five but later moved on to double bass. At age sixteen Lewis became a member of the Los Angeles Philharmonic and remained a member of the double bass section for six years. In 1961, Lewis made national headlines by becoming the assistant conductor of the Los Angeles Philharmonic. But by far the biggest achievement for Lewis was his appointment as music director of the New Jersey Symphony Orchestra in 1968, making him the first Black American to be appointed music director of a major symphony orchestra. He held this post until 1976. In 1972 he was the first Black American to conduct the Metropolitan Opera. From 1960 to 1979 he was married to famed mezzo-soprano Marilyn Horne. After his tenure with the New Jersey Symphony, Lewis had numerous guest conducting engagements with major orchestras like: Boston, Chicago, Cleveland, New York, and San Francisco. His last post was as music director of the Radio Symphony Orchestra in Hilversum (1989–1993).

Paul Freeman (1936–) was born in Richmond, Virginia. He received his B.M., M.M., and Ph.D. from the Eastman School of Music. In 1967 Freeman won the Dimitri Mitropolous International Conductors' Competition. From 1968 to 1989, Freeman held conducting posts with the Dallas, Detroit, and Victoria symphonies. In 1987 he founded the Chicago Sinfonietta. The Sinfonietta's mission has not only been to serve as model for diverse music being presented at the highest artistic level, but to serve as a model for diversity in its participants. As a guest conductor Freeman has led more than one hundred orchestras in thirty countries. In 1996, he was appointed music director and chief conductor of the Czech National Symphony Orchestra in Prague. To date Freeman has made more than two hundred recordings, but is widely recognized for his mid-1970s recording of Black classical composers. This series, produced by Columbia Records, traces the history of black classical composers from 1750 to the present.

James DePreist (1936–2014) was born in Philadelphia, Pennsylvania, and is the nephew of the renowned contralto Marian Anderson. DePreist began his formal training in music at the University of Pennsylvania and the Philadelphia Conservatory of Music, studying composition with Vincent Persichetti. In 1962 DePreist contracted polio while on tour in East Asia, which resulted in paralysis in both legs. During his recovery he immersed himself in the study of orchestral scores. His career took off after winning the 1964 Mitropoulous International Conducting Competition in New York. He was appointed by Leonard Bernstein assistant conductor of the New York Philharmonic in 1965. In 1980 DePreist was appointed music director of the Oregon Symphony. He remained with the Oregon Symphony for twenty-five years. Through his artistic leadership the Oregon Symphony developed from a regional ensemble to an internationally recognized recording symphony. In 2005 DePreist was awarded the National Medal of Arts, which is the nation's highest honor for artistic excellence. DePreist has made more than fifty recordings and has conducted every major North American orchestra and internationally has conducted in Berlin, Munich, Tokyo, Prague, Rome, London, Stockholm, and Vienna.

Isaiah Jackson (1945–) was born in Richmond, Virginia, and started his musical journey at age four on the piano. Although Jackson grew up in a segregated neighborhood, he was far from disadvantaged. His father and grandfather were both surgeons and one of his childhood friends was the famed African American tennis star Arthur Ashe. At age fourteen Jackson was sent to boarding school where he continued his studies on the piano. Jackson enrolled at Harvard with a concentration in Russian history and literature, all the while continuing his music studies. After graduating (cum laude) from Harvard University in 1966, he decided to pursue music and continued his formal training at Stanford University (M.A., 1967) and the Juilliard School (M.S., 1969, D.M.A., 1973). Jackson has held posts with the American Symphony Orchestra, Baltimore Symphony Orchestra, Rochester

Philharmonic, Flint Symphony Orchestra, Dayton Philharmonic, and the Royal Ballet.

Kay George Roberts (1950–) was born in Nashville, Tennessee. At age nine, Roberts began playing violin in the Cremona String Orchestra, which was organized by Robert Holmes, a Black music educator, conductor, and composer. Roberts thrived in this segregated ensemble for several years. When the Youth Symphony in Nashville opened its doors to Blacks, she auditioned and was accepted into the program. Roberts received her formal training at Fisk University and the Yale University School of Music. She received two master's degrees from Yale (M.M. in violin performance and M.M.A. in violin performance and orchestral conducting). She received her D.M.A from Yale in conducting, becoming the first woman to do so. Roberts studied conducting at Yale with Otto-Werner Mueller. She also studied with Leonard Bernstein, Gustav Meier, and Seiji Ozawa at Tanglewood. Roberts is music director of the New England Orchestra and principal conductor of Opera North, Inc.

Thomas Wilkins (1956–) was born in Norfolk, Virginia. At age nine, Wilkins fell in love with classical music when he attended a concert where he heard an orchestra playing the national anthem. He was also keenly aware of the conductor's role at the concert and instantly became fascinated at how his movements were helping to shape the sound emanating from the orchestra. He knew then that conducting was his calling. Wilkins received his formal training at the Shenandoah Conservatory of Music and the New England Conservatory of Music. Wilkins is music director of the Omaha Symphony; principal guest conductor of the Hollywood Bowl Orchestra; and the Germeshausen Youth and Family Concerts conductor with the Boston Symphony Orchestra.

Michael Morgan (1957–) was born in Washington, D.C. He began conducting at the age of twelve. He received his formal training at the Oberlin Conservatory of Music. In 1980 Morgan was awarded first prize in the Hans Swarowsky International Conductors Competition in Vienna, Austria. In 1986 Morgan made his debut with the New York Philharmonic as guest conductor as well as starting his new position as assistant conductor of the Chicago Symphony Orchestra. He remained with Chicago until 1991. In 1990 Morgan was appointed music director of the Oakland East Bay Symphony.

Appendix A: In Memoriam

Hi Dr. Jones,

I spent some time with Milt and Rosemary today, and I think you'll like the attached. We cherry-picked bits of *Along the Cherry Lane* and wove them in with what Milt related today.

I was unable to practice piano for two years in my mid teens, due to a serious illness. I had been playing since I was five, and could not wait to get back to my studies. When the doctors told me that I could start playing again, I was elated—only to discover that I had lost much of my ability. I saw four or five teachers, but could not break through to the level I had been playing at before, and I became more and more confused and upset. My parents, who were good friends with Dean, suggested I ask his advice.

I met with him backstage after a New York Philharmonic concert, which he had just conducted, to great acclaim. Dean listened to my problem with great sympathy. He understood that I was really disappointed that I was not going to be a concert pianist after all. But he showed me my situation in a whole new light.

He said, "You're very, very lucky. Being a concert pianist is not a very nice life. You spend half your nights in a hotel by yourself. You're always on the road. The better a pianist you are, the more people resent you. There are a hundred other ways to make a living in music that don't involve the handicaps of being a concert pianist."

That had never occurred to me before. I'd thought of the life of a concert pianist as all pluses—I'd never thought of it in terms of *handicaps*. Because of Dixon, instead of everything having closed in on top of me, it all opened up. I could stay in music! He really lifted me up and helped me look around—and suddenly there were all these new horizons.

I remember that evening at the Philharmonic so vividly. Almost every member of the orchestra came up to Dean and congratulated him and wished him well, and said what a pleasure it had been working with him. They were lining up; it was very unusual. I'll never forget one violist, a young woman, who said, "I learned more about up-bowing in your two-hour rehearsal than I ever did in all my years of practice." On the Friday morning both the *Herald Tribune* and the *New York Times*, Virgil Thomson and Olin Downes, respectively, gave Dixon rave reviews. And each used the word *genius*. We were all elated—he'd done it! We were so proud of him and thrilled for him. Everyone assumed that he'd now go on to the stellar career he so deserved. He'd break through the color barrier.

A week later, his wife called my parents. Nothing had come up, and they were going to Paris. He hadn't had one single offer.

I never saw Dean again. He died in 1976. But a few years ago, I was listening to the Met Opera on the Saturday morning broadcast. During the first intermission, there was an interview with Ruth Bader Ginsburg, the Supreme Court justice. She is a big supporter of the Washington National Opera. The first question was, "When did she first get interested in opera?" She answered that when she was eight years old, she lived near Brooklyn College. Her mother took her to a lecture/concert given by a wonderful African-American conductor named Dean Dixon. The young Ruth was enthralled. From then on she made her mother take her wherever Dixon was conducting or speaking. And she told how, unfortunately, in those years this great musical talent couldn't get a career in the U.S. because of the color of his skin, so he moved to Europe and lived out his life there.

That Monday morning I called Michelle Krisel, who was Plácido Domingo's assistant at the Washington Opera. I said, "Michelle, did you hear the justice on Saturday?" She said no. I told her the story. She told me that the justice and her husband were coming to dinner at her house on Friday, and I should write and tell her my experience with Dean Dixon. So I did, and a couple of weeks later a very nice letter came back, which is now on the wall of my office, with the gold records. Justice Ginsburg wrote how Dean Dixon was a great man who influenced both our lives enormously, for the better. The way he was treated in his own country, she wrote, was shameful.

I feel honored to have known Dean. I really loved him.

LETTER TO DEAN DIXON FROM CHESTER HIMES ON OCTOBER 17, 1963

Dear Dean,

I am really very happy to hear from you and some definite information concerning your whereabouts. You know, people have you placed everywhere; and although I knew you were conducting the Frankfurt Symphony orchestra in 1962, since then I have had sworn information that (1) You had resigned and were now conducting the symphony orchestra in Helsinki, Finland; (2) That you were conducting the symphony in Australia; (3) That you were spending a year conducting throughout the African nations; (4) That you had gone back to the U.S. to tour the country, etc. Otherwise I would have dropped you a line before now and given you the latest scuttlebutt. In fact I made a flying visit to Frankfurt on the 5th of this month—I arrived at 7:50 a.m., saw my publishers in Frankfurt and Darmstadt, and took the 9:57 that same night back to Paris; and I would have certainly telephoned and tried to reach you, but I had only recently heard (from Phil Lomax, a soul brother) that you were definitely in Helsinki, and I didn't do the logical thing which would have been to inquire in Frankfurt and not pay attention to what a soul brother said.

I fully understand the difficulties presented by your former frau and sympathize with you. As the chicks used to sing in those old after-hour joints: Money-money-money—it ain't funny honey. I'm having severe money troubles myself, which was the reason I couldn't get to Frankfurt in August. My books are being published regularly here in France and receiving a certain acclaim: but French publishers just refuse (bare face) to pay me—I have a new book appearing in a few weeks and I think I will have to go to court—if I can get a French lawyer to represent me. So you can see, I will enter a prayer for you too, dear brother, in these trying times. And I'm not being facetious; I know your problem is serious.

By the way, I suppose you know Ollie was here for a visit this spring, jolly and healthy, and got a new car to take back east. But he gave me the impression that life over there is a bit restraining. But nothing can be as bad as France at this time; I think it is worse now than when they used to scribble the signs on the walls: US go home. For you though, being a guest conductor, it should be nice.

Perhaps you know, too, that Torun had a very successful exhibition at Georg Jensen's on Fifth Avenue in May (with lots of publicity, etc.) and now she's selling in the U.S. and being publicized in *Vogue* and *The New Yorker* and such and is on her way to becoming a very wealthy woman. And Walter is still on the scene (very much) but he's been here for the past month, working for Nicole Barclay who's opening a new firm after her divorce; and Torun has been in Sweden having exhibitions and also supervising Pia's birth of baby. Now Pia has a little daughter and Torun has a little granddaughter; and Pia is staying on in Sweden to grow up.

Well, that's about all the news. I hear Leroy is back in town, but I haven't seen him.

Do you know that Inez Cavanaugh has opened a successful joint in London called The Village (in Chelsea) and she writes that "The Baron" is living it up.

Here's hoping that your difficulties will resolve themselves and all the best to you and Mary. Looking forward to seeing you.

all best
Chester[1]

LETTER FROM EVERETT LEE TO DEAN DIXON
ON DECEMBER 4, 1967

Dear Dean!

This is to thank you again for a wonderful concert. You were really magnificent. It was good too to see you after such a long time, and I trust we will meet again in the not too distant future. On Thursday of this week I am flying to New York, and as I promised I will give your Mother a ring while I am in town. I think I shall be in N.Y. about a week or so then go out to Cleveland to see my Mother and spend Xmas there, then back here (Paris) to work—thank you! When will those Americans ever open their doors really to us? Or will they ever? Will be back in Sweden at least by the 7th of January. Let me take this time to wish you and yours the Merriest of Christmases and a Happy and continued successful '68. Let me also thank you for offering some sort of recording(s) in Frankfurt some time in the future. . . . I appreciate your thought very much.

Yours,
Everett[2]

LETTER FROM JESSYE NORMAN TO DEAN DIXON
ON JANUARY 13, 1971

My dear Mr. Dixon,

My I please say what a pleasure it was to have worked with you again. I cannot wait until we can do it once more. I have derived a great deal of inspiration from you as a person and as an artist. For this experience I must thank you.

I hope that you have had restful and happy holidays!! I had much fun in Munich for Christmas and Vienna for New Year's. I have become a real fan of these wonderful Strauss waltzes!!

Here are some date possibilities: December of '71 (the first week), January 25–30 1972, and February 12–20 1972. Should you need to have a more detailed schedule of possibilities on my part, please let me know.

I am interested in doing "Death of Cleopatra" by Berlioz, but if you come across something more interesting, kindly let me know.

And please, would you do me yet another favor, aside from providing me with a marvelous breakfast idea . . . would you please write a letter of reference for me to the Ford Foundation that must be sent to them before January 31st. They are sponsoring a program for concert artists wherein the nominated persons are asked to send in biographical data and recordings, as well as letters of reference, in order to be considered for selection to actually participate in the program. If chosen I would have the opportunity to choose an American composer to write a work for me, for chamber orchestra or piano, or full orchestra, and I would be obligated to perform this work three times within a twelve-month period. Plus, I would receive an award of five thousand dollars.

I am sending the recording that I did with EMI last year, and I would love to have a copy of the work we just did together, if it is at all possible.

I know how terribly busy you are, but I hope that you can do this for me. (Am I being impossible?)

Enclosed, please find an envelope for your use, as well as an address label for the tape recording, should you have a moment to ask to have it copied, if such a thing is allowed.

The Chinese dinner was fabulous; and I hope we meet again before the end of the year. I would be most interested to coming to some of your concerts. I just need to know when and where. [In her handwriting] Typing was never one of my best things!

Warmest regards,
Jessye[3]

DIXON'S LETTER OF REFERENCE TO JESSYE NORMAN ON MARCH 23, 1971

To Whom It May Concern:

Miss Jessye Norman with whom I have worked often—both in rehearsing for and giving concerts with orchestra and in making radio recordings—is a talent and a voice of extraordinary proportions. In vocal equipment, technique, style, mastery of vocal line, dynamic contrasts, diction, rhythm, case of execution, emotional involvement and control, cleanliness musically, musicality, flexibility, trueness of pitch, vibrato control, lasting stamina, musical intelligence—in all of these areas and more she excels. Any assistance in furthering her career can only be richly rewarded by watching the steady developing art of this most promising artist.

Dean Dixon
Head Conductor
Frankfurt Radio Symphony Orchestra[4]

LETTER TO P. C. HEUWEKEMEYER FROM TIMOTHY REYNISH ON JUNE 1, 1971

Dear Mr. Heuwekemeyer,

I am sorry that we had no chance to thank you on behalf of the students of the [Hilversum] course for the facilities which are made available to the student conductors, and for the smooth running of the course. Between the 9 working students, we must have attended practically every course in Europe and the States, including those run at Salzburg, Sienna, Aspen, Monte Carlo and elsewhere, and there was no doubt in our minds that the N.O.S. course is second to none.

The chance of working with the Radio orchestras is quite unique, the facilities afforded in the way of video tapes, recordings of aural work and the avant garde repertoire, and above all the constant co-operation and advice from the orchestral players themselves all contribute towards this.

Mr. Dixon we found totally uncompromising, utterly ruthless in this search for methods, which would train and teach. At first we found his methods bewildering; we had come looking forward to making music from the scores that we had prepared, but found that he was not interested in how good we were, but only in finding out our bad points, so that he could offer possibilities of extending our technique. His attitude must have caused many problems to the administration, as it did to us. At the end of the first week, with two days of theory arranged for us, those in category I had 15 works or parts of works to learn and prepare, as part of the psychological pressures that conductors must be under in the profession. His techniques were unorthodox and uncomfortable, but I suspect that he is one of the few really great teachers of an art that is so subjective that it is almost un-teachable.

May I once again on behalf of the students, thank you and through you the musicians and administration of N.O.S. for what was for all of us a great experience.

Yours sincerely,
Timothy Reynish[5]

LETTER TO DEAN DIXON FROM JOSEPHINE HARRELD LOVE ON AUGUST 24, 1971

Dear Dean,

I am sending this letter through your manager in the hope that it will eventually reach you and not go through a chain of other persons.

The news that you are at last to visit Detroit has made us very happy. It is an event for which we have looked forward hopefully for many years and one that should have taken place long before this. A group of Detroit musicians and music-lovers have been importuning the management of the symphony for many years on your behalf. Your arrival is a cause for celebration!

You have some old connections here. Canon Frederic Ricksford Meyers of the Episcopal Cathedral recalls you as an alter-boy in his church in New

York. His wife, the former Marjorie Peebles, also recalls vividly that phase of your early life.

Marjorie is our family physician and my closest friend. The two of us have for sometime discussed what we might do in the way of making you welcome here and would like to do something that would be enjoyable for you during your off-hours here. I have talked with Paul Freeman and Marshall Turkin, the manager of the orchestra, about the length of your visit and what times might be available but do not want to make further plans without consulting you first.

It is rather late for me to write you a fan letter—but I have followed your career with great interest during all of these years and should have sent you a letter long before this to say just how proud I feel about your development as a musician and a person, but I am a procrastinator.

Some years ago when my daughter was a student in Sweden, she went to a concert conducted by you and wrote in glowing terms to me about it. I was sorry that she did not go backstage to speak to you. She thought of doing so but was timid about it. I wish that she had. It would have at least been one small connecting link during those years that stretch behind us since student days at the Institute of Musical Arts.

I hope I haven't made us sound too respectable! There is little change actually. In spite of my great advance in years, and the fact that I could easily be a grandmother, I feel very much as I did so many years ago—except that my attitudes have broadened and my outlook has become more radicalized.

With warmest good wishes always,
Josephine Harreld Love[6]

LETTER TO DEAN DIXON FROM ANNETTE SCHUSTER ON MARCH 3, 1972

Dear Mr. Dixon,

I realize that you probably won't even remember me, but I still wanted to write this. I am the young conductress who met you in Kansas City last February when you conducted our orchestra. You were most kind and gave me such good advice concerning my conducting career. I took your advice and really began learning scores inside and out, analyzing them as I went. I also intensified my work on baton technique. At any rate, in June '71, I really got a lucky break and was named student conductor with the K.C. Youth and Jr. Youth Symphony orchestras. In July, I [was selected] as one of the associate conductors with the Olathe Civic Orchestra. I am really thankful that I took your advice. It has proven a great asset. As you know things can get terribly discouraging, but when you love music so much, you can't give it up, no matter how bad things seem. I realize I'm very lucky to have not one but three orchestras to work with and such great learning experience.

I so enjoyed the Young Peoples' Concert you conducted on T.V. last spring. In fact the Haydn "Farewell Symphony" made such an impression on the junior orchestra that I'm planning on programming it soon.

I still hope to study in Germany, and I'll probably go early in 73, but I've still got a lot of studying and work to do.

Once again, thank you Mr. Dixon for your great kindness. I've got a long tough, road ahead of me for sure, but I'm going to keep going and make it.

Continued success for you.

Sincerely,
Annette Schuster[7]

LETTER TO DEAN DIXON FROM RITHA DIXON ON JANUARY 10, 1973

My Darling Love, My Dean,

This should be the one letter that'll reach you first, the one letter that should reach your heart and also the one to wish you from the bottom of my loving heart all the good things that are within the limits of our possibilities and also enough strength to get safely through anything that might not be so very good. I want to wish you good health, I want to wish you success, calmness of the mind but enough activity around to keep you young and content and loveable. Whatever I can to help you, I'll do with all my love and sincere and deep feelings for you. I am very proud to be your woman and thank you for everything you gave me. Let our togetherness still become more together—that is what I should like to try and give you for this first truly together birthday.

Your Ritha[8]

LETTER TO RITHA DIXON FROM BENGT WALLERIUS ON NOVEMBER 19, 1976

Dear, dear Ritha,

I wrote a letter to Dean just a few hours before the message of this sudden death reached me. I expected both of you to Gothenburg at the end of this month and I looked forward to days of talk and undertakings in our old style, with past and present and future in our special mixture. And so this crushing message—not to believe in and still quite incredible. I have been anxious for Dean's health for years and I have at our many partings often suppressed a suspicion, that this could be the last one. And I must admit that I have had a presentiment, that our long friendship should end once just in this way.

Dear Ritha, many persons from the whole world bring you their sympathy in these days, and so do I who had the privilege to be one of your rallying-points in Scandinavia. My thoughts are very often going to you feeling deeply for you in your sorrow.

Even if Dean and I met with very long interruptions during the last decade I had the feeling that our friendship was a continuum—we could always start again at the very point, where we finished last time. Our close co-operation in the fifties was mixed with very much pleasure and many bright adventures and undertakings.

And now all this is put to an end. Dean has left a great blank behind him, and as far as I am concerned I will keep him as a living memory, an unforget-table friend and fellow, to whom my thoughts often have run and still will run, grateful to all he gave of warmth and delight.

Affectionately

Yours,

Bengt Wallerius[9]

LETTER TO RITHA DIXON FROM PERVIL EASTMAN ON NOVEMBER 28, 1977

Dear Ritha:

More than a year has passed since the untimely death of Dean. True, he is no longer physically present with us, but in the hearts of many, including myself, he will ever be remembered and cherished. To you, the loss has been deep and painful. It is hoped that the year, which has passed has brought some measure of softening of the blow, which visited your home at the time of his death. It has often been said that time heals all things. I do hope that the healing process will hold true for you.

It was good of you to take the time to reply to my letter and give me the details of Dean's last happy days as well as his last painful and sorrowful hours on earth. I know how painful it must have been for you to have done so. But, on the other hand, I also feel that the thoughts that during your times together you did so much to make him feel happy that those memories gave you the needed strength and courage to want to continue. From the little that I know, aside from his successes at various concerts, which gave him personal satisfaction, the deepest and memorable happiness he experienced, he had them while with you.

It was most unfortunate that Dean died at the time he did. Had he not done so, he would have accomplished the seemingly impossible task—that of total acceptance. The climate of the world began to change shortly before his death and because he was so able, so very well prepared, so widely experi-enced, so deeply intelligent and had so much to offer, he would now have stood head and shoulders above the crowd. In a very broad and true sense, he never had a real chance to succeed. True, he was able to knock down some barriers, but the bigger forces were still formidable. And in doing so, he had to work harder, longer and surrendered a high price—his health. Had he not been such a superior musician, they would have destroyed him long ago. You mentioned having received only one acknowledgement from the various heads of orchestras in response to your letters. Most of those who did not respond probably feel that the threat to them in the form of Dean has been made easier. Our world can be beautiful and our world can be cruel. In many cases like Dean's, the world is often more cruel than beautiful and appeals to the emotions are more frequent than appeals to the intelligence and common sense. Thus, his passing, while mourned, brought sighs of relief to many. He was no longer a threat or proof to their theories of superiority, accomplishments and achievements. Someday, it is hoped, humanity will come to realize that the important thing is not a person's skin color, but the fact that he or she is a part of the human family and is worthy of all consideration and respect. It is a personal tragedy and a blow to society when people are divided by skin color, by religion and the like. We are all GOD'S people and under HIM we are all one. Think how exhilarating our world could be if people of varied backgrounds were permitted to share all of themselves with each other without thinking of restraint! In many respects, many would experience psychological and emotional emancipation and be free adults in the true sense of the word.

In a short while 1977 will close and 1978 will begin. May beautiful things begin to happen to you in the NEW YEAR and may they continue to happen always. The best and warmest of wishes for lifelong happiness with the hope that each new day bring to you new joys, new hopes and, in passing, leave pleasant memories. Continue to be of good cheer and take a fresh look at the loveliness of each day. May all your days be bright beautiful mornings. Sincere wishes for continuous firm grasp on sound health.

Sincerely yours
Pervil

Appendix B: Conductors Handbook

As Dean Dixon settled into his post in Frankfurt, he began to take on opportunities to teach. In 1962, he taught at the Salzburg Mozarteum program in Austria. In 1963, he taught at the Jeunesses Musicales, Weikersheim in West Germany. That same year he taught at the Radio Hilversum in Holland and returned in 1971. Teaching the art and psychology of conducting was something Dixon took very seriously, because the mentorship he craved while studying at Juilliard never materialized. He wanted to use his wealth of experience to help those aspiring young conductors avoid many pitfalls that he encountered. Over a span of ten years, Dixon compiled a checklist of things that he observed students doing and found himself correcting on a regular basis. This checklist was likely the beginning of a handbook for the young conductor.

- As a rehearsal technique, do not play through the exposition as a repeat.
- Watch "washing clothes" motion.
- More look at the last stands of the strings.
- Not only to always say "together." But also who is wrong and who has the right of way.
- "Angry man" look instead of "co-operating fellow artists."
- Play and then correct in order to stimulate the imagination of the players.
- Use both left and right hand to show architecture phrases.
- No private conversations.
- No clapping for stopping.
- No tapping for stopping.
- Do all of the stand fixing at one time, concentrate on fixed points one after the other, building a crescendo of authority.
- Too much looking around after hands are in start position.

- Eyes in the orchestra for the start.
- More architecture on phrase endings.
- Once putting out the hands leave them out.
- Don't hold on to the stand with the left hand.
- Either wait or do not wait for silence.
- Upbeat always big enough to be seen by the whole orchestra.
- Using only the left hand for attacks while right hand stands still is not advisable.
- If wanting a cutoff, stop at the end of each fermata, then say so and demand it.
- If using the left hand so much, watch that the page turn is not too obvious.
- When saying where to start, i.e. "a tempo" after the orchestra makes its first mistake, then say i.e. "a tempo starts on the fourth beat in the bar."
- Too much conducting, not enough music making.
- Attempt to get the tempo without having to give the whole previous bar.
- Rather than saying, "Last stand in the seconds you are dragging," better to say, "Don't drag seconds."
- Upbeat to upbeat.
- Allow the tempo of the slow to finish completely before taking the next fast tempo.
- Talk over the music only when you can be heard.
- Hold the stick so that you can get more singing into it.
- Give the woodwinds more pizzicato beat entrance.
- Talk to the orchestra rather than to the score.
- When you stop, say something, anything, but preferably something important or something funny.
- Don't clap or tap for quiet.
- Explanations clearer, louder, and finish them.
- The string trouble is often because they can't hear the woodwinds or the brass.
- As little talking over the music as possible.
- Sing the mistake in rhythm correctly under the flute solo rather than saying 1, 2, 3.
- Start at the beginning to better establish contact.
- Better to start at letter L than 22 measures after L—the less counting the better.
- As little talking as possible before playing.
- When you want to say primarily softer, then take up a larger attention calling beat and pull that down.
- Stop in the music stop places.
- Watch your page-turning technique.
- Have pages of your own score fixed to stay open.
- Left hand not always facing up.

- Know when to look at score.
- Never too long a time with eyes in the score.
- Look authority.
- Change tempi [seamlessly] when necessary.
- Give more crescendo, decrescendo in the stick.
- Use preferably international words—Rudolfo [for letter R] instead of reindeer.
- Bending knees for piano.
- In sustained forte passages, one must have more external or internal forte tension.
- In slow movements when orchestra falls apart or even begins to fall apart, then take larger geometric design in the stick.
- You are conducting from the time your name is called.
- Announce [conducting] in 1 or 2 or in 4 if there is any possible confusion.
- Stay still generally in the G.P. bars.
- With short stops try to stop where you are going to start.
- If you are that kind of personality, watch too much smiling.
- Say whatever you have to say to the orchestra in whichever language, but in a loud voice.
- Try to hear more and relate your conducting to what is being heard.
- More leading, less following.
- Know when to pull the orchestra together.
- Eyes steady before beginning.
- Slower talking.
- If changing stick from hand to hand, it is not to be seen.
- Tend to sustain the forte until the next piano.
- More look of the movement in the music—still or flowing.
- Let the pants fall down or leave them alone.
- Play something and then speak.
- Say with or without repeat.
- When two hands are in play, cut off the fermata with the two hands.
- Preferably do not beat fermatas.
- Use the snapping of the finger very judiciously.
- Get more with the orchestra and then take them forward or pull them back.
- Better to say Caesar than letter C.
- In talking voice put more dramatic variety.
- Watch the whistle position of the lips.
- A larger amplitude to slow orchestra down.
- Not too much movement in the pauses.
- When stopping the orchestra in rehearsal, watch out for throwing away orange peel gesture.
- Be conscious of stick holding variety.
- More listening to balance and fixing it while conducting.

- Tend to conduct the subito pianos.
- Better to take the stick out of play while you talk—preferably down by your side.
- Left hand for expression, right hand for beauty; and right hand for expression, left hand for beauty.
- Finish looking at the music, then look at the orchestra, then start.
- Be careful of shaking your head "no" while conducting.
- In making retards with inexperienced orchestras tend to widen the beat.
- Watch in making crescendi that you are not too large too soon.
- When orchestra begins to fall apart, conduct harder, clearer.
- Conduct harder for transition spots.
- Say everything in a loud carrying voice.
- After taking the woodwind or the brass or strings alone, then say something, anything, but something.
- Be careful when you are saying marcato that you sing marcato rather than staccato, etc.
- While conducting have the starting places and correction places in your head—too much time is looking for where to start.
- Restart at larger places.
- When having played a bit, then say something about why repeating it to let the orchestra know why you repeated it, or why it is now better.
- Try to arrive at a certain level of obvious achievement before going on.
- Hold longer fermatas when having difficulty.
- Too much music conducting during new difficult work and when so large a part of the orchestra is resting and trying to count measures is not advisable.
- Better to start with presto after a good adagio rehearsal.
- Conducting in the fermatas not advisable and cutoffs at the end of the fermatas should be in the character of said fermatas.
- While holding the orchestra ready to start, don't roll the eyes around too much.
- Say sixteen, then counting before or after that number.
- Before telling the winds to give pianissimo there, in functional rehearsing it is often more feasible to ask for less forte first.
- Don't start from the beginning too often.
- Remember the stick phrasing possibilities.
- In fugue type music go more toward the entrances.
- Don't conduct the pauses if it is not necessary.
- Your music stand must be high enough to be able to turn the pages without seeming to be turning the pages too much.
- Say "repeats" or "no repeats."
- Have your music stand at a high enough or low enough angle for you to be able to look at the music without seeming too obviously to be looking.

- After telling where to start, give a split second for the orchestra to find the place.
- Try to remember to stop and speak about the biggest wrong first.
- Beware of too much talking.
- Have pull together spots in mind.
- Take orchestra imperceptibly to new tempo within a one-tempo movement.
- When talking to a mixed orchestra, remember to say ladies and gentlemen, not only gentlemen.
- The smaller the beat the more the control.
- Upbeats must be in character of the start.
- Make decision of whether sforzando is in piano.
- Try not to overconduct.
- Try to remember that much music can go on very well without a conductor, once it has been started on the right track.
- Singing stick.
- Try to make a crescendo of a tension before starting.
- Use relatively same stroke in same passage—sforzando in the Beethoven Symphony No. 3, movement no. 1.
- Facial expressions in character.
- Intensity needed in forte, but even more needed in piano.
- In Beethoven Symphony No. 3, 2nd movement, say with or before the double basses before the start.
- Say "the Beethoven, oh sorry!" the first to admit your own mistakes.
- Have both flexible and tight right-hand wrist technique.
- Upbeat always big enough to be seen by the entire orchestra.
- Make accelerando or ritardando for a special section of the orchestra while not disturbing the rest of the orchestra, but be careful to be able to come back to correct tempo when finished with the apparition.
- In the rehearsal tend and try to start at easily findable places.
- Criticize as large a group as possible.
- In stopping the orchestra during rehearsals, unless it is obvious to everyone why you stop, then say something.
- With minimum rehearsal time number every measure of your score.
- Try to by prearrangement have score and parts where you go numbered at least each ten measures.
- Try hardest not to mark your scores, but if you have to then in pencil easy to rub out, preferably black.
- Work from whole to part, primarily.
- Love and respect is higher than hate and respect.
- Know when and where to start, and when and where to stop.
- Memory is necessary, but the superior question is what to memorize.

- Left hand is sometimes a twin sister, sometimes a twin brother, sometimes a whip, sometimes a snake with a bird, sometimes asleep, and sometimes turning pages.
- Try to cue when, where, and how needed.
- Drill the orchestra on things where they need your help.
- Your goal is happy and good performances as a result of happy and good work.
- Without high rhythm no high music.
- Let your rehearsal technique represent a mark of your intelligence and gentlemanliness as well as add a mark of your musicality.
- Ensemble playing (the playing together of an orchestra) is a matter of how large you can get the orchestra to grow their ears.
- Your goal in the field of balance is to get the orchestra to be self-balancing.
- Interest and motivation of the orchestra is your responsibility.
- Intensity is your responsibility, but remember it is not inherent in speed.
- Remember that when you say vibrato to the strings you are stepping into an area in which there are many, many, many different kinds of vibrato.
- Remember as a conductor it is very, very easy to qualify as a god, but very, very difficult to qualify as a good human being.
- When orchestra has no landmarks, then put something in, either letters or numbers.
- Be careful of too much talking, be careful of talking too rapidly, be careful of saying too much often "I want, I do not want, I would like to have, I would . . . "
- Use numbers; then when in the hundreds and above use the terminology one-one-two, rather than one hundred and twelve.
- When holding up fingers for a first or second ending, hold front and sideways and diagonally.
- Tend to watch with the mental eye your mouth position while conducting.
- Tell the orchestra whether you start beating before the music or not.
- To hold your own tempo better, work also with the metronome.
- Watch starting over a private smile.
- Stamping of the foot to get a rhythm is a sign that you are losing.

Notes

INTRODUCTION

1. In this section of Ewen's book, Dean Dixon, Izler Solomon, and Sylvan Levin are listed as "Conductors for Tomorrow."
2. Dean Dixon Papers: Box 1, Folder 1, Doc. 29, Schomburg Center for Black Research and Culture, NYPL.

PROLOGUE

1. Harold C. Schonberg, "Philharmonic Opener Attracts Thousands," *New York Times*, July 22, 1970.
2. Robert B. McElroy, "Dixon and the Philharmonic: Blackface and No Gloves," *Newsweek*, August 1970.

1. WEST INDIANS IN HARLEM

1. List or Manifest of Alien Passengers for the U.S. Immigration Officer at Port of Arrival (Index T715, roll 619, vol. 1321–23), National Archives, Washington, D.C.
2. Nancy Foner, *Islands in the City: West Indian Migration to New York* (Los Angeles: University of California Press, 2001).
3. State of New York Certificate of Marriage of Charles and McClara Dixon, New York City Department of Records and Information Services Municipal Archives.
4. Irma Watkins-Owens, *Blood Relations: Caribbean Immigrants and the Harlem Community, 1900–1930* (Bloomington: Indiana University Press, 1996).
5. Gilbert Osofsky, *Harlem: The Making of a Ghetto, Negro New York, 1890–1930* (Chicago: Ivan R. Dee, Inc., 1996), 120.
6. Osofsky, *Harlem*, 136.
7. D. Antoinette Handy, *Black Conductors* (Lanham, Maryland: Scarecrow Press, 1995).
8. Handy, *Black Conductors*, 105.

9. Kaj Kristoffersen, "Fate in A Baton" (working paper, Dean Dixon Papers, Schomburg Center for Research in Black Culture, New York Public Library), 4.

10. Dean Dixon, interview by Kaj Kristoffersen (hereafter author/interviewer cited in text as KK), 1967, transcript, Dean Dixon Papers, Schomburg Center for Research in Black Culture (hereafter cited in text as SCRBC), New York Public Library (hereafter cited in text as NYPL).

11. Dean Dixon, interview (interviewer unknown), 1964–1967, audio interview provided from private collection of Ritha Dixon.

12. http://www.saintmarkschool.org/.

13. http://www.katharinedrexel.org/Katharine_Drexel.html.

14. Reminiscences of Kenneth Clark (1976), Oral History Research Office Collection of the Columbia University Libraries (OHRO/CUL), 28.

15. "Kenneth Clark was a psychologist, educator, and social reformer who dedicated his life to the cause of racial justice. His groundbreaking studies on race and child development helped end segregation in the United States. He also founded the North Side Center for Child Development in Harlem. Clark was the first Black American to join the New York Board of Regents and to serve as president of the American Psychological Association." Reminiscences of Kenneth Clark (1976), Oral History Research Office Collection of the Columbia University Libraries (OHRO/CUL), 29.

16. Dean Dixon, interview (interviewer unknown), 1964–1967, audio interview provided from private collection of Ritha Dixon.

17. Dean Dixon, biographical sketch (unpublished, Dean Dixon Papers, SCRBC, NYPL), 1.

18. Dean Dixon, interview by KK, 1967, transcript, Dean Dixon Papers, SCRBC, NYPL.

19. Michael J. Lepore, *The Life of the Clinician: The Autobiography of Michael Lepore* (Rochester: University of Rochester Press, 2002), 22–26.

20. Australian interview in the 1960s.

21. Dean Dixon, interview by KK, 1967, transcript, Dean Dixon Papers, SCRBC, NYPL.

22. Dixon, interview by KK, 1967.

23. Dixon, interview by KK, 1967.

24. Dixon, interview by KK, 1967.

25. Dixon, interview by KK, 1967.

26. Samuel Gardner to McClara Dixon, 15 March 1928, Dean Dixon Papers, SCRBC, NYPL.

27. Undated letter from McClara Dixon to Dean Dixon, Dean Dixon Papers, SCRBC, NYPL.

2. DEAN DIXON SCHOOL OF MUSIC

1. Dean Dixon, interview by KK, 1967, transcript, Dean Dixon Papers, SCRBC, NYPL.

2. Until this point, Dean Dixon has been referred to as Dean. From this point on, he will be referred to as Dixon.

3. Dean Dixon, interview by KK, 1967.

4. Dr. Adam Clayton Powell, Sr., who was the pastor of this well-respected and recognized church from 1908 to 1937, sought not only to develop the spiritual health of his congregates, but to also be relevant to the community they served. The latter was exhibited through its kitchen and relief ministry, which was responsible for feeding and clothing a great number of Harlem residents during the Depression.

5. Dean Dixon, interview by KK, 1967.

6. Dean Dixon, interview by KK, 1967.

7. Dean Dixon, interview by KK, 1967.

8. Dean Dixon, interview by KK, 1967.

9. Dean Dixon, interview by KK, 1967.

10. Dean Dixon, interview by KK, 1967.

11. Steven C. Smith, *A Heart at Fire's Center: The Life and Music of Bernard Herrmann* (Los Angeles: University of California Press, 1991), 16.

12. Dean Dixon, interview by KK, 1967.

13. Ernest Dunbar, *The Black Expatriates: A Study of American Negroes in Exile* (New York: E. P. Dutton, 1968).

3. THE DAMROSCH SCHOOL

1. Andrea Olmstead, *Juilliard: A History* (Urbana: University of Illinois Press, 1999), 11.

2. Dean Dixon, interview by KK, 1967, transcript, Dean Dixon Papers, SCRBC, NYPL.

3. Dean Dixon, interview by KK, 1967.

4. Olmstead, *Juilliard*, 138.

5. Dean Dixon, interview by KK, 1967.

6. Dean Dixon Papers: Box 1, Folder 1.

7. Dean Dixon Papers: John Mackey, "Music for the Millions," *Spotlight*, January 1945, 22 (Box 8).

8. Dean Dixon, interview by KK, 1967.

9. Dean Dixon, interview by KK, 1967.

10. Dean Dixon, interview by KK, 1967.

11. Dean Dixon, interview by KK, 1967.

12. Dean Dixon Papers, McClara letter to Dixon, no date (Box 1, Folder 3).

4. PURSUING THE DREAM

1. Dean Dixon, interview by KK, 1967, transcript, Dean Dixon Papers, SCRBC, NYPL.

2. Dean Dixon, interview by KK, 1967.

3. Dean Dixon, interview by KK, 1967.

4. Dean Dixon, interview by KK, 1967.

5. Andrea Olmstead, *Juilliard: A History* (Urbana: University of Illinois Press, 1999), 124.

6. Dean Dixon, interview by KK, 1967.

7. "Programs of the Week," *New York Times*, May 1, 1938.

5. ELEANOR ROOSEVELT

1. Letter, Eleanor Roosevelt to Mrs. Henry M. Roberts, Jr., February 26, 1939, Franklin D. Roosevelt Library and Museum Website.

2. A Comprehensive, Electronic Edition of Eleanor Roosevelt's "My Day" Newspaper Columns, Monday, May 20, 1941, http://www.gwu.edu/~erpapers/myday/.

3. Gail Stockholm, "Dean Dixon: A Return with Laurels," *Music and Artists*, June/July 1970, 12.

4. David Ewen, *Dictators of the Baton* (Chicago/New York: Ziff-Davis Publishing Co., 1948).

5. Stockholm, "Dean Dixon: A Return with Laurels," 7.

6. Dean Dixon, interview by KK, 1967, transcript, Dean Dixon Papers, SCRBC, NYPL.

7. Dean Dixon Papers: Letter to Dixon from Locke, dated June 21, 1941, on Howard University stationery.

8. Dean Dixon Papers: Chotzinoff letter to Helen Harris, September 1941 (Box 1, Folder 8).

9. Dean Dixon, interview by KK, 1967.

10. Dean Dixon, interview by KK, 1967.

11. Dean Dixon Papers: Robert Jacobson, "Lincoln Center Spotlight," March 1972.

12. Stockholm, "Dean Dixon: A Return with Laurels," 11.

6. THE PLASTIC CARROT

1. Dean Dixon Papers: Berger article, "The Moment Is Right for Dean Dixon" (Box 1, Folder 1).

2. Dean Dixon, interview by KK, 1967, transcript, Dean Dixon Papers, SCRBC, NYPL.

3. "Dean Dixon Heads NYA Symphony," *Philadelphia Tribune*, September 20, 1941.

4. Dean Dixon Papers: Chotzinoff letter to Helen Harris, September 1941 (Box 1, Folder 8).

5. Ella Davis, "Conductor from Harlem: Dean Dixon Makes His Way With Baton Despite Many Hazards," *New York Times*, January 11, 1942.

6. Dean Dixon Papers: Walter White letter to Mayor LaGuardia, January 12, 1942 (Box 1, Folder 8).

7. Dean Dixon Papers: Walter White letter to Dr. Mordecai Johnson, February 2, 1942 (Box 1, Folder 8).

8. Dean Dixon Papers: Carl Van Vechten letter to Dixon, February 2, 1942 (Box 1, Folder 8).

9. "American Artists Heard At Concert." *New York Times*, May 11, 1942.

10. "American Artists."

11. A Comprehensive, Electronic Edition of Eleanor Roosevelt's "My Day" Newspaper Columns, Monday, May 12, 1942, http://www.gwu.edu/~erpapers/myday/.

12. Howard Taubman, "Dean Dixon Gives Stadium Program: Young Negro Conductor Directs Philharmonic-Symphony Offering Two Novelties," *New York Times*, July 11, 1942.

13. Gail Stockholm, "Dean Dixon: A Return with Laurels," *Music and Artists*, June/July 1970, 14.

14. Dean Dixon, interview by KK, 1967.

15. Ernest Dunbar, *The Black Expatriates: A Study of American Negroes in Exile* (New York: E. P. Dutton, 1968), 191.

16. Howard Taubman, "Shoestring Opera Makes Its Debut: Presents 'Tales of Hoffmann' at Hunter College, With Dean Dixon Conducting," *New York Times*, January 27, 1943.

17. Dean Dixon, interview by KK, 1967.

18. Dean Dixon, interview by KK, 1967.

19. Dean Dixon, interview by KK, 1967.

7. SEARCH FOR DEMOCRACY

1. "New Orchestra Formed: American Youth Symphonic to Bow at Carnegie Hall," *New York Times*, November 22, 1944.

2. Dean Dixon Papers: Notes from Dixon on the start of the American Youth Orchestra, no date (Box 2, Folder 1).

3. Notes from Dixon on the start of the American Youth Orchestra.

4. Notes from Dixon on the start of the American Youth Orchestra.

5. Olin Downes, "Dean Dixon Leads Youth Orchestra: Negro Conductor Impressive in Debut with New Group—Vivian Rivkin is Soloist." *New York Times*, December 17, 1944.

6. Dean Dixon Papers: Box 2, Folder 1, Doc. 2.

7. Dean Dixon Papers: Box 2, Folder 1, Doc. 2.

8. Dean Dixon Papers: Robert Jacobson, "Lincoln Center Spotlight," March 1972.

9. Dean Dixon Papers: Box 2, Folder 1, Doc. 2.

10. New York Philharmonic Archives, Board of Directors files, Papers of Arthur Judson, Folder No. 006-02-47.

11. Dean Dixon Papers: Review from the *Boston Guardian*, June 1945.

12. Dean Dixon Papers: Script from "Music for You," April 10 (Box 8, Folder 21).

13. Dean Dixon Papers: Letter from Albert Stoessel, March 1942.

14. Dean Dixon, interview by KK, 1967, transcript, Dean Dixon Papers, SCRBC, NYPL.

8. BLACK AND WHITE

1. Dean Dixon, interview by KK, 1967, transcript, Dean Dixon Papers, SCRBC, NYPL.

2. Dean Dixon, interview by KK, 1967.

3. Dean Dixon Papers: Mike Berger, "The Moment is Right for Dean Dixon," not published (Box 1, Folder 1).

9. EXODUS

1. Dean Dixon Papers: W. D. Allen, "Discusses Career As Conductor," *Post* (San Francisco), June 1, 1972.

2. Dean Dixon, interview by KK, February 14, 1967, transcript, Dean Dixon Papers, SCRBC, NYPL (Box 1, Folder 7).

3. Dean Dixon Papers: Box 1, Folder 1.

4. Letter written by Vivian Rivkin on October 6, 1950, from the personal papers of Lavi Daniel.

5. Dean Dixon Papers: Interview by Frederick Woods, 1963 (Box 9, Folder 8).

6. Gordon Parks, *Voices in the Mirror: An Autobiography* (New York: Doubleday, 1990), 185.

7. Dean Dixon Papers: Review by Hufvudstadsbladet, December 15, 1951 (Box 8, Folder 3).

8. Dean Dixon Papers: Kaj Kristoffersen, "The Price of Genius: A Symphony of Bittersweet Success," unpublished. (Box 1, Folder 1).

9. Dean Dixon, interview by KK (Box 8, Folder 3).

10. Dean Dixon Papers: Box 3, Folder 4.

10. MARY

1. Dean Dixon Papers: Anne Dupree, "Love at First Sight," *Woman's Day with Woman*.

2. The Winter War occurred during World War II, between Finland and the Soviet Union. The Soviets were looking to expand their territory and demanded that Finland grant them a lease of the Hanko Peninsula, which was located twenty-five kilometers beyond the Leningrad border, so that a naval base could be constructed. When Finland refused, war broke out. It was a deadly conflict that lasted less than four months. The Soviets eventually forced the Finns to agree to a lease of the Hanko Peninsula. The war showed major flaws in the Soviets' military tactics. Although their military was far superior to the Finns, their casualty count was more than six times that of the Finns, because they grossly underestimated the Finnish terrain and fighting a war in the winter.

3. From 1940 to 1943, the occupation of Denmark was considered by many more of a "political cooperation" that an occupation. Meaning that while a vast majority of the Danish

population was against the occupation, the government, which was still a functioning entity during this period, believed that it could be handled in a more pragmatic manner.

4. Betty Best, *Women's Weekly*, March 6, 1963.
5. Betty Best, *Women's Weekly*, March 6, 1963.
6. Dean Dixon Papers: Kaj Kristoffersen, "Fate in a Baton," unpublished, no date, Box 1, Folder 1.
7. Dean Dixon Papers: Letter to Berger, 1968 (Box 1, Folder 17).
8. Dupree, "Love at First Sight."
9. Dupree, "Love at First Sight."
10. Kristoffersen, "Fate in a Baton."
11. No author, "World's foremost Negro Conductor Dean Dixon Becomes Permanent Director of Symphony Orchestra in Gothenburg, Sweden," *Ebony*, December 1951.
12. Ernest Dunbar, *The Black Expatriates: A Study of American Negroes in Exile* (New York: E.P. Dutton, 1968).
13. Dunbar, *The Black Expatriates*.
14. Dean Dixon Papers: "Woman of the Week, Mrs. Dean Dixon: Exception to Her Own Rule," *Mirror*, November 25, 1962.

11. DRAMA, DOWN UNDER

1. Dean Dixon Papers: C. M. Prerauer, "Matter of Wristwork," *Nation*, December 15, 1962.
2. Dean Dixon Papers: A letter from Sir Charles Moses to Dixon on November 19, 1962, Box 2, Folder 10.
3. Betty Best, *Women's Weekly*, March 6, 1963.
4. As a result of the 1967 referendum, in 1971 Neville Bonner became the first Indigenous Australian to be elected to the Australian Senate.
5. Dean Dixon Papers: Letter to management team, no date, Box 4, Folder 7.
6. Dean Dixon Papers: "Hurt Conductor to Carry On, Left Arm or Eyebrows" *Sydney Morning Herald*, June 23, 1964.
7. Dean Dixon Papers: article from the *Daily Mirror*, "Great Future For Orchestra: The Sydney Symphony Orchestra Would One Day Be a Truly Great International Orchestra," August 24, 1964, Box 2, Folder 9.
8. Dean Dixon Papers: Charles Buttrose cable to Dixon on August 25, 1964, Box 2, Folder 9.
9. Dean Dixon Papers: Sir Charles Moses letter to Dixon on August 27, 1964, Box 2, Folder 9.
10. Dean Dixon Papers: Sir Charles Moses letter to Dixon on August 27, 1964, Box 2, Folder 9.
11. Dean Dixon Papers: Dixon letter to Sir Charles Moses on November 15, 1964, Box 2, Folder 9.
12. Jim Swartzman, "A Flat That's All Harmony," *Woman's Day*, 1967.
13. Dean Dixon Papers: Letter from Dixon describing his September 18, 1965, experience with Queen Elizabeth, 1965, Box 2, Folder 10.
14. Dean Dixon Papers: Resignation letter from the Sydney Symphony Orchestra on July 9, 1967, Box 2, Folder 10. Dixon's 23 Points:

1. Substantially more pay
2. More security, along enlightened European lines
3. A pension scheme geared for musicians
4. Satisfaction with their claims for disability pensions
5. Satisfaction that they are receiving literal as well as theoretical pay on travel days when on tour

6. Tour travel to be counted as work
7. Six weeks' vacation in one period
8. Longer warming-up period on return from vacation
9. More first class transport when traveling
10. An average of a five-hour workday
11. Players of distinction should receive much more opportunity for solo broadcasts with the ABC
12. A five-day workweek computed on the basis of a twenty-day month
13. Severance pay after ten years
14. A permanent official should be primarily responsible for the orchestra
15. A permanent welfare officer for consultation about industrial, health or domestic problems, work frictions, personality clashes, discussion reasons for leaving, etc.
16. Improvements and innovation made by the musical director should be continued in his absence.
17. Studio broadcasts and rehearsal schedule should be planned more firmly in advance and made available to all musicians at least a month in advance.
18. Orchestra members felt the need for better and greater presentation of their work in promotion and public relations.
19. They should receive official announcement that they are employed by the ABC.
20. The orchestra, at its present strength, should not be divided to take on separate engagements simultaneously.
21. Musicians should receive an allowance for the upkeep and repair of their working clothing.
22. There should be fewer public concerts per year.
23. The Sydney and Melbourne Symphony Orchestras should receive decided recognition and be given special status in terms of their much greater workload and responsibilities.

15. Box 2, Folder 9.

12. PRAGUE

1. Dean Dixon Papers: Letter to the Hessischer Rundfunk on November 1, 1967, Box 7, Folder 1.

2. The Warsaw Pact was a 1955 treaty signed by the Soviet Union, Czechoslovakia, Albania, Poland, Romania, Hungary, East Germany, and Bulgaria. The agreement allowed for provisions to set up a unified military command, led by the Soviets, to protect any of its members from attacks from outside governments.

3. Dean Dixon Papers: Letter to Kaj Kristoffersen from Dr. Von Hecker on July 3, 1969, Box 7, Folder 10.

4. This was likely a reference to the French writer and philosopher Jean-Paul Sartre's play *No Exit*, where three people who are condemned for eternity in hell quickly realize that their "hell experience" was not necessarily "fire and brimstone" but dealing with each other's failings; "Hell is other people."

5. Dean Dixon Papers: Letter to Dixon from Dr. Hecker on September 21, 1968, Box 7, Folder 11.

6. Dean Dixon Papers: Letter to Kaj Kristoffersen from Dr. Von Hecker on July 3, 1969, Box 7, Folder 10.

7. Dean Dixon Papers: Letter to Rafael Kubelik from Dixon, November 14, 1968, Box 5, Folder 6.

13. SOJOURN HOME

1. Dean Dixon Papers: June 29, 1966, letter from the American Symphony Orchestra to Dixon, Box 4, Folder 17.

2. Dean Dixon Papers: April 8, 1968, letter to Detroit Symphony from Dixon, Box 4, Folder 5.

3. Dean Dixon Papers: December 19, 1967, letter to Mrs. Adler from Dixon, Box 4, Folder 12.

4. Dean Dixon Papers: No date, open letter to all European contacts from Dixon, Box 4, Folder 4.

5. Dean Dixon Papers: August 21, 1968, letter from Arthur Judson to Dixon, Box 4, Folder 6.

6. Dean Dixon Papers: August 21, 1968, letter from Arthur Judson to Dixon, Box 4, Folder 6.

7. Dean Dixon Papers: June 13, 1969, letter from Martin Taubman to Dixon, Box 4, Folder 17.

8. Dean Dixon Papers: July 21, 1969, letter to Sherman Pitluck from Dixon, Box 4, Folder 17.

9. Dixon joined the organization Subud in the 1960s. The word Subud is comprised of "three Sanskrit words": Susila, Budhi, and Dharma. Dixon described each word in the following way: "Susila is the character of a person in which one finds the true human qualities he should have according to the will of God. Budhi is the higher power of an individual, which can lead him if he is able to discover it. And Dharma is sincerity, devotion, and acquiescence in God." According to Dixon, "Subud is a way of receiving which makes it possible for an individual to bring his life into accordance with the will of God. This cannot be attained quickly or easily; the process causes a long and deep purification which is accompanied by suffering. It demands from a person devotion, confidence, patience and sincerity. Subud is no model for living or philosophy of life. It adds nothing new to that which has already been told to mankind in the great religions, but Subud leads one gradually to a deeper understanding of religion." Dean Dixon Papers: A statement (in draft form) by Dixon dealing with the origin/ meaning/ philosophy of Subud, Box 1, Folder 27.

10. Dean Dixon Papers: December 3, 1969, letter to Pervil Eastman from Maxwell Cohen, Box 4, Folder 17.

11. Dean Dixon Papers: October 13, 1969, letter to Sherman Pitluck from Dixon, Box 4, Folder 17.

12. Dean Dixon Papers: January 3, 1970, letter from Martin Taubman to Sherman Pitluck, Box 4, Folder 19.

13. Dean Dixon Papers: January 3, 1970, letter to Martin Taubman from Sherman Pitluck, Box 4, Folder 19.

14. Dean Dixon, interview by KK, August 17, 1970, transcript, Dean Dixon Papers, SCRBC, NYPL, Box 1, Folder 7.

15. Dean Dixon Papers: July 19, 1970, letter to Martin Taubman from Sherman Pitluck, Box 4, Folder 19.

16. Dean Dixon, interview by KK, August 17, 1970.

17. Dean Dixon, interview by KK, November 1970.

18. Dean Dixon Papers: July 21, 1970, press release from the office of the Mayor, John V. Lindsay, Box 12, Folder 3.

19. Dean Dixon Papers: July 27, 1970, letter to Martin Taubman from Sherman Pitluck, Box 4, Folder 17.

20. Excerpts from an e-mail by Ritha Dixon on August 16, 2014.

21. Dean Dixon Papers: September 15, 1970, letter to Sherman Pitluck from Dixon, Box 4, Folder 18.

22. Dean Dixon Papers: Box 1, Folder 5, October 5, 1970.

14. I'M NOT TIRED YET

1. Dean Dixon, interview by KK, August 17, 1970, transcript Dean Dixon Papers, SCRBC, NYPL.

2. Dean Dixon, interview by KK, August 17, 1970.

3. Dean Dixon Papers: Kansas City Philharmonic program notes, January 19, 1970, Box 3, Folder 4.

4. Dean Dixon Papers: Letter to Sherman Pitluck from Martin Taubman, February 24, 1971, Box 4, Folder 16.

5. Dean Dixon Papers: Letter to Martin Taubman from Sherman Pitluck, March 11, 1971, Box 4, Folder 16.

6. Dean Dixon Papers: Letter to Sherman Pitluck from Dixon, March 11, 1971, Box 4, Folder 16.

7. Dean Dixon Papers: Letter to Dixon from Sherman Pitluck on March 19, 1971, Box 4, Folder 16.

8. Dean Dixon Papers: Letter to Martin Taubman from Sherman Pitluck on May 18, 1971, Box 4, Folder 16.

9. Dean Dixon Papers: Letter to Sherman Pitluck from Martin Taubman on June 8, 1971, Box 4, Folder 16.

10. Dean Dixon Papers: Letter to Sherman Pitluck from Dean Dixon on July 12, 1971, Box 4, Folder 16.

11. Dean Dixon Papers: Letter to Dean Dixon from President Richard Nixon, March 1, 1972, Box 1, Folder 5.

12. Dean Dixon Papers: Letter to Eugene Ormandy from Sherman Pitluck, April 4, 1972, Box 4, Folder 16.

13. Dean Dixon Papers: Letter to Dean Dixon by New York Law Firm on April 7, 1972, Box 4, Folder 18.

14. Dean Dixon Papers: Letter to Bill Judd from Martin Taubman on July 12, 1973, Box 4, Folder 9.

15. Dean Dixon Papers: Letter to Martin Taubman from Bill Judd, on July 26, 1973, Box 4, Folder 16.

15. RITHA

1. E-mail from Ritha Dixon to Rufus Jones on October 16, 2014.

2. Dean Dixon Papers: Letter to Betty Best from Dean Dixon on June 30, 1972, Box 1, Folder 17.

3. Letter to Betty Best from Dean Dixon on June 30, 1972.

4. Dean Dixon Papers: Review by Roger Covell, "Master of the Hall," *Sydney Morning Herald*, November 8, 1973.

5. Dean Dixon Papers: Karen Monson, "Bad Night at Symphony and Trouble is Up Front," *Chicago Daily News*, May 24, 1974.

6. Dean Dixon Papers: Robert C. March, "Dixon Makes Uneven Music," *Chicago Sun-Times*, May 31, 1974.

7. Dean Dixon Papers: Letter from Dean Dixon to the Frankfurt Radio Orchestra on August 15, 1974, Box 4, Folder 16.

8. Dean Dixon Papers: Letter to Dixon from McClara.

9. James Felton, "Dixon's Belated Debut is Brilliant, Exciting," *Evening Bulletin*, April 1975.

10. Dean Dixon Papers: Box 1, Folder 3, May 14, 1975.

11. Dean Dixon Papers: Box 1, Folder 4, November 12, 1975.

12. Letter from Ritha Dixon addressed to Kaj Kristoffersen and his wife, Christa, on November 15, 1975. From the personal collection of Ritha Dixon.

13. Dean Dixon Papers: Letter to Richard Covell from Dean Dixon on January 19, 1976, Box 1, Folder 21.

14. Dean Dixon Papers: Letter to Karl Rarichs from Dean Dixon on May 10, 1976, Box 1, Folder 21.

EPILOGUE: ON MY SHOULDERS

1. Ernest Dunbar, *The Black Expatriates: A Study of American Negroes in Exile* (New York: E.P. Dutton, 1968), 174–75.

2. D. Antoinette Handy, *Black Conductors* (Lanham, Maryland: Scarecrow Press, 1995), 310–11.

3. Anne Lundy, "Conversations with Three Symphonic Conductors: Denis de Coteau, Tania Leon, Jon Robinson [*sic*]," *Black Perspective in Music* 16, no. 2 (Fall 1988): 213–14.

APPENDIX A: IN MEMORIAM

1. Dean Dixon Papers: Letter to Dean Dixon from Chester Himes on October 17, 1963, Box 1, Folder 27.

2. Dean Dixon Papers: Letter from Everett Lee to Dean Dixon on December 4, 1967, Box 4, Folder 4.

3. Dean Dixon Papers: Letter to Dean Dixon from Jessye Norman, January 13, 1971, Box 1, Folder 30.

4. Dean Dixon Papers: Reference letter written by Dean Dixon for Jessye Norman, March 23, 1971, Box 1, Folder 30.

5. Dean Dixon Papers: Letter from Timothy Reynish about Dixon and the Hilversum Conducting Course, June 1, 1971, Box 1, Folder 28.

6. Dean Dixon Papers: Letter to Dean Dixon from Josephine Harreld Love on August 24, 1971, Box 1, Folder 20.

7. Dean Dixon Papers: Letter to Dean Dixon from Annette Schuster, March 3, 1972, Box 1, Folder 28.

8. Dean Dixon Papers: Letter to Dean Dixon from Ritha Dixon on January 10, 1973, Box 1, Folder 31.

9. Dean Dixon Papers: Letter to Ritha Dixon from Bengt Wallerius, November 19, 1976, Box 1, Folder 31.

Selected Bibliography

BOOKS

Abdul, Raoul. *Blacks in Classical Music: A Personal History*. New York: Dodd, Mead and Co., 1977.

Bainton, Helen. *Facing the Music: An Orchestral Player's Notebook*. Sydney: Currawong Publishing Co., 1967.

Bontemps, Arna. *We Have Tomorrow*. Boston: Houghton Mifflin Co., 1945.

Dunbar, Ernest. *The Black Expatriates: A Study of American Negroes in Exile*. New York: E.P. Dutton, 1968.

Ewen, David. *Dictators of the Baton*. Chicago/New York: Ziff-Davis Publishing Co., 1948.

Fletcher, Martin, ed. *Our Great Americans: The Negro Contribution to American Progress*. Chicago: Gamma Corporation, 1954.

Foner, Nancy. *Islands in the City: West Indian Migration to New York*. Los Angeles: University of California Press, 2001.

Gray, John. *Blacks in Classical Music: A Bibliographical Guide to Composers, Performers, and Ensembles*. New York: Greenwood Press, 1988.

Handy, D. Antoinette. *Black Conductors*. Lanham, Maryland: Scarecrow Press, 1995.

Lepore, J. Michael. *The Life of the Clinician: The Autobiography of Michael Lepore*. Rochester, New York: University of Rochester Press, 2002.

Olmstead, Andrea. *Juilliard: A History*. Urbana: University of Illinois Press, 1999.

Osofsky, Gilbert. *Harlem: The Making of a Ghetto, Negro New York, 1890–1930*. Chicago: Ivan R. Dee, Inc., 1996.

Parks, Gordon. *Voices in the Mirror: An Autobiography*. New York: Doubleday, 1990.

Richardson, Ben, and William A. Fahey. *Great Black Americans*. Second ed. New York: Thomas Y. Crowell Co., 1976.

Smith, C. Steven. *A Heart at Fire's Center: The Life and Music of Bernard Herrmann*. Los Angeles: University of California Press, 1991.

Sparks, Richard, and Milton Okun. *Along The Cherry Lane: Tales from the Life of Music Industry Legend Milton Okun/as told to Richard Sparks*. Beverly Hills: Classical Music Today, LLC, 2011.

Watkins-Owens, Irma. *Blood Relations: Caribbean Immigrants and the Harlem Community, 1900–1930*. Bloomington: Indiana University Press, 1996.

MANUSCRIPT COLLECTION

Dean Dixon Papers. Manuscripts, Archives, and Rare Books Division. Schomburg Center for Research in Black Culture, the New York Public Library.

Index

About the Author

Rufus Jones Jr., D.M.A., is director of orchestral and choral studies at Westglades Middle School in Parkland, Florida. He began his formal training in music at the University of Texas at Austin. After graduating with a B.A. in music, he continued his formal training as a Clifford D. Clarke graduate fellow at the State University of New York in Binghamton, where he received the M.M. in instrumental conducting. He completed his formal training at Texas Tech University, where he received the D.M.A. in orchestral conducting. Dr. Jones spent the next eight years as assistant professor of conducting and director of orchestral activities at Georgetown University in Washington, D.C. He has conducted youth, university, and professional orchestras throughout this country and abroad and is frequently invited to national music festivals as an adjudicator and clinician. His research has focused on African American classical musicians. Dr. Jones has written extensively on the music of William Grant Still. In 2009, his three-volume edition *The Collected Folk Suites of William Grant Still* was published and featured at the Inaugural William Grant Still Tribute Conference in Natchez, Mississippi. Dr. Jones currently resides in Miramar, Florida, with his wife and daughter.

9/22/15